Joe & Marie —

May you find inspiration
in these pages & in
conversation with the
many prophets who walk
among us.

Prophets Walk Among Us!

VOICING CHANGE™

VOLUME 1

VOICING CHANGE

INSPIRATION & TIMELESS WISDOM FROM
THE RICH ROLL PODCAST

BY RICH ROLL
& GUESTS

FOREWORD BY JEFF GORDINIER

RICH ROLL
ENTERPRISES

JOHN LEWIS

"Meaningful conversation matters. It's the antidote to what ails us. It's the centerpiece to unlock the better self within. And it's the solution to building a better, more united world."

—Rich Roll

CONTENTS

After the final no there comes a yes
And on that yes the future world depends.
No was the night. Yes is this present sun.

—Wallace Stevens

"What's it like to be interviewed by Rich Roll?"

I've heard that question more than once since I appeared on Rich Roll's podcast in the summer of 2019. If you're holding this book, you know: The dude has a following.

I should start out by saying that I do not represent the, um, *typical* guest on this particular podcast. I am not and will never be an endurance athlete. My idea of physical exertion is to go for a two-hour walk in the woods, preferably not uphill. My idea of endurance is to sit for a five-hour tasting menu in a restaurant with at least two Michelin stars.

Nor am I some trailblazing TED-talking thought leader with a Theory That Will Alter the Course of Human Consciousness. My idea of a cognitive breakthrough is to reach the end of a day in front of my laptop, make sure my twin toddlers are safely in their cribs, and pour an ice-cold martini with three Cerignola olives while listening to the Rolling Stones. I am a food writer, a music lover, a suburban dad, a compulsive and peripatetic traveler, and maybe—if we're being honest here—a bit of an intellectual lightweight.

Nevertheless Rich invited me to appear on the podcast, and I said yes. And to underscore what Wallace Stevens is telling us in that snippet of poetry up there, "yes" was the right call. I live in the Hudson Valley of New York, but I flew out to Los Angeles and steered my rental car up some canyon roads to the house where Rich Roll and his family live. (With its stark white walls and its narrow strip of an outdoor pool, it looks like the set of some lost Hal Ashby movie from the 1970s.) Rich greeted me in his warm West Coast way and we wandered into his home studio and before I knew it we were recording the podcast. And when I say "before I knew it," I mean that—I actually wasn't aware that we'd begun taping the conversation.

But it was too late. We were rolling, we were flowing, we were shooting the breeze. (What's it like to be interviewed by Rich Roll? It's like reconnecting with an old friend who somehow remembers more about your life than you do. The guy does his research.) Both of us used to be competitive swimmers in the 1980s, so we've got that in common, but it's safe to say we have chosen different paths since our chlorinated youth. If you've listened to Rich over the years or you've read his excellent memoir, *Finding Ultra*, you know that his path has taken him through a wasteland of addiction and junk-food gluttony to the state of healthy, open-hearted, plant-based equilibrium that he occupies now. As it says on the back cover the *Finding Ultra* paperback, "he could see where his current sedentary life was taking him—and he woke up." I can see where my current sedentary life is taking me, and, well, I will probably keep on doing that until someone or something forces me to change.

But it's just that—the possibility of change—that percolates beneath the surface of every Rich Roll conversation, regardless of who the guest may be. I view Rich as being part of an American continuum that stretches back to Ralph Waldo Emerson. At our best, we (as individuals and as a country) are constantly in flux, always inching toward a state of grace, diligently working at shedding old selves and welcoming the cleansing scrub of transformation. With that in mind, it's no accident that Rich's audience has surged in recent years. We're in the midst of a period of change more sweeping than anything witnessed in the United States of America in half a century. The #MeToo movement, the #BlackLivesMatter movement, a lethal pandemic, rising consciousness about the damage we keep on doing to the planet, a bewildering carnival of technological traps and delights, a widespread realization that dark chapters of our nation's history have been systematically erased or ignored, a vast awakening to the horrors of factory farming, a persistent challenge to the limitations of "traditional" gender categories—I mean, I've lost track of all the paradigm shifts and inflection points.

A lot is going on.

So what's it like to be interviewed by Rich Roll? It means you're sitting down to exchange ideas with a person who is fully aware of these shifting tides—and humbly open to where they're pulling us. Rich knows that we're never going back. He knows that, to borrow from a much-quoted Bob Dylan lyric, "he not busy being born is busy dying." He understands that if you want to embrace change, you've got to push through that final no to the yes that's waiting on the other side of the wall.

I felt invigorated after my conversation with Rich in California—I suspect that that's not an uncommon response—and so I decided to hazard a curveball. I told Rich that I had a table booked at Noma, which is often referred to as the best restaurant in the world. I had a reservation for lunch. Would he want to tag along? On any given day there could be 20,000 people on the waitlist for such a meal. The lunch would give us an opportunity to hang out with René Redzepi, the most charismatic and influential chef of the past decade, and Redzepi would make sure that his kitchen could prepare a vegan version of the menu for Rich. (I texted Redzepi to double-check.) There were only a couple of minor obstacles. Number one: Noma is located in Copenhagen, Denmark. Number two: The lunch was scheduled to take place in a few days.

I told Rich that I realized it would be a crazy thing to do—to fly all the way to Denmark for lunch. I told Rich, as well, that every meal I had eaten at Noma had transformed me in one way or another. I told him I had gotten used to hearing the word "no," in situations like this.

I don't need to tell you what he said.

Jeff Gordinier is the food & drinks editor of Esquire *magazine and the author, most recently, of* Hungry: Eating, Road-Tripping, and Risking It All with the Greatest Chef in the World. *He lives near the Hudson River with his wife, Lauren Fonda, and his four children, Margot, Tobias, Jasper, and Wesley.*

Tap tap tap. "Is this thing on?" I asked. "Can you hear me?"

"It's working," Tyler replied, his voice echoing throughout the vacuous and humid warehouse. I can't distinguish a soundboard from a preamp, so I enlisted our tech-savvy teen to help kick-start what I was convinced just might be the worst idea ever.

I opened up GarageBand on my beleaguered laptop. Hit *Record*.

The rest is history.

It was over eight years ago, but I vividly recall the moment. Seemingly insignificant at the time, thus began a most uncommon adventure—setting in motion a chain of events that would forever alter the course of my life and ultimately impact countless people across the globe.

It was also a difficult and confusing time.

Earlier that year, I released my first book, *Finding Ultra*. Part memoir, part wellness manifesto, it chronicles my trajectory from insecure child to man in the throes of alcoholism. My path to recovery. My slide into the sedentary complacency of middle age. And my spiritual quest for authentic self-actualization through plant-based nutrition and ultra-endurance pursuits.

I put almost everything I had into creating that book. Even more went into pushing it out into the world. Technically a practicing attorney at the time, I realized that my interest in the law had evaporated. *Finding Ultra* was my opportunity to step into a new professional reality. But making that shift hinged entirely upon the book's success, which, to put it mildly, was very much in question.

My friend Casey Neistat once said, "If Tarzan never let go of the vine he was swinging from to grab the next one, he never would have reached the other side of the jungle. He just would have

sat there, swinging back and forth." It was time to finally let go. It was time for a giant leap of faith.

So, on the day *Finding Ultra* landed in bookstores across America, I officially shuttered my law practice. And, placing my trust in faith over logic, awaited the new path I was certain would soon present itself.

"I didn't reach my athletic peak until I was 43. I didn't write my first book until I was 44. I didn't start my podcast until I was 45. At 30, I thought my life was over. In my 50s I know it's just beginning. Keep running. Never give up. And watch your kite soar."

This is to say that I lifted a line out of the book. A mantra I had come to believe with every fiber of my being: *When your heart is true, the Universe will conspire to support you.*

What followed, however, would test me more than any ultra-endurance race I had braved, any

obstacle I had previously faced and overcome. A period of struggle so difficult, it brought me to my knees—and called into question my very sanity.

The book did fine. Hardly a *New York Times* bestseller, it managed to find an audience. But it didn't put food on the table. And despite my conviction that new opportunities would follow, the phone simply did not ring. Months passed. Bills stacked up. Dead air. A dead end.

My mantra, it seemed, was bullshit.

Gravely behind on the mortgage and teetering on total financial collapse, I saw an email land in my inbox. It was from Chris Jaeb, an entrepreneur I had met once previously, now reaching out with an opportunity: Come to Kauai and help me transition my organic farm into a community space. It was an odd request. But also a godsend. A gift.

Within weeks our family had relocated to the Garden Isle's lush North Shore, dwelling in furnished yurts among the young WWOOFers (willing workers on organic farms), tilling the fertile soil of the property dubbed Common Ground. When the vertigo lifted, I wasn't sure we'd ever return to Los Angeles. Our house inching towards foreclosure, there was no looking back now.

Exploring the Na Pali Coast and daily swims in Hanalei Bay restored my balance and provided a fresh perspective. It also, over time, produced a case of island fever. I was extremely grateful to Chris for the lifeline—without it, I can't imagine what we would have done. But I started feeling uncomfortably disconnected from the world. Pondering my next moves. Anxious for a creative outlet. Itching to make something new. Anything.

Then it occurred to me: a podcast.

Let me provide some context. In 2012, podcasting was hardly the hot medium it is today. A hobbyist pursuit; nobody, save a select few, could reasonably call it a vocation, let

alone a source of any income whatsoever. From a financial perspective, it was a harebrained scheme; a fool's errand.

However, I was a fan of the medium dating back to its earliest days. A time before podcast apps, streaming services, or professional networks. A time when, if you wanted to listen to a podcast, you had to roll up your sleeves and work for it—an onerous process that involved downloading an audio file from your desktop computer and then bouncing it to an iPod or .MP3 player. A time when there wasn't much selection. And very few people were listening. In fact, in 2007, I didn't know anyone other than myself who had ever listened to even a single podcast. By 2012, things hadn't changed that much.

My affinity for the medium escalated in lockstep with my love affair with endurance sports. Training for my first Ultraman in 2008, I suddenly found myself spending an absurd amount of time alone, all day on my bike or lost on a remote trail. Podcasts became my constant and only companion. My training partner didn't just keep me company, it provided an all-expenses paid graduate degree in life.

I couldn't stop wondering, Why isn't everyone listening to podcasts all the time?

Between 2008 and 2012, I easily consumed more than 2,500 hours of people talking. My entire EPIC5 Challenge Hawaii adventure was narrated by Marc Maron, Ira Glass, Dan Carlin, Bill Simmons, and Joe Rogan—unwitting mentors in what I didn't then realize was boot camp for me to one day host a show of my own.

So, on a balmy Kauai afternoon in late November 2012, when that creative spark tickled my frontal cortex, I already knew exactly how to satisfy the itch:

I opened up GarageBand on my beleaguered laptop. Hit *Record*.

I recently relistened to that very first episode, a loose and relaxed conversation with my wife, Julie. A bit formless and certainly rough around the edges, our voices echoed across the makeshift "studio"—a cavernous warehouse designed more for agriculture, less for acoustics (pro tip: avoid podcasting in gigantic rooms with concrete floors and impossibly high ceilings).

Once I got past the amateur nature of the production and my cringe-inducing aversion to my own voice, I was struck by the clarity of purpose. A first stab at continuing a conversation I began with *Finding Ultra*. A baby step in the direction of personal evolution through long-form discourse. A humble intention to broker important ideas too often unaddressed in the limited bandwidth of mainstream media.

Now nearing almost 600 episodes, the show has matured from its humble warehouse roots into a signal that now reaches people all over the world—a reach that provides access to some of the world's most dynamic and forward-thinking minds.

The medium I fell in love with loved me back. And yet so little has fundamentally changed since that first episode. The intent remains intact. Even the theme music ditty—a track composed in mere minutes by my stepsons and nephew and always intended as temporary—continues unaltered to welcome each new conversation. Like many, I frequently fumble the ball, fail, and misspeak. But every once in a while, I get it right. Either way, I always give it back. And together, we grow.

Family aside, hosting the podcast has been the most fulfilling adventure of my life, an ever-evolving experiment in meaningful discourse. It's given me a doctorate in life, a priceless education that

has taught me things no school could and given me countless tools that have made me a better partner, parent, servant, and man.

Along the way I have been both challenged and inspired. Moved to tears and given pause. Elevated in ways I previously could not have imagined. And left forever grateful for all my guests, without whom my podcast would not exist. A collective in the service of humanity, entrusting me with your stories, your truths and your timeless wisdom has been a privilege—and an honor—to amplify.

My gratitude, of course, extends to you—the extraordinary community of devoted readers and listeners to whom I hold myself accountable. I don't take your valuable attention for granted. And I'm profoundly touched knowing that I am not alone but am part of a vast and growing community that deeply cares about things that truly matter.

It is in this spirit that I present this devotional offering—a curated anthology of some of my favorite exchanges. In the pages that follow, you will discover excerpts transcribed from nearly 50 episodes, each respectively accompanied by my considered reflection. Peppered throughout the book you will also find a handful of original, thought-provoking essays contributed by a selection of past guests.

For some, *Voicing Change* presents an opportunity to reconnect with catalog favorites—a coffee-table keepsake for the ardent fan. For others, it's an introduction to new voices that will inspire further investigation. For each appetizer that unfolds in the pages that follow, I invite you to digest the full meal. The entire catalog is freely available on my website to stream or download.

Writing is a team sport. This book reflects that notion more than most. I am indebted to an extraordinary group of artists who ply their talents behind the scenes, week in, week out, to create the podcast—and the exclusive work you now hold.

In closing, I would be remiss if I did not address the many confusing ways in which our chaotic world is changing—rapidly and tumultuously. From political strife to climate change, we are confronted with problems of enormous magnitude, some of which are existential—very real threats to the future of humanity and the well-being of the planet at large. Resolving these issues demands our best selves and our full attention. It's a process that inaugurates simply, with two people sitting across from each other, earnestly seeking greater understanding.

After over 1,000 hours of recorded, intentional discourse—and with every new episode published—I am convinced that meaningful conversation matters. It is the antidote to what ails us. It is the centerpiece that unlocks the better self within. And it is the solution to building a better, more unified world for ourselves and future generations.

May this meditation on the power of conversation unlock the authentic, more fully expressed self within. Because the change we seek demands the best of us. And all our voices are required.

Peace + Plants,

Rich

There is no quest more noble than that of self-actualization freely shared in service of others. It is in this spirit that I make this devotional offering, in reverence and dedication to all who seek to do and be better.

GOING BEYOND MOTIVATION
AND WHY MINDSET IS EVERYTHING

Hands down, David Goggins is the most inspirational person I have ever met.

Forged in a crucible of adversity, David is a man of extraordinary will and charisma, placed on Earth for a singular purpose—to empower people with the tools and hard truths required to face life's obstacles head on, shatter personal limitations, and ultimately self-actualize.

Often referred to as "the hardest man alive," David is the only member of the US Armed Forces to complete SEAL training (including two Hell Weeks), the US Army Ranger School (where he graduated as Enlisted Honor Man), and Air Force Tactical Air Control Party training.

But he's best known for superhuman feats of strength and ultra-endurance.

After several of his friends died in a 2005 helicopter crash while deployed in Afghanistan, David honored their memory by tackling the ten most difficult endurance challenges on Earth to raise funds and awareness for the Special Operations Warrior Foundation—a nonprofit that provides college scholarships and grants to the children of fallen spec ops soldiers.

Thus began a most unexpected yet remarkably storied athletic career as one of the world's most accomplished endurance athletes. David took first place in the 2007 48-Hour National Championship endurance foot race, where he ran 203.5 miles, beating the previous record by 20 miles. In 2013, he set the world record for most pullups in a 24-hour period (4,030). From 2007 to 2016,

he took additional top finishes at dozens of the world's most grueling races, including the HURT 100, Leadville Trail 100, Western States 100, and more. This is a guy who parachuted from 1,200 feet into Kailua Bay during the swim start at the 2008 Ironman World Championships, completed the race, and celebrated by working out *again* later that day.

But David's greatest accomplishment is that, throughout his life, he has faced and overcome a concatenation of seemingly insurmountable obstacles to become the man he is today: obstacles like asthma, sickle cell anemia, psychological and physical abuse, obesity, academic struggles, and even a congenital heart defect that often left him competing—and winning—on a mere fraction of his actual physical capabilities.

The implausible journey is laid bare in David's stratospherically successful memoir, *Can't Hurt Me*.

GINS

Honest and powerful, it's the story of a man who transformed pain into obsession and, phoenix-like, rose from a state of utter desperation to take complete ownership of his life and total command of his mind to manifest a most extraordinary life.

In addition, David has had a profound impact on me personally. Stumbling across his story way back in 2007—a moment long before anyone outside of the small ultra-endurance subculture even knew who he was—his example helped ignite my passion for ultra-endurance and fuel the self-belief required to pursue a new path. I simply cannot repay the debt of gratitude I have for this man.

My two podcast conversations with David are by far the most popular, listened to, and viewed episodes in the history of the RRP. Our initial meeting took place in late 2016 and marked the first time he ever shared the details of his life on a long-form podcast. It's a powerful episode that helped set in motion a series of events that has culminated in David's status as the motivational guru of the moment.

Think of him as an artist. His medium is his life. His message is that we all harbor a masterpiece within. And his example is that literally anything is possible.

It's time to torch complacency. Get brutally honest with yourself. Embrace vulnerability. Callous the mind. Get comfortable with being uncomfortable. And prepare to go to war with yourself

Because your life is not some future event. Your life is now.

—*Rich*

David: The thing that holds people back is the truth. Their truth, the real truth about who they are as a person. I think it all really starts there. You may not be a courageous person, but are you willing to find it within yourself to go through the very hard journey of finding your truth?

When I made the conscious decision to become a warrior, I realized that my mentality had to change. I took my poopy-pants, the world-is-against-me mindset and I flipped it. I became the devil to get out of hell. Through the crucibles of life, I decided to create a guy I was proud of. I built that calloused mind, first in the armed forces and later in the ultra-endurance world. When you put yourself through the crucible, you find out who you are.

Everybody's journey is different. My journey to see who David Goggins was took me into some of the hardest areas a human being can imagine. Now, at 41, I'm the happiest person on the planet because I've climbed Mt. Everest several times. I knew if I could make it, I could look back on my life proudly. That's what kept me going.

Now, goals are important. But the reason people quit or train endlessly without reaching their goals is because they don't look at themselves in the accountability mirror. You may be the most physically fit person on the planet, but if you haven't handled your jealousies, your insecurities, whatever happened to you as a child, and everything in between, they're going to surface when your mind starts to question why you're doing what you're doing when you put yourself in the crucible.

Everybody has issues. You're a human being. You're fucked up somewhere. That somewhere (or several somewheres) is keeping you in the same spot. Most of us sit back and say, "God, I wish I could do that," and we wait and we wait and we ask more questions and ask more questions.

If I'd asked a bunch of questions, I'd still be trying to figure out how to run one hundred miles. Once I had the idea to run Badwater, I did it in four months. I qualified in four days and ran the damn race. I had to lose 105 pounds in sixty days to become a Navy SEAL, so I lost the weight and became a damn SEAL. I wanted to be a Ranger at 41 years old. The second I thought about it, I researched it. I didn't ask questions, I achieved it. We waste tons of time not starting our journey asking questions about how to start the journey. Get an idea, start walking, and figure the shit out as you go. Vision quest.

You can change, but it truly takes you wanting to change. That's the one thing I learned about life: you have to be willing to fail one hundred times to succeed once. If you're not willing to do that, you're not going to get a fraction of what you're looking for.

It's not about ultra-running, being a SEAL, pull-up records, or anything like that. It's not about "push yourself until you die." No, I'm about pushing yourself harder than you think you're capable of. I'm about not giving up when you feel a little pain or when something is uncomfortable. I'm about changing the way you perceive limitations.

In the end, my message isn't about pushing yourself until you can't live anymore; it's about pushing yourself harder than you did yesterday. I challenge you to get over all your excuses and find the truth of who you are. Figure it out. Start your journey.

"When you think you're done, you're only at 40% of your total potential."
—David Goggins

ZACH BUSH, MD

RECONNECTING WITH NATURE IS OUR MOST PRESSING IMPERATIVE

Zach Bush, MD isn't just a compelling pioneer in the science of well-being and environmental health. He's a virtuoso healer. A master consciousness. And a gift to humanity.

Over the course of our friendship—and our four profound podcast conversations shared—Zach has revolutionized how I eat and live. He's forever altered how I interface with the world as a conscious consumer. How I engage with myself, others, and the oneness of our shared biosphere. And—perhaps most profound—even how I think about death.

One of the few triple-board-certified physicians in the country, Zach specializes in internal medicine, endocrinology, and hospice care. He is an internationally recognized educator and thought leader on the microbiome as it relates to health, disease, and food systems. He is also the founder of Seraphic Group, an organization devoted to understanding root cause problems and their solutions in the sectors of big farming, big pharma, and Western medicine at large.

Zach is also the founder of Farmers Footprint, a nonprofit coalition of farmers, educators, doctors, scientists, and business leaders aiming to expose the deleterious human and environmental impacts of chemical farming and pesticide reliance, while simultaneously offering a path forward through regenerative agricultural practices to rebuild living biodiversity and ultimately reverse climate change.

How we treat the planet impacts human biology. Intuitively, we understand this to be fact. But what distinguishes Zach from his medical peers is his holistic application of evidence-based science, humanity, and the intelligence of nature to reimagining this relationship—and transforming the world.

A man with a deep mastery of the interdependence of macrocosm and microcosm, Dr. Bush's brilliance truly shines on subjects like soil regeneration. The connection between intensive farming practices, environmental degradation, and chronic disease. Our unhealthy relationship with material consumption and mortality. And the existential, urgent mandate that

humanity return to a more symbiotic relationship with the planet and all living things.

Among the most impactful colloquies of my lifetime, Zach has a knack for landing our podcasts with unmatched profundity—all mind-blowing master classes in thinking both deeply and broadly about the precious miracle that is both life and death.

I love this man. I'm grateful to call him friend. A critical voice in the most pressing conversations of our time, helping amplify it has been my honor.

May Zach's wisdom leave you empowered and armed with greater clarity to reimagine and actualize a healthier, more sustainable, purposeful, intentional, and fulfilling life experience for yourself.

Because the change this world needs most rests not with those comfortably nestled in the seats of power, but instead with you and me.

—*Rich*

"If we don't reconnect with nature, we will just destroy it again."
—Zach Bush, MD

Zach: Now that we have seven billion souls on the planet, the ultimate political control is around the food chain and whether it delivers health or not. The politicians are not the solution. You and I are the solution as consumers.

In the late 1990s and early 2000s, diseases in what seemed like completely different organ systems in the population began to go epidemic simultaneously.

An example of this is autism. We had one in 5000 children with autism in 1975. Today we have one in 36 children with an Autism Spectrum Disorder. Then to further emphasize that, the fastest acceleration in that growth pattern happened between 2012 and today, where we're seeing a doubling in time every two to three years. At this current rate, we'll see one in three children with autism in 2035.

There is also a rise in skin cancer and bone marrow cancers. Then in 1996, a sudden rise in Alzheimer's in women. We have species-specific, gender-specific, organ-specific diseases in the brain and peripheral cancers all of which took off at the same time in the mid-1990s. Autoimmune disease and unbelievable epidemics started in the late 1990s.

Put simply, I believe this phenomenon is caused by one thing: chronic inflammation. Inflammation is actually a normal biologic response to an injury. The immune system lies throughout your body in different shapes and forms, but 80% of the work done by the immune system is done in your gut lining. It is your barrier system between the outside world and what you breathe, drink, eat, and so on.

If you plucked a human hair and cut that in half, that's the thickness of your gut membrane. You have this half a human hair's cellophane layer that protects you from every bite of food you eat. This tells us something big about what we're engineered for—we need to be inherently in contact with the ecosystem and nature around us. If we start to tinker and screw with that nature, the membrane is going to become very vulnerable and start to leak. If we have a chronic inflammatory epidemic in the world, which is a better definition of lots of diseases, then we must be overwhelming the immune system of all of the public for some reason at the same time. Sometime between 1982 and 2000 we did something to the environment to totally decimate the protection system of our immune systems.

It comes down to what started to happen after World War II: we began making chemical-based fertilizers for the first time. Farmers started using chemical fertilizers, and it and it was revolutionary for them. But the plants treated with these fertilizers began to lack nutrients and became weak. They became prone to viruses and pests. To solve this issue, the industry created a new chemical weedkiller, and the farmers became trapped in this codependent relationship with chemical fertilizers and weedkillers.

The most famous of these, of course, has become Roundup. We currently sell and use four-and-a-half billion pounds of glyphosate, which is the active ingredient in Roundup. That chemical was never patented as a weedkiller. It's only been patented as an antibiotic and then was re-patented as an antiparasitic, an antifungal.

So here's where it connects: think of the essential amino acids in your body like the alphabet. Nine of them can't be made by the human body, so those nine have to come from your food chain somewhere. It turns out that they're only made by bacteria and fungi in plants. Imagine treating a food chain with a chemical that blocks the ability of plants to make the building blocks for a healthy human body. We literally subtracted out the ability to build a healthy human body from our food because we changed those 26 letters.

The other side effect of glyphosate includes direct injury to the protein structure that holds your gut lining together. This would be bad news if that was it, but it turns out that every macro-membrane in your body, the blood vessels that fuel your entire body with oxygen nutrients are held together with the same tight junctions. The blood-brain barrier that protects your peripheral nervous system and your brain, same tight junctions. The kidney tubules that are held together to detox your body, same tight junctions.

Since we introduced a chemical that is directly toxic to this Velcro-like protein, we have turned into leaky sieves. Every time we breathe, every time we eat, we're starting to leak and our immune system gets overwhelmed.

Then you get to the blood-brain barrier—it can be compromised by glyphosate. That's exactly when we see this steep increase happening in autism, Alzheimer's, Parkinson's, neurodegenerative conditions like multiple sclerosis, autoimmune diseases and all the rest. We are losing the identity between the outside world and our immune system by the breakdown of these membranes. We get leaky. That's literally taking away self-identity from the immune system and

so we get autoimmune disease, where we're starting to react to our own body as if it were foreign. In the same way, at the macro level, I believe we're losing our self-identity as human beings as we start to leak.

We start to get majorly depressed. We start to get anxiety. We start to get lost down these rabbit holes of doubt, insecurity, fear, guilt. We have spiritual crisis. We have relationship crises that's on an epidemic level equal to cancer and beyond. The ability to stay in human relationships seems to be the most complicated thing that we could possibly endure right now. It's because we are literally losing self-identity at the cellular level because we are eating a chemical that breaks our self-identity at the cellular level.

Fortunately there are bacteria and fungi that can eventually digest the glyphosate. The downside is we need to stop spraying it so that they can return. All of this may sound like a lot of bad news, but figuring out the problem is the first step. Let's keep the solution simple. Let's start thinking about mechanisms for you to reintroduce the microbiome to your body. Number one, get fermented foods back into your diet. Ferment your own food if you can. Number two, breathe as many environments as you can. It turns out we can repopulate our microbiome not just by eating it through fermented foods, but by breathing the bacteria and fungi in our environment. Get out of your house, go on a hike, go near a waterfall, go to a swamp, go to the mountains, go to as many macro-ecosystems as you can and breathe there for a few hours.

It's really that simple. Grow your own food. Get back out in nature. Together we can rebuild the greatest farming nation in the world. Together we can grow the greatest food on earth.

"The politicians are not the solution. You and I are the solution as consumers."
—Zach Bush, MD

A ROADMAP TO RECOVERY FOR THE HUMAN SPECIES

BY ZACH BUSH, MD

Terminal Condition

In this modern day, one in every two males in the US is diagnosed with cancer before they die. Women are just behind at one in three. Cancer rates have doubled in just 25 years, the measure of just one generation. Globally, cancer is now the second leading cause of death.

The word "cancer" is loaded with emotional programming of fear and hopelessness that has been galvanized by ancestral, societal, academic, and philanthropic story telling of this mortal enemy of life. This emotionally charged diagnosis of cancer crashes on the unprepared human psyche to cause a mix of all the facets of grief: shock, denial, anger, resignation, and even guilt. As the emotional dust settles into our cracks, physicians and patients alike are trained to respond with an action plan that any military strategist of history would recognize. A combination of defensive and offensive action that begins with a thorough surveillance and assessment of the enemy, then deployment of resources and weapons to contain then kill the offending intruder that is threatening. The war on cancer.

This rhetoric has been galvanized over the last 50 years by the unanimous voices of academic, philanthropic, and pharmaceutical enterprises. The US now ranks 35th in the world for health outcomes, far behind all the wealthiest countries, and lagging behind smaller countries and economies like Croatia and Chile. Among developed nations we have the highest rates of neonatal death on day one, and some of the highest rates of developmental, metabolic, autoimmune, vascular, and neurodegenerative disorders of any nation in the world. We lead the charge in the global epidemics of childhood and adult cancers.

This war is more lucrative than any warfare in history, the current US medical system generates $3.7 trillion in annual spending to manage chronic disease, with cancer being among the most profitable, and is expected to balloon to $5 trillion by 2025. Our entire US military and defense budget (the most expensive military complex in the history of the world) is five times less at $0.68 trillion dollars. The economic stimulus of war has often buoyed failed empires, but wars for oil, territory, or political gain have proved inadequate in magnitude to stabilize the massive scale and instability of today's US economy. Disease warfare is the last bastion of economic stimulus that can buy us time in this modern empire. We are fools. Our only hope for delaying the collapse of the empire is continued rapid growth in GDP over the next decade. This is a terminal condition. We are economically codependent on our own rise in chronic disease. We have necessitated an enemy from within.

The rise and fall of empire is an age old story, but as Western economies rapidly increase our exportation of the worst of what we produce— from soda and energy drinks, to GMO and chemical agricultural technologies, the growing global health crisis poses a new question: Will humanity birth a next empire? Sperm counts in males of typical reproductive ages have declined by 52–57% in Western nations over the last 40 years. One in three males now has sperm counts in the infertile range. The trend is not slowing. Without a change in direction we can see the extinction of our species on the horizon, in less than 100 years. We are in our hospice moment as a species.

But, there is a poetry of grace in the science of cancer that reveals a path out of fear for a different future.

Isolation

The engineering of your biology is dependent on your connection to the greater ecosystem of life around us. Biology collapses rapidly when isolated. Consider how much we need contact with other people in our lives. For centuries military and prison systems have utilized solitary confinement as one of the most extreme forms of human torture. Within days of isolation every mind begins to create hallucinatory realities so that something can be seen, heard, experienced. With prolonged isolation self-identity erodes and the individual becomes prone to manipulation and codependence. From Stockholm syndrome to your typical abusive relationships, from sexual abuse to substance abuse, isolation of the mind and social experience is a critical ingredient. The biologic dis-ease that results from macro-isolation is only a mild version of the biologic chaos that ensues when we create microscopic isolation. This is where we create crippling depression, anxiety, obesity, infertility, autoimmunity, diabetes, heart attacks, organ failure, and ultimately cancer.

For more than a century, medical science has believed that the health of the human body wholly depended on the immune system's capacity to beat back the outside world; a belief that was exemplified and reinforced with the antibiotic, antifungal, antiviral era of the latter half of the 20th century. In these years it seemed inexplicable that this mass chemical warfare against the world of the germs might be the very cause of the chronic disease epidemic that exploded across the developed world in those same years. But, the last twenty years of scientific discovery has revealed the devastating scale of the human collateral damage in this war. The discovery of epigenetics and the advent of rapid genomic sequencing, coupled with the exponential acceleration of computational capacity of computers, has revealed an extraordinary new reality of human life: one in which the human is not at the center.

As we push into the single cellular environment of the healthy human body, we find every compartment teaming with biodiversity. Microbial diversity of bacteria, yeasts, and viruses have been discovered in every healthy organ system of the body, from the colon to the breast, from the prostate to the kidneys, from the liver to the brain. The healthy human body is an ecosystem of biodiversity. As we sterilize this system with antibiotic herbicides in our food and water systems, hand sanitizers, air filtration systems, and the ever-advancing antimicrobial armament of Western medicine, vitality declines, and extinction approaches.

We have been working for years in our laboratory to understand the relationship of the microbiome to the seemingly unique human biology within us. The discoveries are humbling. The sequence of events leading to any type of chronic disease in the human begins in the ecosystem of the bacterial microflora that thrives throughout the body, but in the greatest abundance in the gut. The massive surface area of the human gut has been estimated to be the equivalent of two tennis courts. This vast terrain is inhabited by thousands of species of bacteria whose population out numbers the human cells in your body at least 10:1. This ecosystem of microbes produces a diverse molecular family of metabolites from your food that creates a wireless communication network to power cell-cell communication within the human organ systems, and across species of the microbiome. When antimicrobial pressure occurs, microbial diversity is lost (A single course of oral antibiotics

can lead to an 80% loss of microbial diversity), and the communication network is diminished. Consequently we see a rapid decline in cellular repair and energy production. The barrier function of the gut and vascular cell systems within the body are compromised, cells become isolated, and the gut and vascular systems begin to leak. Within minutes we can see the development of pre-cancerous features in these newly isolated cells. If the microbiome and its communication system are not restored, the cells remaining in isolation will continue down the cancer pathway.

In the example of the human breast, we find a unique species of bacteria, *Sphingomonas yanoikuyae*, as the predominant member of a diverse microflora, but with chronic antimicrobial stress and toxicity within the breast tissue, this species is lost, and the microbiome adapts with the emergence of *Methylobacterium radiotolerans* as the predominant species within a different microflora diversity in that breast. Interestingly, the original healthy microbial flora can still be identified in the other breast of the same woman that does not yet have cancer. If the population of *Methylobacterium* declines under continued toxicity and antimicrobial pressure, the related breast cancer becomes increasingly malignant and the likelihood of mortality of this woman increases. Simply stated, cancer is the terminal result of a collapse of the microbiome.

Reconnection

You are alive. This is a fact that defies mathematic, biologic, and philosophic comprehension. It can only be understood, and therefore appropriately marveled at, in the experience of being alive. My concern is that we

forget to notice. Our collective behavior would suggest that we are oblivious to this daily miracle of life, so we become distracted and lose sight of the beauty. So we must strive to reconnect. We need to dive deep into this sensual beauty of our Look at the back of your hand as it rests on the table for five minutes. Sit quietly and marvel at it in all of its complexity. You have learned to hold a smart phone at all times, and now, for all of its supposed familiarity, "the back of your hand" is as often seen as the dark side of the moon. When you realize that your mind wanders, bring your attention back to the hand. See the texture of the skin, the knuckles, the nails, the hair. Become aware of the extreme order that underlies the structures, an extremely carefully controlled order that reveals the inherent self-awareness of each component that understands its structure and function within the greater system. The fingernail knows just where to spring from the fleshy bed at the end of each digit that is the compilation of lanky bones, various connective tissues and padding, fluid filled joint spaces, vascular, lymphatic and neurologic bundles, all meticulously organized and suspended in the web of the extracellular matrix and more macro fascial systems. Finally, this perfect package of subspecialized tissues and cellular structures are wrapped in the multilayered epidermis of the skin, capable of producing multiple function-specific variations, for example, observe the extreme difference between the skin of your palm and the back of the hand, and the bizarrely well demarcated boundary along the side of your hand and each finger between the two skin types.

The sloughing layers of dead and desiccated cells that make up the skin are surprisingly animated by a neural web that allows you to sense with extraordinary detail the textures and characteristics of the world that you live within. Once you are beginning to experience being alive within a multi-dimensional biologic system through the observation of your hand as it sits on the table, then you should move your hand. Roll your fingers as if on a keyboard, slowly for a bit then faster, recognize the coordination you are capable of moving this astronomically complex biologic instrument. Once that psychedelic experience begins to normalize, then touch the face of a baby, or the bark of a tree, or the texture of the fur of your favorite pet, or press your face against the face of your lover.

Mind blown.

Then move to your other senses. Smell, taste, hear, see . . . you are capable of multi-dimensional connection with the world around you. The complexity of the beauty us overwhelms the senses if we will take the time to be completely present in our observation. Be a good witness for a moment. Then breathe it all in. Now exhale completely, so you can breathe it in deeper. Feel your chest and lungs filled with the beauty around you. We are sentient beings, the pinnacle of our extraordinary engineering devotes itself to the multi-dimensional connection to life around us. We are here to connect.

As we reintegrate the human experience into the nature that we developed within for millions of years, we see restoration happen. It begins with the microbiome. As we disrupt our daily pattern of programmed sterility and repetition with a perfect meandering through a field of wildflowers, or a path in the woods, or the cold smooth stones in the floor of the mountain stream, life begins to take root in our bodies again. Nature is always ready to reseed our bodies with the vast microcosmos of archaea, bacteria, fungi, and protozoa that are the necessary living aspect of the soil beneath our feet, and within the diverse ecosystems of our body. The power of this reconnection demonstrates that grace in mother nature's design that I previously eluded to. Our laboratory and clinic have been among the very first in the world to witness the healing power of a restored communication network from the microbiome. Within minutes of this exquisite reconnection we get to see diverse cellular systems that have been damaged and isolated by acute or chronic herbicide exposure begin an eloquent process of reconnection. Cells with all the features of a cancer just minutes before, are rejoined to the human system either to repair their accumulated damage for restored function within the multicellular system, or to eliminate themselves peacefully to be replaced by healthy cell division or stem cell recruitment. The complexity of healing is mind boggling. It seems impossible that these human cells, isolated in a petri dish, many decades separated from their deceased human donors, have a memory of their identity within that human body. With communication restored, they rapidly reorient to their structure and function, revealing their unique purpose within a vast macrocosmos.

Over thousands of years of industrialization and technologic advancement man has learned to conquer every facet of the living world that we inhabit. Most recently it is the annihilation of the microbiome of our soil, water, and air systems of the planet, as well as within our own bodies. As a result, we have become the consumptive cancer on the planet. We have consumed more than half of life on the planet over the last 50 years alone. We are estimated to be causing the extinction of one species on earth every 20 minutes. In our domination we have failed to understand that there is no manifest destiny, only a malignant destiny in our striving for complete isolation. We have undermined the foundation of life on this exquisitely beautiful planet. As we see the approach of our own extinction, we have the opportunity to envision a different path. It will begin with reconnection.

Get out in that nature today—get dirty, ignite your senses, be fully alive today—to realize a different future tomorrow.

SHUT UP AND RUN

Powerful female role models abound. But, as a father of two young girls, I began to notice that culture fails at properly celebrating them. Part of my podcast mission is an effort to help change that.

Let's start with Robin Arzón—the ambassador of sweat and swagger—and one of my all-time favorite queens of self-empowerment.

At the height of her corporate law career, Robin fearlessly left it all behind to embark on new adventures in the health and wellness space. She soon discovered her passion for coaching athletes, bridge running across New York City and tackling 100-mile runs. She even ran five marathons in five days across Utah. And she's the author of *New York Times* Best Seller *Shut Up and Run*. A toolkit of practical advice and motivation to help every runner cultivate miles of sweat, swagger, and frienaship, it is the ultimate expression of all things Robin.

Now vice president of fitness programming and head instructor at Peloton, Robin hosts massively popular indoor cycling experiences. More than a gym class grind, think self-empowerment after party doused in sweat.

But it's not what she does that makes Robin special. It's who she is.

There was the time she was kidnapped and held at gunpoint—a near-death experience that reformed her perspective on life. And the fact that she lives with Type 1 diabetes—a disease that persistently threatens to sideline her active lifestyle. But Robin isn't interested in playing the victim. She's interested in telling a different story. A story of greatness writ large that involves constant reinvention and tenacious commitment to persona growth. A narrative that aims to redefine, reform, and rethink possibility through movement.

Human performance art in motion, Robin is a powerhouse of positive vibes. Confident, colorful, and courageous with a no-bullshit attitude and NYC street cred for days, she is inspiration personified.

And she's got a message for you: *Sweat transforms lives.*

—**Rich**

"*Set your life on fire. Seek those who fan your flames.*"
—**Robin Arzón**

Robin: Lacing up ill-fitting shoes at 10 at night and running with my motley crew of friends like a pack of miscreants out of the movie *The Warriors* . . . that was how I fell in love with running. It was very simple.

When I was first becoming a runner, I was so intimidated by all of the running bibles and the compendium of information available. Since then, I've trained for dozens of ultra-marathons and my hundred-miler, and I've realized something along the way:

It's all bullshit.

You don't need a $700 Garmin watch for your 5K. Like, chill bro. Westerners live in a culture where we're seeking shortcuts and hacks and apps, like time-saving genie machines. So there's a lot of noise that intimidates people unnecessarily.

Runners feel the need to apologize for being newer, slower, bigger, smaller—whatever adjective you want to apply to it—and that makes them feel "lesser than."

But I'm here to tell you: be unapologetic about who you are. And it starts with the drive. How badly do you want it? And how many issues of *Runner's World* are you going to go through before you actually lace up and get out?

Real talk.

I think by now you can see why I titled my book *Shut Up and Run*.

The thing is—if you're not enjoying the experience in the training miles, then it doesn't really matter what the finish line looks like.

But if you do enjoy it, really think about how badly you want it. Because, like anything worth having, you must make sacrifices to be good.

So get out the door. Sacrifice watching your favorite TV show tonight. Sacrifice going out for a late-night dinner.

Our entire lives are made up of micro-decisions and micro-moments. If we're simultaneously celebrating tiny victories while pursuing the next ones, we're going to be just fine.

"I so believe in unchecking all the boxes and then creating your own or just living in that fluid space where you're redefining yourself everyday."

—Robin Arzón

I've been publicly sharing my personal journey with alcoholism and sobriety for over a decade.

From inception, my podcast was deliberately and consciously created as a storytelling vehicle to elucidate the pernicious nature of addiction. It's a vehicle to better educate people on solution-based paths to overcoming a disease that indiscriminately kills countless annually. A lifeline for the desperate many that struggle alone and in silence.

I do this to underscore that there is always hope, no matter how lost you find yourself.

But what if you're not an alcoholic? What if you, like millions of people, occasionally drink just a little too much?

Booze may not be destroying your life like it did mine. But you can't argue that it leaves you feeling off your game. Hungover, tired, and lethargic. Unfocused and unproductive. And more often than not, depressed.

You'd prefer to stop. But it's fun. A way to blow off steam and connect with colleagues and friends. Plus, because drinking is fundamentally integral to so many people's social or professional lives, opting out seems impossible. What then?

Andy Ramage faced this very real and relatable predicament. The only difference? He decided to do something about it.

A former professional footballer (as they say in the UK), a career-ending injury prompted Andy to hang up the cleats and enter the world of finance. Channeling his hard-earned, athletic work ethic, conventional success soon followed in the form of two co-created multimillion-dollar city brokerage houses.

But doing well in banking "required" (or so he thought) drinking. Lots of drinking. Long *Mad Men* style booze-soaked client lunches. Countless happy hours, foggy pub crawls, and giddy cocktail soirées, followed by clubbing and the occasional after-party.

Work hard, play hard. That's the job.

Andy didn't necessarily have a drinking "problem." But the lifestyle left him drained. Listless. And looking for a change.

Bucking the unwritten rules of his professional environment, he decided to take a

> *"Alcohol is like kryptonite to your dreams."*
> **—Andy Ramage**

ANDY RAM

AGE

break from alcohol and instead expend his energy on a quest for peak performance and well-being. It stuck. Not only did Andy feel markedly better, his work performance improved. His relationships became more meaningful. He fell back in love with the simple things that brought him joy as a young lad. Slowly, a new world of life opportunities began to emerge.

Transformed, Andy enthusiastically began sharing his experience, challenging friends and colleagues to quit the booze for 28, 90, or even 365 days. What he didn't know then was that the friendly contest he concocted among peers would soon explode into a full-blown international movement he ultimately dubbed *One Year No Beer*.

Today, Andy and his friend Ruari Fairbairns have parented OYNB into a world-leading behavioral change platform that has helped over 70,000 people boot the bottle and invest instead in well-being.

Their companion book, *The 28-Day Alcohol-Free Challenge* is a UK bestseller. And Andy's solo-authored *Let's Do This* is a motivation playbook for making any type of personal change.

I first met Andy two years ago when he turned up for our Plantpower Ireland retreat. Fast friends from the outset, I found his story inspiring—and certain to resonate with the RRP audience.

Alcoholism is a self-diagnosed disease. Left untreated, it will always progress and ultimately lead to one of three places: jail, institutions, or death. If you are a true alcoholic, or a sober member of a certain unnamed 12-step program, Andy's message isn't aimed at you.

This one is for the average drinker, those a bit closer to "normal" (whatever that is) on the alcohol spectrum who find themselves abusing the booze from time to time. It's for those who started drinking in their teens and never really stopped. And it's for people who have maintained a slow and steady pace of consumption without any given thought to addiction or the negative side effects of alcohol on a daily basis.

This is to say that Andy's message is directed at the majority of our society.

Because quitting alcohol isn't just for alcoholics.

—*Rich*

Andy: I reached conventional nirvana. I had a successful career, a house, a family. I was having a good time, working hard and playing hard. I made it, but I was still unhappy. I discovered that looking good on paper is not really what life is about. I was quite sick. I didn't feel well, I was always 5 out of 10. I was overweight, unfit, unhealthy. My relationships were strained. My mental health was suffering. It wasn't surprising to find out I had heart disease at 35.

I decided to do things differently. I wanted to be successful, but on my terms, not society's. I wanted to get fit, I wanted to get healthy. I wanted to be energized, I wanted to be motivated, and I wanted to nurture my relationships at home. To do this, I had to quit drinking alcohol. I wasn't an alcoholic, I didn't hit rock bottom. I was just a moderate drinker and I drank no more than my peers. It didn't affect my career. I wasn't in trouble at home, but I knew in my gut I was drinking too much, and so was the rest of the planet.

To put it plainly, alcohol is awful for your health, even if you don't consider yourself a problem drinker. It's carcinogenic. In over 50 studies, it's shown to be linked directly to cancer and to over 60 different diseases. This doesn't just apply to the addicts; it applies to the average drinkers too. But the thing is, the average drinkers will never hit a breaking point like the addicts often do. They just keep grinding it out and wearing away.

This is my message to the moderate drinkers: quitting alcohol isn't just for alcoholics. Going alcohol-free will radically transform your life. If you want to be an even better athlete, take a break from alcohol. If you want to be an even better parent, take a break from alcohol. If you want to be an even better entrepreneur, take a break from alcohol. Just think about it: even if you only drink once or twice a week, you're always slightly under the cloud of alcohol. You may not be displaying the classic signs of nausea and all that sort of stuff, but you have a slight hangover and disrupted sleep. It's awful for your productivity, for your motivation, for your mental health. People are under-performing all the time and don't even realize it.

We're all time-poor. It's a modern-day disease, right? Stop drinking. You will get a ton of time back. For the last 10 years, I would be in a constant wrestle with my alarm clock every morning. There was no time. It was work, stress, family, repeat. But it's not that we don't have a lot of time, we just waste so much of it. Why would I ever waste a day on a hangover? I've

> "Quitting alcohol isn't just for alcoholics. Going alcohol-free will radically transform your life. If you want to be an even better athlete, take a break from alcohol. If you want to be an even better parent, take a break from alcohol. If you want to be an even better entrepreneur, take a break from alcohol."
>
> **—Andy Ramage**

built this vibrant, healthy lifestyle that's alcohol-free, and I would never put it in danger by having a drink. That just doesn't compute in my brain anymore.

When you're drinking, you're never consistent. Your diet, exercise, and productivity are all never consistent. But when you remove the alcohol, you're on the ball every day. You're confidence skyrockets. It catalyzes all these other changes. You'll find your diet improves, you'll lose weight, you'll be more present for others and your life will amp up in so many more ways. You don't need alcohol to be cool, fun, sexy, and successful. That's total bullshit. To have the ability to step away from the crowd takes an immense amount of courage. It was empowering for me.

To be a father to my two girls and to not drink makes me feel strong as a person. It makes me feel manly to know that I can deal with everything life throws at me with a clear head, and deal with it effectively and vibrantly, rather than bury myself in alcohol. Knowing that you can deal with the stress and heartbreak and harder parts of life without drowning in booze is one of the biggest benefits of going alcohol-free. But for so many people, it's become so ubiquitous in their lives, that for every occasion there's an excuse to drink. But we're not authentic when we're drinking—we turn into a false person. So many of us have created these identities around alcohol that can be difficult to let go. We hide behind them. If you can take a break from alcohol, you will discover your true self, your authentic self, and it will be the greatest discovery you'll ever make.

BRUCE FRIEDRICH

INNOVATING THE FUTURE OF FOOD

Currently, 7.5 billion people currently share this spinning blue planet we call Earth. By 2050, that number will escalate to 9.7 billion. By 2100? The population will be 11 billion.

How can we possibly feed 11 billion people sustainably?

To answer that question, rest your gaze upon the massive industrialization of animal agriculture. On the surface, what we commonly call factory farming appears incredibly efficient, creating titanic economies of scale. But peer just below the surface and you'll discover a government subsidized complex of mass suffering that is irreparably polluting the environment, eviscerating our dwindling natural resources, and destroying human health to boot.

It's an apparatus that is beyond wasteful. Utterly unsustainable. And indefensibly cruel.

Not only is our food system in dire need of innovation, it's an existential threat to the future of humanity and planetary well-being.

Bruce Friedrich is a man who has committed his life to solving this problem by innovating the future of food and food systems.

The executive director of The Good Food Institute, Bruce is also the founding partner of New Crop Capital, organizations both focused on replacing animal products with plant and culture-based alternatives. He graduated magna cum laude from Georgetown Law and Phi Beta Kappa from Grinnell College, holds additional degrees from Johns Hopkins University and the London School of Economics, and was inducted into the Animal Rights National Conference Hall of Fame in 2004.

A popular speaker on college campuses—including Harvard, Yale, Princeton, Stanford, and MIT—Bruce has appeared on NBC, CNN, Fox News, MSNBC, and Court TV.

Despite the profound systemic ills of our current food system, extraordinary technological innovation, extreme urgency, and public demand are rapidly converging to create healthy, sustainable, and compassionate solutions.

In other words, Bruce is optimistic.

—Rich

"Unless the governments of the world address climate change, we won't be able to feed 9.7 billion people in 2050."

—Bruce Friedrich

Bruce: 9.7 billion. That's how many people we're going to have to feed in 2050. And we're simply not going to be able to do it with the degree of inefficiency that is inherent in growing crops to then feed them to animals so that we can eat the animals. It's a vastly inefficient system, and, moreover, it's directly attributable to global climate change. But times are changing. At our nonprofit, the Good Food Institute, we're helping the meat industry transition away from animal-based meat and toward plant-based meat and clean meat—both of which have less of a carbon footprint, are more sustainable, are friendly to animals, and taste good.

You see, every meat consumer is thinking about taste and price. If we can create products that compete in those two ways, we can save a ton of animals, cut back on carbon dioxide, and create a healthier food system. But unless the governments of the world address climate change, we won't be able to feed those 9.7 billion people in 2050—and that's a scary thought. One thing to note is that a lot of meat consumers who don't change, don't change because it's difficult. There are social pressures when you're out to eat meat because that's what everybody else is eating. But if we create products that are taste and price competitive, it makes it so much easier to raise awareness and encourage people to change because it makes sense to change.

At the Good Food Institute, we are making products to transform the default choice of food into the option that's good for animals, the environment, sustainability, and global health. And that's just the beginning.

There's a colossal market opportunity and a lot of good to be done in this space by entrepreneurs, food scientists, tissue engineers, and plant biologists. In their hands they hold a tremendous amount of good—and the ability to save the world. Truly, it's a really cool time.

Millennials legitimately care in a way that previous generations didn't, and our hope is that this will translate to more of the best and brightest taking these kinds of jobs and being part of the transformation. For the people with lots of energy, smarts, dedication, and ambition, it's the perfect time to get involved.

For individual consumers, the healthiest way to help the environment and themselves is through a whole foods plant-based diet. For friends and family who are not yet vegan, there's fantastic transition food, like Tofurkey, Field Roast, and Boca Burgers, that are just great. There are plant-based options that meat eaters simply haven't tried, but that they will try if you encourage them to. I am extraordinarily optimistic. And there are an awful lot of people who are a heck of a lot smarter than I am, who are extraordinarily optimistic.

For me, it's just incredible to be part of this movement of so many beautiful people doing so many beautiful things. Because veganism isn't just about an ingredient list. Veganism is an ethic.

RYAN HOLIDAY

EGO IS THE ENEMY

Our culture is currently mired in an unprecedented epidemic of ego—a societal blight of apocalyptic proportions precipitated by the advent of selfie-crazed social media, self-esteem parenting, and spurious self-help gurus fomenting an illusory sense of entitlement.

The result is a woefully misplaced celebration of ubiquity over meaningfulness. Of endless distractions over devotion to work ethic. Of self-congratulatory passion over fidelity to process. Of unbridled hubris over humility. And of rampant self-seeking over service.

We often equate ego with confidence, self-assuredness, and ultimately success. The domain of the great visionary.

But what if this notion is utterly false? A personality trait that, at every turn, thoroughly undermines that which we seek most? And what if modesty, humility, and self-honesty are not actual weaknesses but in fact our greatest asset?

Ask Ryan Holiday and he will tell you bluntly: ego is the enemy.

An autodidact who dropped out of college at 19, Ryan has matured into one of the most important thinkers of his generation. Now 33, he is a media strategist, prolific writer, and public intellectual with six perennial bestselling books to his name, including *Ego Is the Enemy, The Obstacle Is the Way,* and *Stillness Is the Key.*

Best known for pioneering Stoicism to mainstream adoption, if Ryan has a niche, it's exalting the modern-day practicalities of ancient philosophy to live more optimally.

Measured and self-effacing to a fault, Ryan's work and counsel is currently coveted by some of the world's most successful CEOs, political leaders, world class athletes, and NFL coaches.

In a culture of loud mouth bloviators, click-bait agitators, and white-noise shrill, Ryan is the welcome and sober voice we need.

I have a great fondness for this human. Plus, he's a very good runner. I can't come close to keeping up with him intellectually or athletically.

—Rich

"When you remove ego, stillness emerges. You need stillness to overcome life's obstacles."

—Ryan Holiday

Ryan: *What is the meaning of life? How do you deal with a world that you don't control? How do you find purpose? What's right and wrong? What is the path to the good life?*

These are the most critical questions Stoicism grapples with.

I based *The Obstacle Is the Way* on one line from Marcus Aurelius which is, "The impediment to action advances action. What stands in the way becomes the way." You don't control what happens in life, but you control how you respond, so you might as well respond in a positive way. It's not about some sort of delusional positive thinking. It's about understanding what objectively is the case and choosing to do something about it.

The first thing that most people do when something happens is decide whether they like it or not, whether it's fair or not, things that the Stoics would say have no actual bearing on the event itself. You have to first decide whether what happened is in your control. The things that are require a full amount of your effort and energy and passion. The things that are not, you have to let go.

Freud said the ego is the rider on the back of the horse. But the ego, as we use it colloquially, is the wild horse that needs to be tamed. Ego is the problem. Ego prevents you from doing the important things you need to do. I use ego as a synonym for arrogance, and selfishness, and endless competitiveness, and greed, and recklessness. Your ego pushes out good things in your life because it expands. It's constantly taking up space—to your detriment.

Cyril Connolly is this obscure British writer who says, "the ego is like a cell which by over-assertion of itself causes cancer." Ego is what propels someone to greatness, and it is what propels people past the point of reasonable utility.

Aristotle's golden mean states that a virtue is between two vices. We need to be right in the middle of "I hate myself" and "I'm a God." It's based on your inherent worth as a human being, and an objective understanding of your capacities and your assets as a unique individual. Every human being has certain dignity and worth, and you can't deprive yourself of that. Everyone deserves to live, and is entitled to certain inalienable rights. You've got to combine those two things. That's where you find grounded confidence. That's where you reign in your ego.

John Keats has this concept called negative capability. He says the mark of genius is to be able to hold two conflicting or somewhat contradictory thoughts in your head at the same time. You have to be able to do that. You have to know that you can do something and be humbled and scared by it at the same time. You can't dwell on things in life because it prevents you from growing.

A great way to let go of your ego is to leave your office, or your house, or whatever space you're in, and go outside. Look up. You aren't the center of the world. You don't even matter in the universe. You are a puny, weak speck in an incredibly large universe.

The overwhelming superiority of nature will tame your ego. And that's a good thing.

> "You have to know that you can do something and be humbled and scared by it at the same time. You can't dwell on things in life because it prevents you from growing."
> —Ryan Holiday

ASSENT TO CHANGE
BY RYAN HOLIDAY

As I write this, I am undergoing change—as of course, you are too. The Stoics would say that life is change. That we are constantly being worked on. Scientists call this entropy, which is just a fancy way of saying things fall apart and chaos reigns.

If you had asked me at the beginning of this year if I was willing to experiment with a life without childcare, without travel, without meetings or meals out, without speaking publicly, with my income dropping significantly, without leaving my house at all really, I'd have said no way. Who could afford that? How would it even work? Yet, at the same time, because of that attitude I always was unaware of what life not missing a bed or bath time for months on end was like. I found it inconceivable that I could live with so many fewer impositions and pointless obligations—they were just unavoidable parts of reality.

Thankfully—gratefully—life disabused me of this notion. This pandemic of 2020 is a radical forced life experiment. It's not been cheap or easy. It's been tragic in many ways for many people. I would never want to diminish that. It's also been transformative for me and for a lot of people too.

I guess what I am saying is that when we think of change, particularly as ambitious people, we think of change we *make*. We think less of the change that happens *to us*. But really, it's this change, what we would call fate or luck (good or bad) is actually much more powerful and usually much more eye opening.

There is this word that, when I first came across it in Marcus Aurelius as a headstrong teenager, that I didn't like. He talks about "assent." Assent? Isn't that weak? Isn't life about *asserting*? But in fact, assenting is a better way to go through life. Stuff happens and instead of getting angry, instead of trying to force it to be different, you *assent* to it. You accept it. You deal with it. You integrate it in your life. You approve it.

You can even love it. That's what "amor fati" means—a love of fate, whatever it is.

We make change, but also change makes us. If we let it. If we love it.

Or at least, that's what I tell myself.

GURU

Inspiration. We crave it. We need it. We love it.

But inspiration alone is a salve that does not cure. Like tissue in a flame, it rarely translates into positive lifestyle adaptations sustained over time. For that you need a more sustainable fuel. For that you need something called "purpose."

What if I don't have purpose? How do I find it?

Purpose derives from a keen awareness of self. An awareness that cannot be found in externalities but instead emanates from the deep recesses of your soul—a place far removed from the dopamine-inducing inspiration hits we restlessly seek outside ourselves.

Indeed, purpose is an inside job.

A favorite steward for such diaphanous, inward-seeking expeditions is Guru Singh, my treasured friend and favorite wizard of all things mystical.

A master spiritual teacher who has graced the podcast more times than I can count, our many conversations on spirituality, awareness, humanity, love, grief, loss, intuition, consciousness, self-care, and other topics both earthly and ethereal always leave my mind edified and my soul enlivened.

A celebrated third-generation Sikh yogi, for the past 40 years Guru Singh has been studying and teaching Kundalini yoga. In addition, he is the author of several books, a powerful lecturer, and behind-the-scenes guide to many a luminary, including Fortune 500 CEOs, athletes, and artists.

A peer of rock legends like Janis Joplin and the Grateful Dead, Guru Singh is also a talented musician who began his recording career on Warner Bros' Reprise label in the 1960s. When he isn't recording tracks with people like Seal,

he's bringing down the house on the daily at Yoga West, his Los Angeles home base.

Imagine a modern-day rock star Gandalf dropping mad guitar licks between pearls of timeless wisdom that beautifully fuse Eastern mysticism with Western pragmatism, and you start to get the picture.

Having spent many hours with this human—both on mic and on the mat—I can promise his wisdom will catalyze a desire to peer more deeply inward. His easy presence will spark a yearning to more thoroughly cultivate your latent intuition. And his gentle, guiding hand will help celibate your trajectory towards the ultimate superpower—unlimited awareness.

To rise up, you gotta lay down. It is there that you will find purpose.

—Rich

SINGH

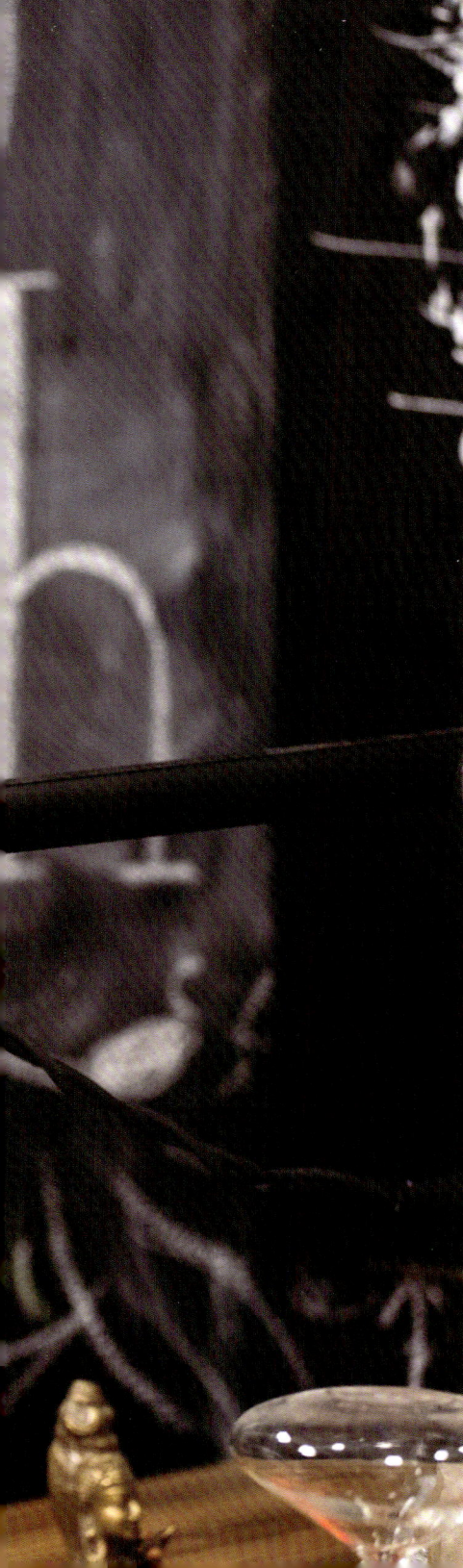

Guru Singh: Are you a ball on the field being moved to wherever the play is taking you, or are you a player? A coach? The owner of the team?

At what level are you willing to play the game?

Yoga is not an Olympic contest. We're not here to prove what we can do.

Kundalini yoga, for instance, is the yoga of awareness—raising your awareness so that you are in tune with your physical, emotional, mental, esoteric, and spiritual bodies.

If I'm standing next to a person off the mat, I have to find some way of creating a yoga—or, creating a connection with them. The easiest way is to constantly be aware of our breathing.

For instance, I remember the alley where I learned to ride a bicycle. Very vivid memories. For the next few days or weeks, I was very conscious of every move I was making on that bike. I became comfortable. That's the same thing that happens with Kundalini yoga—you become aware of your breathing, even though you're still doing other things.

You've got bandwidth. You have an awareness that you're not just talking to somebody—you're conversing. When you start to be aware of these bandwidths in your consciousness, the world of relationships becomes so much richer.

But, the greater your awareness of everything, the greater you're plagued by the devastation, the garbage, the insanity . . . We have inundated the world with such waste that we cannot escape it. This, in and of itself, is creating a crisis.

I'm optimistic, however, because I'm alive. I'm going to help lead it through, like you're going to help lead it through. Knowing that in a physical world—according to physics—for every action, there is always an accompanying equal reaction. This is Newton's Third Law of Motion.

That means that in this moment there is an equal reaction to the demise that is taking place. A wave is sweeping. Under the surface of this extreme superficial nature of bigotry and xenophobia and gender attitudes and homophobia is extreme tolerance. Tolerance is very widespread.

Get involved, but also balance it out so that you're not just involved in reaction, but deep understanding—so that when you do react, you don't react in an unmerited or unconscious way.

Always have hope. Then go from there. Ask yourself: "What are the ways in which I can help to instill hope?"

Athletes talk about getting into the zone and breaking into that zone. That is your higher consciousness. That is the realm in which you're in communion with God. The time to get real is now.

"May you live more in your devotions than emotions."

—Guru Singh

47

WE ARE THE EARTH KEEPERS

The collective Soulforce of the "Earth-Keepers" and "Earth-Restorers" is the power and compassion of saviors. People from all walks of life—all over the world—like spiders, patiently, purposefully and imperfectly connecting their webs of benevolent spaces through the networks of perfect timing . . . an overwhelming task in an underserved moment.

These "Earth-Keepers" and "Earth-Restorers" invite and unite the positive, negative, and neutral aspects of human consciousness, which witnesses the corruption and destruction as a call to action. When woven together, this Soulforce forms the brilliance of balance and equilibrium in a new creative to save the planet. This is who you are, just because you're handling this book.

Like the construction of any web, these more conscious lifecycles and lifestyles join forces to serve the collective of life. Just as fire is contained within wood; water is contained within air, and light is contained within darkness—all spaces are contained within the infinite nothing. When these critical times arrive, the "Earth-Keepers" become an omnipresence of good within the challenged spaces. It's a Cosmic law—perfect balance must permeate everything everywhere.

We craw this together with our hearts and our guts . . . the vast intelligence of our physical bodies when there's proper diet and nourishment to show off our connections and reliance upon each other. Each individual within these networks is brilliant, but together—as a collective—we're beyond imaginable. This permeates amongst us as we instinctively and intuitively work to "keep" this sacred Earth and "restore" her as our nutritious Mother.

This moment in time is like a sailboat in strong winds, we can leave the sails down and drift with the currents—life without a connecting web—or we can raise the sails with an attitude of "together we've got this." This is such a moment, and we're in need of such insistent willingness to believe we know exactly what to do.

This is Soulforce—we're the "Earth-Keepers"—we're the "Earth-Restorers"—we're the way forward. It's time to come together in these stormy winds, raise our sails, and serve each other and the Mother.

With Deep Gratitude,
Guru Singh & Guruperkarma Kaur

ROBYNNE CHUTKAN, MD

LIVE DIRTY, EAT CLEAN

"There is no question that the number one food to eat to grow a good gut garden is plant fiber, and there really can be no debate about that."

—Robynne Chutkan, MD

Our bodies are comprised of more than 30 trillion cells. But the contents of our microbiome—all the bacteria, viruses, fungi, archaea and protists that live in or on our bodies—vastly outnumber human cells.

In reality, we are far more microorganism than human.

We believe that we are sentient beings, responsible for our health, moods, and decisions. But the crazy truth is that the quality of our emotional state, propensity for disease, and even our specific food cravings are all inextricably linked to the nature of our gut ecology.

Most of these microorganisms are symbiotic. Maintaining a diverse and healthy culture of the "good bugs" is fundamental to good health. But should the quality of your microbiome go awry, health havoc ensues.

An integrative gastroenterologist (and avid marathoner), Robynne Chutkan, MD lives at the cutting edge of this fascinating and quickly evolving field of medicine.

A graduate of Yale, Dr. Chutkan received her medical degree from Columbia University College of Physicians and Surgeons in New York, where she completed her internship and served as chief resident. She completed her fellowship in gastroenterology at Mount Sinai Hospital in New York and has been on the faculty at Georgetown University Hospital since 1997.

In 2004, Dr. Chutkan founded the Digestive Center for Wellness, an integrative practice that incorporates nutritional optimization,

exercise physiology, biofeedback, and stress reduction as part of the therapeutic approach to digestive disorders.

Consistently named her one of the top physicians in her field by *Washingtonian* magazine, Dr. Chutkan is the author of three bestselling books: *The Microbiome Solution*, *Gutbliss* and *The Bloat Cure*. She appears frequently on *The Dr. Oz Show*, *Today*, *The Early Show*, and *The Doctors*.

Although the science is complex, Dr. Chutkan's message is simple. The standard Western diet and lifestyle are wreaking havoc on our microbiome, depleting our bodies of the productive biota that keep us healthy and encouraging overgrowth of exactly the wrong type of bacteria. This imbalance is making us sick. More prone to obesity. And creating a litany of negative downstream complications on our metabolism, hormones, our cravings, immunity, and even our genes.

The good news is that there is a solution. A solution that begins with maximizing the diversity of plants in your diet.

One of my most powerful and empowering podcast conversations, Dr. Chutkan will change how you eat. How you shop for consumer hygiene and cleansing products. How you bathe (or don't bathe) and simply, how you live.

Change your microbiome, change your life.

Or as Dr. Chutkan is fond of saying: *live dirty, eat clean*

—Rich

Robynne: Your microbiome is composed of trillions of bacteria that live in and on your body. It reflects everything about you—how you were born, whether you were breastfed or not, where you've lived, the food you've eaten, the drugs you've taken, your hormones, even your stress levels. Your human cells are outnumbered 10 to one by your microbial cells and genes. You are more microbe than human.

My area of expertise is inflammatory bowel disease (IBD), Crohn's disease, and ulcerative colitis. Like most autoimmune diseases, these have yet to be fully understood, but myself and others in my field have begun to notice a common thread: a huge proportion of patients with these autoimmune diseases and GI symptoms all have frequent antibiotic use at some point in their lives.

We have been creating diseases and not even realizing it. This antibiotic connection wasn't in the minds of the patients, and it certainly wasn't in the minds of the doctors who were prescribing them—we have been conditioned to think of our microbes as foes rather than friends.

I'm not anti-medicine, and I'm not an anti-antibiotic. I'm for judicious use of them. There are times where these medications need to be used as a prophylactic, but there's also many instances in which doctors—and patients—just don't have enough information. I didn't know every time I prescribed a broad-spectrum antibiotic that I was removing a third of my patients gut bacteria in five days, potentially setting them up for things like food allergies and asthma and autoimmune diseases.

Even if you're not taking antibiotics from a doctor, you're getting them by eating animals. Antibiotics have been used for animal fattening since the 1950s, but much more aggressively in recent times. We know that giving animals antibiotics can increase their weight by as much as 15%, which mean 15% more profit. The current statistic is that 80% of all the antibiotics sold in the US are used in the animal industry.

I've been in operating rooms when plaque is pulled out of the coronary arteries—that's not kale. That's lard. You can make such a significant difference in your risk for disease through your diet. That's real—that's not wishful thinking. What I think is wishful thinking is the idea that you can continue to eat a diet high in refined sugar and animal fat and take a pill and protect yourself from disease.

If you want to support your microbiome, start with the simple things. Eat more plants. Get a filter for your water so that you're drinking water with less chlorine in it. Open your windows more often instead of using your air conditioner. Plant a garden or even have something growing by the sink so that you can put your hands into the soil and have contact with those amazing microbes. Form a stronger relationship with nature where you're touching it on a daily basis. Eat real food grown by your hands, or by a local farmer's.

There's no pill or microbiome hack where you still get to eat Cheetos and hot dogs and have a good gut garden. Period.

WIM

"THE ICEMAN" ON WHY BREATH IS LIFE, COLD IS GOD AND FEELING IS UNDERSTANDING

Hailing from a houseboat in Holland, there is ruddy-faced, gnome-like man who will challenge everything you thought you knew about human potential and leave you with one indelible, ineradicable truth:

We are all sitting atop vast reservoirs of untapped, almost superhuman capabilities.

Meet Wim Hof, a.k.a. the Iceman.

A Dutch-born world record holder, adventurer, daredevil, and human guinea pig, the Iceman is best known for his preternatural ability to withstand extreme cold. Perhaps more compelling are his experimental findings with specific and teachable breathing techniques. Rooted in the ancient yogic tradition of Pranayama and canonized for a modern audience as the Wim Hof Method, Wim asserts that he can "turn his own thermostat up" and consciously control his sympathetic nervous system by using his mind through yoga.

This may sound far-fetched. Bananas, even. Before you shrug him off however, hear me out:

- Shirtless and adorned in nothing but shorts, Wim scaled above death zone altitude (22,000 ft) on Mount Everest.
- Again adorned in only shorts, Wim completed a full marathon above the polar circle in Finland—barefoot.
- He summited Kilimanjaro in less than two days (yes, shorts only).
- He swam a world record 66 meters under a meter of ice located above the polar circle.
- He can sit submerged in ice for almost two hours.

Oh yes, there's more. Under doctor supervision in 2011, Wim was voluntarily injected with a poisonous E. coli endotoxin certain to make any human being very ill. He contended an ability to neutralize the threat by using meditation and breathing techniques to control his autonomic immune system response. All I call tell you for sure is that Wim did not get sick.

In addition, beyond his countless feats of incredulity, Wim is a longtime vegetarian who hasn't eaten any food before 6 p.m. for over thirty years.

It's all seemingly insane. But Wim is hardly a carnival sideshow act—his stunts merely a means of attracting scientific community attention for purposes of study and documentation.

Ask Wim and he will tell you that he is nothing special. He declares his feats replicable and his methods entirely teachable—a curriculum that holds the potential to unlock a battery of human superpowers that extend well beyond extreme temperature tolerance to include control over a wide array of sympathetic nervous system and metabolic "reptilian brain" functions previously considered beyond conscious manipulation.

Case in point? After a mere four days of instruction, Wim led a group of brave volunteer students through his doctor-supervised endotoxin exposure experiment. Not one of them got sick either. And he routinely and successfully takes groups of students, most of whom qualify as non-athletes, up summits like Kilimanjaro—in nothing but shorts, of course.

—Rich

> "We are so successful at being comfortable that comfort is becoming the enemy of success."
>
> **—Wim Hof**

Wim: It could have been the heat. Could also have been situations of oxygen deprivation, like when I climbed Mt. Everest or Mt. Kilimanjaro (in nothing but shorts), or when I swam 66 meters under a meter of ice above the polar circle. It could have been anything that triggers the deepest part—the survival part—of the fight, flight, food, the fuck, and the freeze. But I was drawn to the cold. The cold brought me this deeper connection because I had to reconnect consciously into my physiology to endure it.

You see, our consciousness gets into our system and into our cells; it becomes neurological. The patterns enable us to control whatever makes our mood happy and our condition healthy. So, we become alchemists. Anybody can do it. We change our neurology with better breathing. By breathing, I'm always charging. Mostly, I always follow my feelings. And what I feel right here, right now, is insight.

The purpose of being is to make the soul ascend to expanding consciousness. If we follow that path then there is no tension—you just live like a kid: open, simple, clean. Nature in all its beauty, is there, but some people don't experience it because their consciousness gets narrowed. People write me off and say, "Ah, you're religious," or "You're a hippie," or you're this and that. And that's the thing. They are no longer open to nature. But there's a gift to understanding.

The right motivation is found in discovering how beautiful this planet really is, and therefore the energies and nature of yourself. Then you're ready. It's already inside. We just need to apply it consciously so the neurology changes; then, we are not only able to increase our performances, but we also get a sense of spirituality. We begin to understand the real purpose . . .

> *"I think a man's masculinity is tested by how much love he is able to spread. When spreading love, he becomes the protector of emotions, softness, while being present with everyone—that's what it means to be a real man."*
>
> **—Wim Hof**

THOUGHTS ON EGO, TAKING BIG SWINGS,
AND SPEAKING TRUTH TO POWER

Edward Norton is undeniably one of the greatest actors of our time.

Over the course of his extraordinary career, Edward has reaped three Academy Award nominations starring in some of the most extraordinary films of our era—*Primal Fear, American History X, Fight Club, Birdman,* and *25th Hour* among them.

The occasion for our conversation was *Motherless Brooklyn*—a long-gestating passion project in which Edward not only starred, but a film he also wrote, directed, and produced. A period crime noir that confronts the shadowy malevolence of power in 1950s New York City, Edward embodies as a twitchy Tourettic detective determined to find his boss's killer. Evocative of *Chinatown,* it's a towering achievement and terrific watch.

Unfamiliar to most are Edward's many off-screen interests and achievements as an entrepreneur, investor, philanthropist, and environmentalist.

In 2010, he co-founded CrowdRise, a crowdfunding platform that raised over $500 million for nonprofits and was later acquired by GoFundMe. He is the co-founder of an advanced data science company called EDO, which provides audience analytics to media companies. In addition, Edward is an avid pilot. He is also the founding board president of the Masai Wilderness Conservation Trust, a Kenyan conservation and community development organization. To raise awareness for the organization in 2009, he ran the New York Marathon alongside a group of Masai, completing the race in a very impressive time of 3:28.

That's just the tip of the iceberg when it comes to this famously private, hyper-intelligent polymath—a man with more than a few thoughtful opinions on filmmaking, creativity, environmentalism, and the nature of power.

Expanding upon the themes explored in *Motherless Brooklyn* and their relationship to issues of modern-day concern, our discussion mines the perils of ego in both entertainment and politics. We discuss disenfranchisement and the implications of weaponized social media in our politically divided culture. And Edward provides a master class on the state of environmental activism.

On the subject of creativity, we explore the importance of gestation—distancing yourself from the noise to reboot artistic originality. How to balance art against other life priorities. And how to separate the product of creative labor from the vicissitudes of audience reception (a point he illustrates with a great story about *Fight Club* and Brad Pitt).

Finally, Edward provides a compelling perspective on the nature of power—and how this theme underscores his latest work.

They say never meet your heroes. I disagree. A pinch-me moment, it was an honor to talk with a man I respect and admire tremendously.

—Rich

EDWARD NORTON

"I think ego is the deepest addiction there is."

—Edward Norton

> *"In this country there's dark shit going on.*
> *And not knowing that it's going on*
> *puts you in danger."*
> **—Edward Norton**

Edward: I'd suggest that we have a core conflict as to whether we're going to prioritize corporate well-being over human well-being, and that this fundamental argument is the underpinning of many—if not all—of our major social challenges. It's basal to our healthcare problems. It's basal to our environmental problems. It's certainly basal to income disparity, poverty, and the hollowing out of the middle class. If we can't recognize that the rights and welfare of corporations are not, in fact, more important than those of people and prioritize human interest over corporate interest, we are going to see all of our really serious problems intensifying. The degree to which humans are increasingly valued only as corporate consumers is terrifying. We're being spoon-fed entertainment that's really just sort of a burger and a Xanax blended together and all it's really doing is priming us to buy non-essential products and technology that itself is primarily designed to loop us back to the content.

Facebook and Instagram, their whole business model is to be an ad platform. They're in the business of selling ads. But now too they get paid to promote ideas and the manipulation that's taking place that's really dangerous is not a manipulation to get us to buy anything. It's the manipulation literally of how we feel about each other. Russian military intelligence is using these platforms in a concerted effort to foment antagonism within our society to cause chaos and social unrest and to corrode faith in our democratic elections. This sounds like it's out of a James Bond movie, but it's happening. Their agenda is to destabilize us with rage, put us into such a state of information confusion and such anger with each other that we can't function. And it's working.

This is all related to why I love noir films. They don't just acknowledge the shadow in American life—they dig into it. They basically say there are things going on under the surface of what we call the "American narrative" and if we're not paying attention, it will do us harm, really serious harm. Really good noir films hypnotize you. They force you to experience an inability to understand what's happening and yet they don't alienate you because they're sexy. They take you through a portal. There's an aesthetic pleasure of listening to language and watching people, but then slowly they remind you that you really don't know what's going on.

In this country, no matter what anybody tells you, there's dark shit going on and not knowing about it puts us in danger.

DON'T FEAR WORK THAT HAS NO END

SCOTT

From the outside looking in, he was living the dream. Killer SoHo loft. Private jets to exotic locales. Rolex, cover model girlfriend, and cash. Lots of cash.

But 10 years living decadently as an extravagant nightclub promoter in New York City took it's toll.

By 28, Scott Harrison *had become the worst person he knew.*

Utterly lost, mired in a crisis of conscience and desperate to rediscover his sense of purpose, Scott decided it was time for a drastic change. So he left New York City and decamped to West Africa, volunteering as a photojournalist aboard a hospital ship off the coast of Liberia.

During this time, Harrison documented levels of poverty and illness he never knew existed. As one year turned into two, he came to understand that many of the infections and diseases their group treated were waterborne and thus easily prevented if people had access to what should be a basic human right: clean drinking water.

Scott couldn't understand why nobody seemed focused on solving this important problem at scale. So he decided to tackle it himself.

Upon returning to New York in 2006, Scott turned his full attention to the global water crisis and the (then) 1.1 billion people living without access to clean water. The manifestation of that commitment is charity: water—a revolutionary for-purpose endeavor that to date has raised over $450 million to fund an astounding 51,000-plus water projects that deliver clean water to more than 11 million people all across the world.

Along the way, Scott literally reinvented how we give and rejuvenated how we think about giving. He did it by creating an aspirational brand. He did it by restoring public trust in charity. And he did it by leveraging technology to deeply connect each and every giver with the gift's specific result and impact.

Thirst, Scott's *New York Times* bestselling memoir, recounts his redemptive tale of transformation and the twists and turns that built charity: water into one of the most trusted, disruptive, innovative, and admired nonprofits in the world.

One of the most impressive people I have ever met, Scott reminds us that each and every one of us holds the power to positively impact the life of another. And that life is more fulfilling, meaningful, and rewarding when we are persistently engaged in the pursuit of service.

His mantra? *Don't be afraid of work that has no end.*

—Rich

"I think there's a real freedom that comes with service, but so many people are enslaved in the service of themselves."
—Scott Harrison

HARRISON

Scott: At a very young age I went into this caregiver role for my mom. I was a good kid. I was the good Christian who didn't smoke, drink, or cuss, and I played piano in church on Sundays. I played by the rules.

Maybe it was not having the normal fun life. Maybe it was that religion felt a little oppressive to me. But when I moved to high school, little transgressions immediately seemed like a lot of fun.

So, I joined a band, and soon after became a nightclub promoter. It was 10 years of very predictable models, bottles, 45 Clubs, and flying around the world to chase fashion week in Milan, Paris, and London. I went from not doing anything to having problems with nicotine, gambling, pornography, and drugs. It got dark in a hurry.

The whole thing—it sounds so silly now, but it was what I thought was important at the time. More money, more girls, more things. We were selling a dream.

Eventually I realized that there would never be enough of the things I was looking for to satisfy me. There would never be an end to the self-serving sycophantic nature of climbing the social ladder.

It was like a veil had lifted. There was so much sadness and wreckage—the value system was just off. Deeply hungover on a trip, I began to read this piece of deep theology called *The Pursuit of God* by A.W. Tozer. I felt like I was reading the opposite intention of my life. And what would the opposite of a hedonistic, self-serving life look like? A life of serving others, with virtue and purity.

So I went on a drive, not really sure where I was going. I started to pray and talk to God. I got this idea to just explore the opposite of my life in a tangible way. I had this moment where I was staring up at a hospital ship, about to walk up the gangway and sail to Liberia. It was almost this prophetic moment that I could walk away from my old life and leave it on the shore and sail across the ocean to a new adventure.

I worked as a photojournalist that first year in Liberia, and I was moved by the stories of the people that I met and photographed. I put together an exhibition and raised about $100,000 through my photos.

I'd bought a motorcycle and started traveling off the ship into the deep rural areas of Liberia. I saw people drinking dirty water for the first time. I had never seen human beings drink from swamps and having green, infested water crawling with bugs and parasites. Children were drinking water that we wouldn't let our dogs drink.

When I came back, my core vision was to reinvent charity. I wanted more people to have a redemptive experience of giving their time and talent and money. I wanted to invite people to try unselfishness versus selfishness and do that through clean water. I wanted to spread the transformative human experience I'd gone through with others through giving and generosity.

Because one out of every 10 people alive today is drinking bad water. This is a profound concept that I've wrestled with over at charity: water. Now my charity has raised a quarter of a billion dollars and accumulated the largest dataset of rural water supply in the history of the world.

So, know that no one is past redemption, and that there's hope. My favorite quote goes, "Do not be afraid of work that has no end." I look at our mission like that; it will have no end. That is what's truly fulfilling.

"Let's build a culture of giving. Not out of guilt, shame or obligation, but because it's an opportunity to share our blessings with others."
—Scott Harrison

FROM EATING DISORDER
TO OLYMPIC GLORY

We tend to think Olympic athletes live perfect, charmed lives. Genetically gifted, they gracefully inhabit a world beyond mortal challenges—physical specimens oozing talent so rare, it effortlessly skyrockets them onto the global stage.

This is not the experience of any Olympian. And it's certainly not the story of Dotsie Bausch—an Olympic silver medalist with a very human story of struggle and pain that underpins her improbable athletic accomplishments.

A seven-time US National Champion, former world record holder and two-time Pan American gold medal winner in track cycling, Dotsie earned silver in team pursuit at the 2012 London Olympics. Not only was she a long-time vegetarian at that time (now vegan), she was almost 40 years old when she won that medal—the oldest ever in her discipline

and one of the oldest athletes to ever compete in an Olympic Games.

Dotsie's accomplishments are extraordinary. But more remarkable is the hard-fought road this exceptional athlete trudged to achieve such heights. Because Dotsie's greatest achievement isn't athletic. Instead, it's the battle she waged and won to resurrect her life from the depths of an eating disorder so severe, it very nearly claimed her life.

Now retired, Dotsie is a public speaker, mentor to aspiring female professional cyclists, and color commentator for NBC Sports. In addition, she is a lighthouse for women and men around the world in their battle to return to healthy eating as an ambassador for The National Eating Disorders Association.

A staunch advocate for animal rights and the health benefits of plant-based eating for

DOTSIE BAU

SCH

health and performance, Dotsie was appalled by athlete-driven dairy industry campaigns slinging milk as a performance enhancer. So she founded Switch4Good, a nonprofit education platform and community that advocates for the benefits of a dairy-free lifestyle. You might have caught one of Switch4Good's anti- "Got Milk" campaigns, a series of commercials that aired nationally during the closing ceremony of the 2018 Winter Olympic Games. Or the more recent series of national spots that ran on NBC during the *Today* show.

Surprisingly common, disordered eating afflicts close to 30 million Americans and 70 million people worldwide. It's a disease so formidable, it drove Dotsie to a suicide attempt. Her experience as both a sufferer and survivor is as powerful as it is instructive.

My conversation with Dotsie explores the bewildering nature of this often- misunderstood disorder and the process she undertook to rebuild her life—from fashion model to athlete. It's an excavation of her unlikely route to Olympic glory. It's about eating plant-based for performance. And it's about advocacy—what it means to live in service to your ideals.

If you suffer from an eating disorder or know someone who does, Dotsie's words are a lifeline.

Delightful, engaging and strong, the world could use more role models like Dotsie.

—Rich

> *"When you're deep into addiction or disorders, you feel like there's no way out. It's especially true with eating disorders because you have to continue to eat, right? But there is a way out. There is freedom on the other side, and there are many pathways you can choose to have freedom from it."*
>
> **—Dotsie Bausch**

Dotsie: I was in a significant amount of pain in my life after graduating college. I felt confused and afraid, powerless. I had a dysfunctional relationship with myself which transformed into anorexia—it made me feel like I had everything under control.

But the feeling of wanting to be in control slowly turned into a feeling of wanting to disappear. I didn't want anyone looking at me. I didn't want any attention. I didn't want people talking about me or how I looked. I just wanted to be so small that I would dissolve.

I had this moment where I knew that if I kept going, I would die. It was a sobering moment of thinking, so what? How could I do that to the few people I had in my life that really loved and cared for me? Recovery has to come from within, but it doesn't necessarily have to be the first catalyst. My catalyst was my family. It would have been so wildly selfish for me to kill myself, so I accepted I might not get better, but I would to try for them.

I found a therapist, and began accessing my feelings, which I had never done before because that's what you avoid as an addict, right? Whether it's drugs, or an eating disorder, you're doing it so you don't have to feel anything. It took a lot of work until I finally knew I was better, that I would never go back. My therapist recognized that there was a competitor in me and before I finished therapy asked, "What's something you've never done before?" And I said, "What about riding a bike?"

My first bike was a mountain bike, but I got slick tires put on it so I could ride on the street, but I was still bouncing around with the shocks. I began to notice on my rides groups of really fast people would speed by me and I was able to stay with them. Some of the guys I met on those group rides invited me to do the California AIDS ride, and I thought, "I can do that. Something good."

The ride went from San Francisco to LA, and I was at the front with the leading guys, on my mountain bike, with the slick tires. The fourth day in the guys asked me, "Who are you? What are you doing?" Once we finished the race they told me I should do a real race, and get a license with USA Cycling. These guys literally bought my license for me. I tried my first race, and the rest is history.

The suffering that I went through in my eating disorder was just so much more massive than any suffering I could ever experience on a bicycle, and the best part of cycling is knowing the suffering ends, knowing there is a finish line. That ability to dig extremely deep and suffer really hard was cultivated in my eating disorder years and it's what ultimately led me to the Olympics. I brought so much perspective to that experience—I had almost died, and being in the Olympics felt like a complete gift. I couldn't believe that I was even in the realm of possibilities that I could experience in my life.

When you're deep into addiction or disorders, you feel like there's no way out. It's especially true with eating disorders because you have to continue to eat, right? But there is a way out. There is freedom on the other side, and there are many pathways you can choose to have freedom from it.

If you let this disease run its course and you die from it, you're not going to be able to do anything. You're not going to be able to have an impact on the world, you're not going to be able to have an impact for the greater good. Allow that to be your bright, shining light out of this.

There is a way out, and you can do it.

CLARITY IS POWER

What is the relationship between history and biology? What is the essential difference between *Homo sapiens* and other animals? Is there justice in history? Does history have a direction? Did people become happier as history unfolded? What ethical questions do science and technology raise in the 21st century?

These are the queries that compel Yuval Noah Harari—a man unafraid to tackle the biggest questions of our time.

A renowned historian who received his PhD from the University of Oxford in 2002, Yuval is currently a lecturer at the Department of History at the Hebrew University of Jerusalem.

But Yuval is best known as the author of three groundbreaking, massive bestsellers. *Sapiens: A Brief History of Humankind* is a narrative of humanity's creation and evolution—a number-one international hit that explores the ways in which biology and history have defined us and enhanced our understanding of what it means to be "human." A worldwide sensation recommended by Barack Obama, Bill Gates, and Mark Zuckerberg, *Sapiens* has sold over 15 million copies, been translated into nearly 50 languages, was listed on the *Sunday Times* bestseller list for over six months in paperback, and was a *New York Times* top-ten bestseller.

Whereas *Sapiens* peered into our past, *Homo Deus: A Brief History of Tomorrow* tunes Yuval's perspicuity on his estimation of our species' future—specifically our quest to upgrade humans into gods. Within two years of publication, the book has sold in excess of six million copies and been translated into over 50 languages.

Yuval's latest work is *21 Lessons For the 21st Century*, a probing and visionary investigation into today's most urgent issues as we move into the uncharted territory of the future. Here he stops to take the pulse of our current global climate, focusing on the biggest questions of the present moment: What is really happening right now? What are today's greatest challenges and choices? And what should we pay attention to?

I can't adequately express the profound extent to which Yuval's work has impacted my perspective on humanity's past. The bizarre future that will undoubtedly reshape our species. And the unprecedented predicaments we currently face—acute problems that if not adequately solved will harken the end of humanity as we currently understand it.

Yuval's work is defined by his perspicacious ability to see things clearly—at a distance and with a rare objectivity that provides a welcome and much needed expanse to explore big ideas.

It's a clarity he credits to meditation, a ritual he diligently practices two hours daily with an annual 60-day silent retreat.

Over the course of an hour, Yuval graced the podcast with a variety of profound insights on a wide variety of topics, including the plight of humanity should we fail to craft solutions to

YUVAL NOA

the existential threats we face. The problem of
disinformation and distraction. How artificial
intelligence is rapidly reshaping our world. And
why Big Data harkens the end of humanism.

In addition, we explored the implications of
our outdated education system. The importance
of professional flexibility in the age of automation.
Why clarity is the new superpower. And the
practices Yuval relies upon to deploy his
prodigious intellectual acumen.

It was truly an honor to explore humanity's
urgent questions with one of the great minds of
the 21st century.

Also, I made him laugh.

—Rich

H HARARI

Yuval: It's common to say that information is power and knowledge is power because it's been true for much of history. Information used to be scarce and censorship worked by blocking the flow of news. But now we live in a very different age. We are flooded by enormous amounts of information. We have far too much of it and we don't know how to make sense of it. Censorship now works by distracting people with an overflow of irrelevant information. In this age, clarity is more important than ever before because we need to know where to direct our focus. Attention is the scarcest resource of all.

Fake news is not a new problem created by Facebook, Twitter, Putin, or Trump. It's been around since the very beginning of time, and in many ways, it was much worse in the past. What is new is that now we are surrounded by devices designed to hack our brains in a way that was never before possible. Until today nobody could really manipulate us. Yes, we are sentient; yes, we have agency; but something is changing. Back then you were truly a free agent, nobody could look into your brain, nobody could understand your mind, nobody could predict what you were going to do next. This is no longer true. Humans are extremely complicated animals, but they are not infinitely complicated. The devices don't need to know us perfectly. They just need to be better than the average human, and this is not so very difficult because most humans know very little about themselves, their desires, and their minds. If the yardstick is to build an algorithm that knows you better than you know yourself, that's not impossible. We are very close to the point where Amazon or even the Chinese government will be able to create systems that are smarter than most of us.

The only thing that can counter the feelings of a human being is the feelings of another human being. But this is now threatened by a Big Data algorithm. We have the potential to create a system that can predict people's feelings. What happens if you have a system that knows what someone wants better than you do? What happens if the system can predict and understand someone's feelings so well that it starts to manipulate them too? The oracle becomes a smartwatch, and then authority completely shifts from human emotions to technology.

We don't have any idea what human life is going to look like when more and more decisions are taken by algorithms. For thousands of years almost all religious, and political, and artistic traditions depicted life as a drama of decision making. Whether it's a Shakespeare play, a Jane Austen novel, a Hollywood comedy, or a theology book, all of these describe life as a kind of road you are walking, and every few miles you reach an intersection and you need to choose which way to go.

You have small decisions, what to choose for lunch, you have big decisions, whom to marry, whom to vote for, whether to start this career or that career, whether to go to war or to make peace. The whole drama revolves around making the right decision. Now how does life, art, and theology look like when whenever you reach the intersection you just take out your smartphone and say, "Okay Google, what should I do now?"

AI is not even near its full potential. It's just in its infancy. We haven't seen anything yet. Every 10 years you are likely to lose your job or your job is going to be completely transformed by the new wave of the latest machine learning wizardry. If you want to stay in the game, you will have to reinvent yourself, not just once, but repeatedly. You might need to reinvent yourself five or six times during your lifetime. The idea of having a profession for life is going to be completely obsolete.

The human mind is a factory for generating fictional stories about yourself, about your family, about your country, about the world. It's so difficult to tell the difference between the stories we invent and objective reality. This is why meditation is the most important thing anybody has ever taught me in my life. Without meditation, I couldn't have survived these last few years. Without the peace of mind that meditation brings I simply couldn't have done it. Meditation brings such powerful clarity and focus and acceptance. It gives me the ability to see reality as it is, and to tell the difference between what is really happening and what is not. The truth of reality versus stories generated by the mind—this is the one thing that algorithms are not even close to telling you.

"The most important thing about living in the 21st century is realizing that we are hackable animals."
—Yuval Noah Harari

RUSSELL

THE AWAKENING

Every podcaster has their dream list—guests they fantasize interviewing. From day one, Russell Brand occupied my top slot.

Our conversation exceeded my expectations, and birthed a friendship.

Officially, Russell is one of the most recognizable and best-loved comedy performers in the world. He's also a phenomenally successful actor, columnist, political commentator, mental health and drug rehabilitation activist, and author with a series of global bestsellers to his name.

Now a devoted dad and husband, when he isn't writing, touring or performing, Russell can be found hosting his wildly popular podcast *Under the Skin* where he probes a diversity of thinkers from Eckhart Tolle to Brené Brown.

Unofficially, Russell is iconic for his very public awakening. A recovering heroin addict, his struggles with drugs, sex, fame, money, and power were custom tailored for tabloid fodder. And his satirical but always probing takes on politics, celebrity culture, and religion often find him in the crosshairs of controversy.

I think of Russell as a hyper-intelligent master of modern discourse and disputation. Perpetually armed with a most delicious turn-of-phrase, he is a philosopher of the extreme. A verbal gymnast who has voyaged to the brink of overindulgence, he has returned to share the unique personal wisdom gleaned from such surfeit with razor-sharp musings on the broader humanity we collectively share—and have a laugh along the path.

With a sui generis brew of eccentric wit, subversive candor, and extreme charm, Russell grapples fearlessly and out loud with, as he describes it, that which lays beneath the surface. With the ideas that define our time. Of the history we are told. And the ulterior truth behind our constructed reality.

What is truly real? How can we craft a more fair and just society for all? How can we live a more intentional life of meaning? What does it mean be a spiritual being in a human existence?

A magical, modern-day mystic, Russell invites us all to voyage beyond the walls of our constructed dimension and, to borrow his phrase, *lick the walls of the hologram.*

—Rich

"We've been taught that freedom is to pursue our desires, but true freedom is freedom from our desires."

—Russell Brand

BRAND

Russell: Fame is an abstraction. It's like someone else's conception of me, so I try not to be involved with it because I'm too greedy. It always leads me somewhere bad. Looking at the comments always leads me somewhere bad. Caring and comparing myself to other people always leads me somewhere bad. I'm living in Los Angeles. I don't have to look very far to see people that are more successful, more famous, better looking than me.

I believe that the way to liberate myself from the belief that I can only be happy if I get what I want is to be of service. My relationships with other people are opportunities to be of service. They're not opportunities to be served. This is what I have to maintain.

I was blessed to receive a hug from the Hindu spiritual guru Amma. She is known as the hugging saint by her followers. After you get a mantra and a hug from her, one of her brahman reminds you of the mantra in case you didn't notice it in the giddy bliss of the hug. When the brahman gave me the mantra, he said, "The material world has nothing else to give you now, Russell. The material world can only take from you." It made my stomach pull in.

It's been a blessing because it means I don't need to go through life needing. I don't need approval or a pat on the back, I don't need material things like automobiles and toys. There's nothing to get from anyone. I tell myself, relationship to relationship, exchange to exchange, "you're not in this car to get something from this driver. You're not going on Rich Roll's podcast to get something from Rich." I have to continually remind myself of this. We've been taught that freedom is to pursue our desires, but true freedom is freedom from our desires.

My deepest belief is that people are all the same. The fact that we are individuals is an attractive argument because we really do seem like we are single beings wrapped in bags of skin. It's hard to imagine that it is perhaps more we are one, that the consciousness that you experience

and the consciousness that I experience, and the consciousness of all of us are experiencing is the same phenomena merely disrupted by more superficial apparel. We're the same, we are one. We don't need to concern ourselves with autonomy. We just need to open ourselves to, in my language, God, and we'll be laughing.

I spoke to the physicist Brian Cox, who doesn't think there's a God. He thinks that everything can be understood rationally. Rationalism is bloody good to understand engineering, good to understand materials, good to understand science and to organize things but to allow it to become the preeminent philosophical perspective is dangerous because it excludes the unknowable. The unknowable is almost everything.

I tried to say, "Look, when people said the earth was flat, they actually thought it. When people thought that the sun went down and up, they actually thought it." We keep discovering deeper and deeper truths. We don't know what we don't know.

There are limitations to what we can see and hear because of the limits of the instruments for which we receive information. If space is infinite, if knowledge is infinite, if wisdom is infinite then beingness itself is infinite. Perhaps society is organized in the manner that it is because not enough people have a scent of the sacred and divine.

Thank God I'm a comedian. I know it's all ridiculous. Life is ridiculous. It's funny to me. I suppose if I can bring anything to this world, into this conversation, let it be that none of us are ever going to be fulfilled by trying to augment our identities and acquire material and status attainment through one another. The thing I think I can contribute is sincerity and humor. This life is so ridiculous. This life is so stupid. This is happening in limitless space. Don't take it too seriously.

A MOVEMENT OF AWAKENING
BY RUSSELL BRAND

Rich Roll's Calabasas ranch, out there in the red oblivion, splits the nothingness like a Hockney painting. A sudden modern building, beautiful partner making inconceivable vegan cheese, glorious children and spiritual fetishes illuminate the cubist space. Then there is Rich himself, the lithe and lovely athlete rishi; kind and contemplative, a conversational facilitator, a space holder.

As well as being a guest on his impeccable podcast, I once had a chat onstage with Rich in Nantucket on the brink of Ahab's ocean for an audience of "influencers." I came off stage after a hoot with RR into the welcome company of Malcolm X's daughter, Ilyasah Shabazz, and Nelson Mandela's grandson, Ndaba Mandela. I only attended the event because of a call from this book's hero and before I knew it my life was suddenly all white whales and Black activism. This man may be a great connecter, a necessary participant in the movement of awakening.

Like all territory the online domain is now primarily possessed by powerful interests but still it can be a space for connection and important conversation, for collaboration, and for the development of ideas that directly oppose the corporatism and commercialism of the internet's silicon leviathans. Through Rich I met John McAvoy, an Ironman athlete who only learned that he was the world's best marathon rower when burning calories in the gym in the UK's most hardcore high security prison, Belmarsh. Rich introduced me to John, the bank robber and career criminal turned saintly triathlete, and he is as good an example as any of the potential for metamorphosis that can occur when good ideas are received. In each of us there are unlived lives, unexplored universes waiting to be inhabited. Are the communities and relationships that grow around podcasts like Rich's, with their global reach and unimpeded good intention, a way in which more people can experience profound change comparable to John McAvoy's?

A friend of mine said if Jesus came back today, he'd have a podcast, which after I'd moved past my own tendency to search for confirmation that I am the risen messiah makes a kind of sense. It is a medium where we are unshackled from the oppressive and corporatized grammar of mainstream media, where we have a genuine opportunity for dialogue between increasingly polarized communities. Of course, podcasts play a part in further cementing the distinct emergent cultural enclaves that come with the capacity we now have for communication. Certainly, spending two hours listening to Eckhart Tolle unravelling the baffling mesh that stifles modern spirituality makes you think the Prince of Peace could have a podcast. Eckhart explained the complex breakdown and renewal process that the world is currently experiencing as being the consequence of institutions built on egoic principles.

Increasingly I feel that our material reality is a superficial breach, the tip of a submerged, all-encompassing oneness. That indeed we do live within systems predicated on individual need, the culmination of un-evolved primal impulses. Our greed, fear, lust, and shame underwrite the architecture of our theatrical politics and our numbing media. We have lost our collective medicine. We have lost our individual connection. Whilst this time often seems defined by a diffuse and entropic nihilism, I believe we are governed by clear yet concealed ideals, concealed perhaps because of our own unconsciousness, but also because the ideology of capitalism, particularly in its "late" and artificially sustained form, is no longer clear or explicit. On the one hand we have truly intercommunicative global society; on the other we have disparate and localized worlds, parochial to the point of solipsism.

The pandemic has provided a time for contemplation, a holy time of reflection (con-templ-ation, it has a temple in it) but we appear to be emerging from this more polarized than ever. The noble intention to end police brutality seems to be leading to further fragmentation. Generations reared on nationalism and exceptionalism are being asked to discard the ideas that they were fed to rally them into compliance and sometimes violence overnight. In a way it's bloody obvious that trying to make a planet function as a single economic entity for the benefit of an elite will lead to apocalypse. As obvious as the inability of a finite set of physical resources to go on generating infinite growth. The pandemic created a microbial medical emergency and an imaginary economic one. The fact that we are willing to prioritized the latter over the former demonstrates the power of our collective imagination.

How are we to give birth to a new order when the statues have been pulled down and the old ideas erased? How are we to construct a new, evolved way of organizing and flourishing? And what role will be played by conversations like the ones midwifed by Rich?

My hope is simple, that the way that the internet provided a global platform for endless voices (causing in some cases consolidation and in others fragmentation) that we will recognize that we can no longer centralize political and economic power. That

while we are all connected, all have the same basic wants and needs, it is impossible for us to have freedom as individuals or communities as long as power is aggregated through powerful institutions and hierarchies. Gandhi dear beloved, obstinate, mad Gandhi said, "There is no point getting rid of the British then emulating the structures and subjugation that they imposed but with Indians in the dominant positions." He continued, "India is a country of 70,000 villages, each of them should be fully autonomous, trading only where necessary, self-sufficient when possible." He added, "We must end our obsession with gadgets and trinkets." This he wrote in the 1940s, and approaching a century later our fetishization of objects has reached fanatical levels.

We are consumers above all else. In fact, the production of the devices that facilitate our access to podcasts and endless connection and entertainment come at the expense of the freedom of workers, in some cases child workers, throughout the developing world. Put simply to make an iPhone affordable you have to have component parts mined by children. The fact is, capitalism has now provided us with the instruments to overthrow it. My hope is that

will not be to toy with some globalist solution but rather to create more democracy, equality, and ecological responsibility. I believe this can only occur in communities that mimic our indigenous condition: small self-sufficient communities. If we fling off the parasite of consumerism that rides on our backs and lives in our minds, then it is possible to reimagine society entirely. For this to happen we need to keep talking and keep listening (not at the same time, that would be mental, a cacophonous ordeal). We can engage in a global conversation to share the information, resources and new de-centralized institutions that reflect our diverse needs and beliefs, as well as our underlying, universal connection.

"No matter the risks we take, we always consider the end to be too soon, even though in life, more than anything else, quality should be more important than quantity."

—Alex Honnold

ALEX HONNOLD

THE FREE SOUL OF FREE SOLO CLIMBING ON FEAR, RISK, MINDSET, AND WHAT IT MEANS TO BE TRULY ALIVE

Envision climbing the storied 3,600-foot sheer vertical rock face known as El Capitan. The trick? You have to do it without any ropes, harnesses, or any protective gear whatsoever.

Just imagining it makes me quiver.

Unthinkably impossible, even the tiniest mistake or unexpected intervening variable could cost you your life—a life that hinges moment to moment upon otherworldly preparation, meticulous focus, and a preternatural relationship with fear.

And yet this grand achievement is but one aspect of the life of Alex Honnold, a renowned professional adventure rock climber, avid environmentalist, and philanthropist whose audacious free-solo ascents of America's biggest cliffs have made him one of the most masterful and compelling athletes of our time.

A global icon of athletic mastery, the lore of Alex Honnold truly transcends sport. His astonishing El Capitan feat, breathtakingly captured in the awe-inspiring documentary *Free Solo*, enraptured audiences around the world—and landed the film an Oscar for Best Documentary Feature of 2018.

I imagine most of you are familiar with Alex. With palms sweaty and jaw agape, you were riveted by the documentary, or by one of his many stunning climbing videos. Perhaps you saw him profiled on 60 Minutes, or read profiles about him in the *New York Times*, *National Geographic*, or *Outside* and, like me, were left to wonder:

How does that guy do what he does? And more importantly, why?

The answer isn't as elementary as you might imagine. It can't be reduced to simple genetics, strength, drive, or even his most unusual relationship with fear.

I think the answer is far more complex and, frankly, much more interesting. Of course, fanatical preparation plays a role. As does his fidelity to incremental progression. And his unique kinship with risk.

But I think what truly sets Alex apart is a profound and unbridled sense of awe and wonder. An uncanny facility to meld his body and mind with his spirit. And the ability to become absolutely one with his quest.

Inarguably, what Alex does is both staggering and astonishing. But it's who he is that I find most impressive.

We can all learn from Alex's commitment to personal truth. His earnest curiosity. His minimalist lifestyle and passion for environmental conservation. And, perhaps most of all, his principled and selfless allegiance to leveraging his success for the greater good.

—*Rich*

Alex: If your foot slips off a hold at the crux—the most difficult section of El Cap, you would fall 2,500 feet. Falling 250 feet alone would kill you. But the crux also has some low angle terrain beneath it, so if you fell you might also hit this sloping ledge 60 or 80 feet below you and then shoot out and land on El Cap Spire. Or you would miss them both, still alive as you free fall to the ground.

I know there is danger in what I do, I've accepted it. Most people think it's super risky, but it's actually just high-consequence. If I slipped I would for sure die—I free solo giant walls. But it's not necessarily risky, because the risk is actually the likelihood of me falling off, and you can't determine that from seeing a picture or seeing a video. Only I know how solid I am on the wall; how likely I am to fall off it or not.

When was the last time you thought about your mortality? Or made choices that could potentially lead to death? The average person avoids these kinds of thoughts and decisions. But the way I see it, it shouldn't be that uncomfortable because we're all going to die. It's part of being an animal.

My father's passing gave me a sense of urgency. It reminded me that life is finite and that you have to do the things in life you are called to do. So I dropped everything and pursued climbing. I took a semester off from college and never went back. When you're on the right path, it feels like you're not following a path at all. I was living in a car, living in tents, climbing a lot. It didn't feel meaningful until many years later when I looked back and realized just how committed I was to rock climbing.

There is no secret to free-soloing El Capitan—just 20 years of hard work. I knew all the holds that mattered. I still know almost everything about it. I thought about it and imagined it for so many years. It took me eight years to just wrap my brain around it, to really believe it was possible.

I've never meditated and I don't know mindfulness techniques, but when I visualized routes, I'd just let my mind wander. So for the harder parts of the climb, I'd think my way through certain sequences. Then I'd imagine what it'll feel like. I'd daydream and think about how happy I'd be when I grabbed the final hold, how amazing it would be to get onto the summit.

I just knew I was ready. My shoes were perfectly broken in. I was strong, I was confident, I had perfected everything. I'd spent all my years of climbing looking at El Cap as the ultimate objective, the pinnacle of rock climbing, and I just knew I could do it and I felt obligated to try.

What goal is most important to you? What are you willing to put in the work for? To me, it was El Cap. Free-soloing it was something that was extremely important to me. It was something I had to do in my lifetime and I was willing to put in the work for it. The moment when I realized that I had done all the work that I needed to do, I felt ready. I had put in the effort that was needed, therefore being able to do it naturally followed.

There is no life hack to mastery. If it was easy to do, then everyone would do it. So whatever challenge you want to do, break it down into steps. Layout your work. And keep making progress.

"What is the thing that's worth it to you? What is the work you need to put into that?"
—Alex Honnold

> *"True behavior change is really identity change."*
> **—James Clear**

JAMES

HABITS ARE THE COMPOUND INTEREST OF SELF-IMPROVEMENT

What stands in the way of becoming the person you aspire to be?

Maybe it's circumstances. Access or opportunity. For many its bad habits, exacerbated by the unsuccessful war waged to replace them with good habits—a rinse-and-repeat process that generally leads to failure and discouragement.

Why is it so hard to overcome negative patterns?

The problem isn't you. The problem is your system.

Evolving from stuck and unsatisfied into the person you wish to become is equal parts art and science. Science helps explain the root causes of our behaviors and how to modify them. But the application of said principles into practice is very much an art.

James Clear is a man who has spent the better part of his career attempting to understand and master this blend of art and science to improve human habit formation and decision-making.

A regular speaker at Fortune 500 companies, James's work is used by teams in the NFL, NBA, and MLB. He has been featured in the *New York Times, Entrepreneur, Time,* and on *CBS This Morning.* His website receives millions of visitors each month.

Hundreds of thousands subscribe to his popular newsletter. And over 10,000 leaders, managers, coaches, and teachers have built better habits in life and work via his Habits Academy online program.

The culmination of James's evidence-based quest to understand self-improvement is *Atomic Habits,* his sensational *New York Times* bestselling deep dive into what actually works when it comes to behavior modification, and the transformative power of making small changes. Packed with implementable takeaways—including many strategies I have myself employed with great success—it's a must-read for anyone looking to take their life to the next level.

One of my most popular podcasts of 2018, my conversation with James explores the psychology and neuroscience behind behavior change. We discuss the relationship between overly ambitious goals and failure. And why most people make the mistake of optimizing for the finish line when we should instead focus on getting to the starting line.

Bottom line: establishing systems is critical. And focus should always be placed on practice over performance.

Emotional drivers like motivation capture our attention. But they are temporal. The key is breaking reliance on such unpredictable impulses and invest instead in practical actions.

In other words, you're more likely to act yourself into feeling rather than feel yourself into action.

Or, as I like to say, *mood follows action.*

But if you want to really move the needle, stop obsessing on goals and instead put focus on identity.

It sounds counter-intuitive but the research is clear. Long-term results are best derived not from achieving the goals we set for ourselves, but instead by slowly adopting and imitating the daily practices and characteristics of the person we aspire to become.

May James's game-changing insights reframe how you contemplate identity. Set in motion a better method for achieving your ambitions. And create the ultimate roadmap for becoming the person you aspire to be.

—Rich

CLEAR

James: A habit is a behavior that has been repeated enough times to be performed more or less automatically. But the way I like to think about it is: As you go through life, you face different problems, and some of those problems are big and some of them are small. As you come across solutions to the recurring problems, you start to automate them. So every morning, you wake up and you put your shoes on and you've got this little problem that you need to solve: tying your shoes. Pretty soon after you tie your shoes a hundred times or five hundred times or a thousand times, you can do it on autopilot.

You don't necessarily have to rely on a single habit to solve a recurring problem. If you come home from work each day and you feel stressed and exhausted, you might play video games for an hour and that's one way to resolve that problem. You get in the habit of doing it and picking up your controller without even thinking about it. Another person might go for a run for 20 minutes or meditate for 10 minutes. A third person might smoke a cigarette. These are just different solutions to problems we all face. But your original habit is not necessarily the optimal one.

Habits are also defined as behaviors that follow your prediction of interpretation of how you should act in a given context. For example, one person might see their couch as the place where they read for an hour each night. So their interpretation of seeing a couch is, "I should open up a book." For another person, they might see the couch as the place where they turn on Netflix for an hour and eat a bowl of ice cream. That's a different interpretation of the same physical cue. In that way, habits follow. They're this lagging measure of how you predict you should respond to the different contexts in your life. Outcomes are just the manifestation of the behaviors that preceded them. For example, your weight is just a lagging measure of your eating habits. Your bank account is a lagging measure of your financial habits.

Your clutter is a lagging measure of your cleaning habits. You get what you repeat.

In a sense, you could say that every behavior is driven by the desire for a change in state. When you smoke a cigarette or eat a bag of Doritos or pick up your phone, what you really want isn't the nicotine or the calories or the likes on social media. What you want is to feel less anxious or to feel validated. You didn't come out of the womb with a desire to check Instagram—there's nothing evolutionarily wired there. It's just a modern manifestation of an ancient desire to gain respect and approval.

Your habits are also the way that you embody a particular identity. So every morning that you make your bed, you embody the identity of an organized person. Every time you go to the gym, you embody the identity of someone who is fit. In that sense, every action you take is like a vote for the type of person that you believe you are. As you take these actions, you build up evidence of a particular identity.

True behavior change is really an identity change. Don't make it your goal to run a marathon, make it your goal to become a runner. Don't make it your goal to write a book, aim to be a writer. Once you identify as a certain type of person, you're not pursuing behavior change anymore. You're just acting in alignment with the type of person that you believe you are. It's one thing to say, "I want this." It's something radically different to say, "I am this."

One way to break bad habits is through a strategy I call environmental design. The idea is just to restructure your physical environment to make the cues of your good habits obvious and the cues of your bad habits invisible. In many cases, the behaviors that are attractive to us are dependent on the people that we are around. We are all members of tribes. Some of the tribes are big, some of them are small. Big ones might be what it means to be American, or what it means to be French or something like that. And small ones could be what it means to be a neighbor on your street, or a member of a CrossFit gym, or a volunteer at your local high school.

All of these tribes, large and small, have a set of shared expectations for what it means to be part of the group. When you want to fit in with a certain community, you adopt habits that align with the shared expectations of those people. Habits that go against the grain of shared expectations are very unattractive, so one of the ways to make habits more attractive to yourself is to join a group where your desired behavior is normal behavior. Be with a crew where the habits that you want to embody are the standard.

You have to be willing to experiment with your life. You can use science to inform your strategy—it's a good way to make educated guesses and nudge yourself in the right direction. But ultimately you have to be willing to perform these n-of-1 trials to see if a habit is right or wrong for you. This can be frustrating for people because they just want to be handed a book that gives them all the answers. I tried to write that book for habits. But the truth is you need to be willing to run these personal experiments to figure out who you are and who you want to be.

Start off by finding a way to get 1% better every day. It doesn't need to be something radical or huge. The difference between studying Spanish for an hour tonight and not studying at all seems like nothing because regardless, you won't have mastered the language. The difference between eating a salad versus eating a burger and fries seems like nothing because the scale is the same at the end of the night. It's only when your habits have compounded over two or five or 10 years that the impact of those small choices becomes fully apparent.

JULIE PIATT

WE ARE SPIRITUAL BEINGS IN A HUMAN EXPERIENCE

The woman who goes by Sr Mati has lived a life.

Reared in Alaska by a taciturn Texan bush pilot and an elegant Chilean matriarch (think *Green Acres*), Julie Piatt grew up the youngest of five. Often left to fend for herself, it was a childhood imprinted with nature's impossible majesty. Glaciers that extend as far as the eye can see. Solo forest hikes with only a tin can rattle to fend off the bears. And rickety, single-engine seaplane excursions with dad, lost on remote lakes untouched by civilization.

But the anarchic, Wild West sensibility that defined Anchorage in the late 1970s also left a mark. Relatively lawless, it was a town where the mayor and the madam would unapologetically cavort in public. Where money and drugs flowed, courtesy of the roughneck powered Trans-Alaska Pipeline. And a place where high school students clubbing with their teachers was normal.

An education in the polarity of light and dark, Alaska sculpted Julie into a warrior of the wilderness—and a woman equally adept at navigating the street and the boardroom.

Thawing her bone chill in the desert bake of Arizona State University, upon college graduation Julie decamped for destiny in Los Angeles. Initially making a name for herself as a fashion designer— Julie Piatt Collection once adorned racks from Nordstrom to Neiman's—her creative aperture would soon expand to interior design, painting, sculpture, music, cuisine, writing, and other parts unknown, led only by her inner muse.

For an artist like SriMati, everything is art—and the world her canvas. And yet Julie, ever-defiant, would bristle at the restriction. When asked about herself, she's most likely to respond, *I'm a multi-dimensional being having a human experience.*

Formally, Julie is an accomplished yogi and healer. She's a recording artist with two albums to her name and a mom to four children. A podcaster herself, she hosts *For the Life of Me*. And she is master of *Water Tiger*, her online spiritual community where she muses on all matters metaphysical and divine.

In addition, Julie is the author of three perennially bestselling vegan cookbooks: *The Plantpower Way*, *The Plantpower Way: Italia*, and *This Cheese is Nuts*. A doyenne of all things non-dairy, she is also the founder and CEO of the artisanal plant-based cheese company SriMu, a direct-to-consumer line of next-evolution plant-based delights.

Oh yeah, she's also my wife.

Over the two decades of our relationship, I have met and overcome many obstacles to become the author, podcaster, athlete, husband, and parent I am today.

The young man I once was now unrecognizable, every aspect of my transformation—physical, financial, professional, mental, emotional, and, most importantly, spiritual—is attributable to Julie. A strong and ethereal being, she has always been able to see through the character defects, emotional baggage, and imprinted patterns of my youth. Taking my hand, she helped me believe in the best version of myself lurking within. And it is only by dint of her guidance that I was able to surface a more authentic expression of who I truly am.

I stand today a product of Julie's unconditional love and spiritual mentorship. Her extraordinary patience, clarity of purpose, and convicted belief in me, and in humanity at large.

A constant presence on the podcast, over the years Julie has expounded wisely on a myriad of subjects from plant-based cuisine to unschooling. We've walked you through our marriage relationship, parenting philosophy, and even our financial collapse. In between, we've covered it all: creativity, devotion, communication, gratitude, authenticity, risk, balance, surrender, personal sovereignty, faith, community, and the importance of ceremony.

My intention in sharing the wisdom of Sr Mati is simple: that you enjoy an imprint of what I have been privileged to experience. And that your life be similarly, positively impacted by her presence. Because, as SriMati is fond of repeating, *the divine in me bows to the divine in you.*

—Rich

"Transformation is not for the weak at heart. It is the warrior path."
—Julie Piatt

THERE IS ONLY ONE OF YOU IN THE ENTIRE MULTIVERSE

Understand that we are living a collective experience of life that contains billions of entirely *unique* life forms. There is not another one of you in the entire Universe or anywhere in creation. This means that if you don't fully realize your life potential—what I call your *unique life print*—no one else will actualize it for you. As a consequence, the life form that is "you" will never be fully realized unless you embody it yourself.

NO ONE IS COMING TO SAVE YOU

We have been trained to believe in powers outside ourselves that promise redemption in some future time-space where we will receive deliverance by a chosen verified "holy" one who can solve all the problems of the world along with our own. But in truth, no one can perform your evolution for you. We are born alone and we die alone—and the life experience you came here for is about you and your relationship to it. We are all *potentially* divine humans, all co-creators fully equipped and designed by nature to fulfill our missions. No life form is more or less valued in the eyes of creation. The sun is shining on all of us without edit or discrimination. Can you feel it?

THERE IS NO CONSENSUS IN CREATION

It is curious that we tend to seek consensus regarding the "right" way to live, do and be via intellectual analysis. The result is "group think" opinions that rotate in and out of the narrative pole position regarding what we collectively consider to be the "best" approach to varying aspects of life. Inevitably, after some years, months, or even weeks, the very concrete ideology that informed previous popular thought will shift to the next new "best" opinion. What was previously gospel suddenly collapses, and we migrate to a new position.

There is a phrase in Vedic teachings that the universal reply to every query of "What is right or wrong?" is "For whom and when?" This prescription speaks to the wisdom that recognizes the vast array of colors in creation and the futility of agendas vying for consensus. The true health and vitality of life is found in its diversity. It's the many perspectives and experiences that make life vibrant and thriving. The deeper realization of this awareness is that there is nothing inherently wrong or lacking within you.

YOU ARE A DIVINE LIFE FORM

How can you experience yourself as divine life form if you spend your life drowning in guilt, insecurity and unworthiness? Begin by receiving yourself with unconditional love and acceptance. Let go of the shame and self-judgement. The fact that you are alive at all is an absolute miracle. All experiences from the past have led you to where you are today. You are already enough. You have all that you need to fulfill the life existing inside of you. You need only command it for it to come to fruition.

When you finally understand your inherent sacredness and stop comparing yourself to others, you will experience an opening followed by a relaxation of internal tension and self-judgment. A master of mine described this tension as even having an unpleasant odor. Now you can finally begin the journey of cultivating self-love. Yogic practices of meditation, asana, mirror gazing, Ayurvedic nourishment, and Abhyanga, a form of nurturing self oil-massage and living in harmony with the natural life cycles, are practices that provide shelter from the storm and lead you into greater levels of relationship with yourself. Eating organic living whole foods as much as possible connect you with the sacred desires inside your own heart. As you love yourself more and more, you are in turn able to love others and meaningfully contribute.

"The most important relationship in your life is between you and consciousness."
—Julie Piatt

"Even if no one else believes in you, I believe in you to find your way into realizing your greatest life mission. How could it be otherwise? For you are a divine emanation of God!"

—Julie Piatt

DEDICATE YOUR LIFE TO WHO YOU ARE

As you continue to push past your perspective boundaries, you will begin to discover deeper personal truths and life capabilities. We are fractals of existence, each of us containing the Universe within. This means that you literally have it all! Life is about evolution. It will always present a myriad of experiences designed for your growth. Like a ripple effect, as you access greater levels of self-connection, you in turn begin to bless everything in creation. It's a spontaneous arising rather than a conceived directive. What a blessing of life, to be able to explore yourself as a beloved and unique life form and in so doing, bless everything and everyone around you.
Life is beautiful!

TRANSFORM YOUR SHADOWS INTO TREASURES

When we incarnate on Earth, we take on layers of ancestral trauma. This is part of the collective human experience. Our lives then provide the necessary trials and tests to evolve out of these lower vibrating energies and experiences. Our cultural overlay is one of quantifying life experiences as either "good" or "bad." When we buy into this narrative, we then relentlessly seek only the pleasing aspects of life. How we judge our experiences become the barometer of our value. Yet, in truth, all experiences are divine. And most often, we gain the greatest evolution and expansion from our darkest moments. If you are truly blessed in your life, you will experience at least one "sacred moment" that brings you to your knees with no other option but to deepen reverence for life itself.

TAKE RESPONSIBILITY FOR YOUR EVOLUTION

This may be the most transformative act one can take to truly evolve and contribute to the collective experience of creating a more meaningful world. Stand up and take your post. The time is now. If not you, then who? If not now, when? You are the one you've been waiting for.

CALL OUT YOUR TRAUMAS TO REWRITE YOUR STORY

It's important to face our darkest experiences. To create a safe space to confront and call out our pain. We all have an inner child that needs to be held and comforted. This is essential to claiming our power. But if we want to truly transform, we can't remain quivering under our bedsheets. After some dedicated time spent consoling our little child—along with a lifetime commitment to put them first in our care—we must call upon the greater being within in order to step into our sacred power. By expanding our perspective with reverence for all our experiences, both light and dark, all events are understood to be divine. From this higher vantage point, we transform from victim into powerful creator.

PERSPECTIVE IS YOUR SUPERPOWER

As Universal creators, it is within our power to choose a divine perspective in every experience. All events are neutral until colored by perspective. What life are you creating? One of lack ? Or one of expansion? You are the master artist. Choose wisely. When you envision yourself as the architect of your own life, you begin to freely express your unique nature. Give yourself that permission and live with everything you've got.

YOUR JOURNEY IS UNIQUE TO YOU ALONE

Your path is yours and yours only. Gather inspiration and courage from your friends and community, but in the end it's all on you. No one else can realize your mission. When you lay your head down on your pillow at night, let it be your life you lived. Let this effect expand into every moment of your life. Live it with each breath.

MEANING DERIVES FROM SHARING OUR GIFTS

Uncovering the many layers of my own life form has been an ongoing process of self-discovery. The more I drop what I think I know and instead feel into life, the greater awareness I develop. And the more I grow and expand. We are all required in this life experience. It is a great privilege to be alive during this time on planet Earth. We are in the VIP seats and this transformation is what we signed up for. I'm honored to share this path with so many amazing humans.

Please be more of who you are. Because all of us came here to play our part in the grand symphony of life. And because all are divine. You are valued, you are needed, you are loved.

IN-Q

INQUIRE WITHIN

As we endeavor to mindfully navigate the perils of the world, may we find some sliver of grace. May we reckon with our privilege. Choose beauty and curiosity over rigidity. Compassion and fullness of heart over closedmindedness. And social connection over isolation.

Difficult times across history have always resulted in explosions of creative expression: Art as a means of better understanding our shared human condition.

Few people embody this ethos more thoroughly than Adam Schmalholz, one of my very favorite people breathing air on planet Earth.

Generous, present and deeply curious, he goes by the moniker IN-Q.

A National Poetry Slam Champion, award-winning poet, spoken word artist, and multi-platinum songwriter, IN-Q has shared the stage with everyone from Barack Obama to Eminem. Named to Oprah's SuperSoul 100 list of the world's most influential thought leaders, he's the first spoken word artist to perform with Cirque Du Soleil and has been featured on A&E, ESPN, and HBO.

Inspiring audiences around the world through his live performances and amazing storytelling workshops, IN-Q's poetry videos have a habit of going viral, clocking over 70 million views and counting.

IN-Q crafts verse that not only entertains, but challenges listeners to take a deep look inward to consider their place in the world, their impact on the environment, and to recognize the threads of loss, forgiveness, transformation, and belief that are woven into all of our lives.

His most recent creation is *Inquire Within*, a wholly original, deeply authentic, and inspiring book of poetry and musings that takes the reader on a journey directly to the center of the soul.

It's been my honor to share IN-Q's story and unique gifts on four podcast occasions, including an epic stage performance at my live event in Los Angeles.

Shining a light on the shared human condition, IN-Q provides a dynamic lens through which to think about ourselves and the world—something we need now more than ever.

It's my turn to shine a light on him.

Provocative, entertaining, and refreshingly honest, may IN-Q's presence, wisdom, experience, and poetry help you reimagine your truth.

—Rich

FATHER TIME
BY IN-Q

I'm staring at the number wondering if I should call. I can hear the tick-tock from the clock on the wall as it meshes with the thump-thump beat of my heart, sometimes getting something started is the hardest part. I didn't meet my dad until I was 15. I'd seen his photograph, but his image was sickening. A coward with a dick, but no balls to back it up. See when he left me as a kid, I had cause for acting up. The funny thing about hate is the person you hate doesn't feel that hate. You feel that hate, but wait, the weight can be too much for a person to take and personally, I was hurt so I just locked it away.

I was angry all the time and I didn't know why. I couldn't handle my own rage, so I would hide it inside. Pretending everything was fine, became a daily pass time. Time passed and I started to believe in my own lies. I took it out on my mom because she raised me alone. The rage that I couldn't own had left me totally numb. It was like landmines in my mind that I didn't understand. So when the boy inside cried, the young man outside, yelled.

I think I learned about my masculinity from TV. The people weren't real, so I knew they couldn't leave me. I would sit there for hours right in front of the tube, the images that I saw were my depiction of truth. It was manhood in a box and I bought into it. The censorship of anything inside of me that's sensitive, the sentence is a lifetime of tears suppressed in a stone face, an overblown ego they've distracted through a paper chase.

Back when I was nine I imagined in my mind that my father was a spy working for the FBI, and that's why he couldn't stop by, write or drop a line. He was off saving our lives from the bad guys, but that was just a lie that I used to get by so that you wouldn't see the tears welling up in my eyes. When you're rejected by the person that you're created by, you secretly feel like you don't have a right to your life. I thought if I confronted him and it would make it alright, but since I couldn't forgive him it just recycled my spite.

I remember meeting him for the first time. Every time a person passed by, I would ask, "Mom, is that him? I look a little like him, right? No? Oh. What about that guy?" And that was what it was like to meet the man that gave me my life. To shake his hand and look into his eyes. We talked till he apologized then said our goodbyes. I walked away on my own. Then I began to cry. Now for years after that I acted like it was all resolved. I told him what I thought so I figured, "Problem solved," but it just re-evolved. My insecurities were eating at my mental health. I took it out on the world because I hated myself.

That's when I finally decided I needed some help. I opened up. I started writing and sharing about my past. I got honest with myself and I started chipping at my mask. I looked into the mirror and confronted what I saw, accepting the reflection by embracing every flaw. Then directing the connection into breaking down the walls by reflecting the perfection of the God inside us

all. I stopped focusing on everything that I had been hateful for and started focusing on everything that I could be grateful for. And personally, there is a lot I can be thankful for.

If pain is dragging you down, just cut the ankle cord. That's when the weight lifted and I really started living. That's when my hate shifted and I really started giving. It's when my fate twisted. It was like an ego exorcism. Your mind-state can be the most powerful of prisons.

My father never played catch with me or gave advice, but if nothing else, that man gave me my life and that's enough for me if that is all he could ever give, because I'm appreciative for every day I get to live. And even though I don't need my dad to validate me, I thought that I should write this poem to thank him for

creating me because every moment that we are alive is like a gift. And if that's not enough to forgive, then what is?

I'm staring at the number wondering if I should call. I can hear the tic-tock from the clock on the wall as it meshes with the thump-thump beat of my heart. Sometimes getting something started is the hardest part. I pick the phone up, the dial tone begins to sing. I punch his number into it and it begins to ring, ring, ring. "Hello Mike?" "Hey man, it's it's Adam, your son."

"If you're not inspired by life, you're not paying attention."

–IN-Q

IN-Q: Poetry has forced me to be self-aware in a way that nothing else has. That's how I write poems in the first place: I just pay attention.

If something inspires me or moves me or annoys me, that's the beginning of a poem. I consider myself the vehicle and the obstacle for them to come into the world—poems emerge through me and through my perception, but I also have to get out of the way in order for them to manifest in the way that they want.

Poetry isn't just about creation, it's about sharing. There is a completion in the giving away. There is a release when you allow it to not be yours anymore, when you allow someone else to interpret it in whatever way they choose. That's why I don't strategize how I want my audience to feel when they hear my work. However they feel it, whatever it is that happens to them, is what they needed.

Technology gives us all of these incredible opportunities … but it's also very isolating. People are not connecting in the same ways that they used to and they're not taking time to be on their own. We're basically trained by consumerism—everything wants something from us. It wants our money, it wants our time, it wants our attention, it wants our likes, it wants our love.

There's a difference between you using a tool and a tool using you. So be silent for a while and to listen to your own true voice because it's going to be the compass that moves you forward in life. That's the lesson I've learned over and over with poetry is to be quiet enough to hear my own voice because it always tells me what I need and where I should go next.

And most importantly, you have to find your creativity—people need to use their voices now more than any other time in history. And we have the ability through technology to do that. Everyone absolutely needs to be pursuing their creative voice in any way they can.

I don't give a shit about money. I don't give a shit about success. I care about somebody being a good person and striving to be a better version of themselves daily. I care about people who seek, ask questions about themselves, their environment, and humanity as a whole. Those are the things that really light me up.

Life is really fucking beautiful. It's hard and it's painful, but it's beautiful. I want to be living in that curiosity, living in that beauty, living in that possibility, until the day I die.

LEARNED FEAR
BY IN-Q

Learned fear can be overcome when you realize the voice inside your head is not yours. It's an imitation of the voices from before repeating on a loop inside your quiet core. Receiving since your youth, when your choices weren't even yours, perceiving was the proof, but reality has many doors. So why are we still fighting other people's wars? Learned fear can be overcome when you realize the voice inside your head is not yours.

It's an imitation of the voices from before repeating, repeating, repeating, on a loop inside your quiet core. And you can't tell the difference because it sounds the same. But trust me when I tell you most of what you think is from somebody else's brain. They have us trained, shackled by imaginary chains, imaginary rules for imaginary games, but they don't know the reasons either.

So where should we place the blame? And who is they anyway? When we're all the same. Our parents had parents, and their parents, had parents. Apparently it hurts to see so I'll be transparent. The world is so much bigger than your insecurities and they don't speak on your behalf without your soul's authority. The world is so much bigger than your culture or community. And they don't speak on your behalf without your soul's authority. Because if it's all a story, then nobody else can tell it for me.

Since I'm always transforming, I defy a category. When you do the same thing the same way, it's habit forming. But nothing in this land of mortal man is mandatory. It's all just transitory. Our world's a laboratory. Experimenting on today can change tomorrow morning. And since matter is mostly empty space, we're in a sea of consciousness where the boundaries are erased. So I stared at my reflection until I couldn't see my face. Then I picked myself and put the flowers in an empty vase. If you came for validation, then you're in the wrong place. The only certain satisfaction is becoming what you've chased. And there's no running from the inner voice, so it's important that you choose. But it's more important that you know you have a choice.

You have a choice. Are you living someone else's life? You have a voice. Does it haunt you in the dead of night? Would you fly if you weren't convinced to be afraid of heights? And who convinced you anyway? They had no fucking right. Right? No one can dim your light. You shine within so bright that you could blind the sun from sight and scare him back into the night. No one can dim your light. I said it twice because you're greater than the circumstances that surround your perfect life. You're not your nature or your nurture. You're a prototype. And if you hone it right, eventually you'll hack your satellite. At first, it's nothing. Then nothing turns into a whisper. Turn the dial and it gets crisper in your transistor. Wait a while and the whisper turns into a scream. It overwhelms your system and you won't know what it means. But pump the volume up and it can tell you all your dreams til pretty soon, it's the only voice you'll ever need. Now you have to do is listen when you want to lead. Your fear disintegrates when you decide to stop and breathe. It's your authentic voice. No matter where you go it never leaves. And that's God. No matter what religion you believe, I'm starting my own religion and everyone is welcome but nobody can join. If you did, you'd miss the point.

JUD BREWER, MD

TREATING ADDICTION WITH MINDFULNESS

Addiction is tenacious. We're all craven animals, vulnerable to habits that don't serve us. Whether it's constantly checking social media, binge eating, smoking, compulsive shopping, or excessive drinking, most of us fall prey to compulsions we feel powerless to arrest.

Why is this? And what can neuroscience teach us about the nature of cravings and how to overcome them?

Dr. Judson Brewer, MD, PhD has devoted his career to answering these questions. His discoveries just might change your life.

A psychiatrist, neuroscientist, thought leader, and scientific researcher in the field of habit change and the "science of self-mastery," "Dr. Jud" (as he is affectionately known) lives on the cutting edge of brain research, leveraging his findings to reduce suffering and help people make deep, permanent, and positive life changes.

The director of research and innovation at the Mindfulness Center and associate professor in psychiatry at the School of Medicine at Brown University, Dr. Jud is also a research affiliate at MIT. Before that, he held research and teaching positions at Yale University and the UMass Memorial Center for Mindfulness.

The author of numerous peer-reviewed publications and book chapters, Dr. Jud has trained US Olympic coaches. His work has been featured on *60 Minutes* and on the pages of *Time*, *Forbes*, BBC, NPR, *Businessweek*, and many other media outlets. His TED talk, "A Simple Way to Break a Bad Habit," is the fourth most viewed TED talk of 2016 with over 15 million views to date. And his app-based behavior-change programs have helped thousands of people overcome bad habits.

As a longtime recovering alcoholic prone to a myriad of thorny compulsions, it's fair to say that habit change is an obsession. I believe in 12-Step. It saved my life and continues to do so twenty-three years since my 100-day rehab stint. And I persistently recommend "The Program" for anyone and everyone struggling with an addiction. But I also remain open to expanding my sobriety toolkit beyond the church basement.

On that note, I came across Dr. Jud's book, *The Craving Mind*, which profoundly impacted me with its concrete distillation of why addictions are so tenacious. A scientific primer on the mechanisms of habit and addiction formation, it also makes a powerful case for how mindfulness can help us transcend cravings, reduce stress, and ultimately live a fuller life.

The nature of addiction is both psychiatric and neurological. Overcoming it is complicated. But there is a science to it. A science that has nothing to do with willpower. And everything to do with mindfulness.

We all experience unhealthy thoughts and behaviors that elude our ability to better control. In kinship with my conversation with Gabor Maté, Johann Hari, and James Clear, my hope is that Dr. Jud provides the gentle and nonjudgmental prodding required to finally face and ultimately overcome the compulsions that don't serve you.

—*Rich*

"On a very basic level, we're probably all addicted to something."

—Jud Brewer, MD

Dr. Jud: When most people think of addictions, they think about substances like alcohol, cocaine, heroin, and whatnot. But when we look at the science of our habits, we can virtually be addicted to anything. We can have everyday addictions to our cell phones and technology, to Instagram or to sugar. There's this very simple definition of addiction: continued use despite adverse consequences. The dominant paradigm to break addictions has been willpower, but it's proven to be more myth than muscle. The prefrontal cortex, which is involved with willpower, is the weakest part of the brain from an evolutionary perspective. It's the first that goes offline when you're stressed, when you're angry, when you're sad, when you're tired.

If you look at the people who have "good willpower" there are some really interesting things to learn. One is that, what we think they are willing themselves to do are things that they simply enjoy doing. Whether it's eating healthy, exercising, or physically challenging themselves. If you ask them why they do it or how they've gotten so good at it, they'll say it feels good, not that they want to get their body in shape for the beach. It's reward-based learning, not willpower. They do it for the reward of doing it. Reward-based learning combined with mindfulness is incredibly powerful. We did a study with people who were trying to quit smoking using mindfulness and taught them to pay attention to their behavior, to study the way smoking made them feel. They noticed the smell, the taste, the feeling of the superheated smoke going into their lungs. When they actually paid attention to their habits, they realized that smoking is gross. It tastes like shit. They received this information through their direct experience. Their brains recalibrated and learned

that smoking wasn't rewarding anymore. Here's the neuroscience: there's a part of the brain called the orbitofrontal cortex. It stores and updates reward value. It's always looking for that bigger, better offer. If we can give our orbitofrontal cortex information through awareness, especially if we do it in real time, it gets accurate and updated data. Accurate being "When I smoke a cigarette, is it that rewarding? No, I didn't realize it's not that rewarding." You can use mindfulness to rewire your brain to find rewards that feel better.

There's no secret behind the curtain to reward-based learning. Identify your triggers, notice your habitual behaviors, and most importantly, pay attention to the rewards or the results. That's where awareness actually can become your friend rather than something that just spirals you into shame and self-doubt. The key there is again looking at the reward because that's what drives behavior. When that value from the old behavior drops, you can find value in something healthier that actually feels good. Be curious and be kind. These are the two key elements of awareness. Curiosity helps you take moments when you're really struggling and allows you to bow to them as a teacher. This helps to calm the cravings that are all-consuming, that make you feel like a prisoner, and instead allows you to step back and just notice what they feel like. Paradoxically, when you turn towards your cravings, they start to dissolve. When you notice your cravings, you'll learn that simple physical sensations have been driving your entire life. When you train yourself to actually be with that discomfort instead of numbing it, you open up the possibility for true and deep healing.

KNOX ROBINSON

RUNNING IS AN ACT OF REBELLION

Against the backdrop of a global pandemic has emerged the most powerful civil rights movement of our lifetime—a historic moment that will indelibly shape the economic, political, and social fabric of our country for decades to come.

Knox Robinson is here help untangle the rhetoric behind our country's supercharged division—and the role running plays in better understanding the Black experience.

A writer, athlete, coach, and national-caliber runner, Knox is an eminent curator of running culture—a passion informed by his many years steeped in Black history, art, literature, music, and poetry. And from his world travels as an ambassador of the sport he loves. For Knox, running has little to do with splits and podiums. It's about movement as an art form. Running as a means of personal and philosophical expression. The physical voice of literature. Poetry. Music. And Politics.

Inhabiting a space in defiance of labels, Knox is the kind of human who, when asked to describe himself, effortlessly pulls the perfect quote from the poetry of Amir Baraka: *"[I am] a long-breath singer, would-be dancer, strong from years of fantasy and struggle."*

Knox's education formally began under the tutelage of Poet Laureate Maya Angelou at Wake Forest University and has continued to mature throughout the many chapters of his life. As a spoken word artist and music manager. As editor-in-chief of *Fader* magazine. And more recently as co-founder and captain of Black Roses NYC—a diverse collective of amateur, often tattooed, New York City runners who gather to hammer out intervals across Brooklyn and the caverns of downtown Manhattan, then go slurp ramen and spin vinyl.

For Knox, urban culture is lifeblood. And running as an act of rebellion—a means to unshackle oneself from pressures and expectations both external and internal. Freedom from the lies others tell us and the lies we tell ourselves. Running is a revolt against the static self. And a stand against civic injustice— the tectonic plates of systemic oppression hellbent on maintaining a status quo well past its expiration date.

One of the most interesting and multifaceted humans I have ever met, Knox's unique life experience informs an important perspective on America's crossroads. On the culture shifts caused by the pandemic and protests alike. On the intersection of sport, politics, and civil rights. On Black American representation in athletics. And on how we can productively move forward from here.

Put plainly, it's going to take more than virtue signaling or performative allyship.

My relationship with Knox is special. I'm a better man for it. I hope his wisdom leaves you similarly impacted, and thinking more deeply about your role and responsibility in positive culture change.

—Rich

"This is our chance . . .
to think beyond
what the mainstream media is
telling us."
—Knox Robinson

"*I just want to keep thinking about love and I would hope that this would be a moment for people to reset and reflect on what that is.*"
—**Knox Robinson**

Knox: What side of history do you want to be on? That's the question I would love for all of us to ask.

It's imperative that we think long and hard about who we are where we're we stand. We're at a pivotal moment in history—lives are literally at stake. Things are super crazy, and they're probably just going to get crazier. Where are we headed collectively as a culture? This is our chance to see beyond speeches that politicians are making. This is our chance to think beyond what our mainstream media is telling us. We can argue about politics, but on some level, there is a crisis of consciousness happening right now. We need to raise the floor on how we port ourselves and how we treat our fellow, man. It starts with our own individual behavior.

I can't stop thinking about the murder of Ahmaud Arbery. His death was so impactful to us runners. I've been Black my whole life, so I'm well familiar with the extrajudicial killings of Black American men in the United States. But Ahmaud Arbery—I just can't shake the image of him in my head. I can't stop thinking about the dramaturgy, the almost theatric staging of his last minutes. The video of his murder is devastating to watch, but it's important because it will expand your aperture. It will show you the truth—how much can you take in? How much can you hold?

I can't get over the way Ahmaud's body moved as he ran. It didn't look like he was trying to escape death, it looked like he was just trying to finish his run. I can't stop replaying those last moments when he goes to the right, the way his hips and knees cut. It's so engrossing to me because his body is my body too. It could've been me.

As I've thought more about what it means to run, I've come to understand that the Black body moving through space and time is such a wild image to people. I see the reactions that strangers have when I run past them, and it doesn't matter if I'm in a Black neighborhood or a white neighborhood or in a different country altogether. A Black man running is one of the most visually arresting images because it symbolizes freedom. Not just freedom of the Black body, but freedom of the mind. You can figure almost anything out through running. We all know that as runners—it's a vehicle for us to see, to imagine, and dream of the future.

But the thing is, society doesn't want you to run. You're supposed to just be a digit. You're supposed to just be a cipher. You're supposed to be like a one or a zero in the code. You're not supposed to get out and think for yourself, you're not supposed to feel. Running is the most crucial thing in the world because it forces you to feel. It may be good and may be bad. It may be hot, and it may be cold. It may be hard, it may be easy. Running is one of our oldest tools, and it's there for all of us at our disposal. Feeling is freedom.

When I say running is an act of rebellion, what mean is that it's a way to throw off all your pressures and all your expectations and all the lies that other people have sold you, and all the lies that you tell yourself, all your self-hatred and your self-doubt, and all your whack relationships and mistakes that you've made in the past, whether it was last night or last year or 10 years ago—running gives you a chance to do something new, to be someone else.

That's rebellion.

TONY RIDDLE

REWILD YOUR LIFE

Screens and cubicles. Shoes and chairs. Fluorescent lights and air-conditioned offices. Processed foods. Netflix and chill.

Disconnecting us from our essential human nature, the comfort and conveniences of modern living aren't making us happier. Ironically, they're driving an existential crisis of unprecedented proportions—rendering us more sick, immobile, lonely, depressed, and unfulfilled than ever.

It's time to stop. It's time we reconnect with that which is most essential.

Nature. Movement. Community. Love.

To do that, we must adopt a more naturalistic approach to lifestyle.

Tony Riddle calls it *rewilding*.

A natural lifestyle coach and barefoot running enthusiast, Tony has devoted his life to studying what makes us human and how to live unprocessed in an artificial world. Through the adoption of simple practices—many of which defined humanity for millennia—he aids people in living healthier and more connected lives by changing our relationship to ourselves, to others, and to our personal environments.

Putting his life philosophy into action, in 2019 Tony ran the entire length of Great Britain, barefoot. From UK's southern tip at Land's End to John o'Groats, the northernmost village of mainland Scotland, Tony's 30-day, 900-mile trek entailed a daily 30-mile run followed by meeting with sustainability experts along the way.

I was initially introduced to Tony through the Happy Pear twins. Enamored with his instructional Instagram tutorials on natural lifestyle practices, I wanted to know more.

My day with Tony began with a running technique tutorial, followed by a trail run (which of course Tony did barefoot despite the sharp rocky terrain), and culminated in one of my most popular episodes of 2019.

Vibrating with positive energy and infectious encouragement, Tony makes plain a variety of simple daily practices—from breathwork and sitting positions to posture and running techniques—to help us live more connected to our environments, our loved ones, and ourselves.

May Tony's wisdom and experience leave you inspired to live more naturally and mindfully.

—Rich

"It's just about becoming and being. Once you strip all the stuff away then you realize you can live authentically."
—Tony Riddle

Tony: We can't all live in nature, but it doesn't mean we can't live naturally.

What I mean is that there is a natural way of doing things. There is a biological norm we should be striving for—abiding by—the closer you get to it, the less likely you're going to encounter injury or disease.

There's a natural way of running for instance, which is just finding posture. Natural runners and natural beings aren't compromised by seated furniture, or sedentary lifestyles, or compromising footwear. Natural runners perform the appropriate task of running without the risk of injury. Running is just a micro element of movement. There's an entirely natural way of moving.

In fact, there's an entirely natural way of existing. 83% of people in the UK live in urban environments and spend 90% of their time indoors. They spend 10% of their day outside, if they're lucky. What do you do in those hours? Eight of them are spent in the bedroom, so first things first, you've got to clean up the air. You've got to get air purifiers and plants.

Change the materials in your space so you're not breathing in and out crap. If you understand sensory genomics, you understand that depression, Alzheimer's, dementia, all these things basically can be coming through neurotoxins which are found in the paints, the mastics, the glues, the carpets, the mattress, all the soft furnishings. If you have the money, go and buy stuff that's made from natural fibers.

Change the lighting so you can get the natural experience of light, which means your metabolism, hormones, and everything can be regulated by the sun. We also know that a lot of time is spent at work.

Start incorporating movement into your day. If you're in an office and your HR department won't allow you to have a standing desk, slide your chair away and do some squats throughout the day.

Everyone loves banging on about 10,000 steps. But for me, if you have 10,000 poor steps that might lead you to an injury, it's probably not the best model. If you're wearing compromising footwear with a dodgy heal and a pointed toe box, it's not the best model. Eat high vibrational foods. Clean up your diet. The cleaner it gets, the more innate things will become for you. Your intuition will get stronger.

I came to this conclusion that I didn't want anything in my life to be about an "ism" or become attached to, "I'm a paleo, I'm a plant-based, I'm a vegan, I'm this." I see things differently within the nutrition world now. I've tried to get this understanding of what I really need on a day-to-day basis. And so if each and every person understood exactly what they needed I think things would be very different. And we wouldn't have labels for anyone and we wouldn't have thousands of books on shelves trying to convince people what they should and shouldn't be eating. The cleaner my diet got, the more I understood exactly what I felt like I needed to eat and the more in tune I could become with that innate ability.

So clean up your diet. Move towards plant-based. Fast. Naturalize your home and clean up your space. These are the best things you can do for yourself to develop an understanding of what it is you need as an individual and that supports the way that you move, the way that you sleep and your own individual digestive system.

MICHAEL

HOW NOT TO DIE

When it comes to reliable nutrition information, the internet is a war-torn, metastasizing mushroom cloud of toxic half-truths and misinformation.

How do we sort through the tribal wars? How do we separate fact from fiction?

Let's start with seeking out the experts. And digging deep into the best, most objective science available.

This is the life's work of Dr. Michael Greger MD, FACLM.

A graduate of Cornell University and Tufts University School of Medicine as well as a founding member and Fellow of the American College of Lifestyle Medicine, Dr. Greger is a nutrition science wizard with a library of scientific journal publications to his name. He has testified before Congress; lectured at countless symposiums and institutions; and was an expert witness in the infamous Oprah Winfrey meat defamation lawsuit.

His massively popular books, including *How Not to Die, How Not to Diet,* and their cookbook analogues, all became instant *New York Times* bestsellers and crowned Dr. Greger a media darling, his excitable face popping up everywhere from *The Dr. Oz Show* to *The Colbert Report.*

When Dr. Greger isn't speaking, crafting high-level policy initiatives, or penning perennial bestsellers, he scours thousands of medical journals in search of the world's best, most objective nutrition research to bring you free, impeccably researched, and straight-to-the-point videos and articles every single day at NutritionFacts.org—the world's most authoritative, nonprofit, science-based public service destination for all things nutrition, health, and disease prevention.

Finally, it's worth noting that 100% of all fees and proceeds he receives from speaking and book sales are donated to charity—his effort to avoid all conflicts of interest.

Whether you're looking to lose weight or simply learn more about nutrition, separating fact from fiction can be daunting for even the most well-intentioned, conscientious consumer.

Why? Because most medical doctors have no training in nutrition science. And because well-funded commercial interests cloud nutrition science with conflicts of interest. Truth becomes obscured by profit motives. Unwittingly, public consensus bends to that will. The result is Big Food's ultimate product: confusion.

To effectively separate evidence-based science from confirmation bias, we need a trustworthy guide. Dr. Greger is that guide.

One of the most delightful, relentless, passionate, and service-minded humans I have ever met, it's been my honor to host several podcast conversations with this man.

May he encourage a new perspective on nutrition and the body's miraculous ability to heal and thrive.

—Rich

GREGER, MD

Michael: What we eat is the number one cause of death and disability in the United States. The most important decision we make every day is what we put in our mouths. If there's any decision that should be built based on the evidence, shouldn't it be this one?

There are about 13,000 articles published on human nutrition, at least in the English language, every year. There's a new drug, there's a new medical procedure or a new medical instrument, but you only hear about these because there's a profit motive behind their marketing. But let's say a new article pops up on the wonders of broccoli, it just gets buried. There's just no incentive to spread that kind of information out to the masses because you can't brand broccoli. No broccoli grower is going to pay to put ads on TV saying how wonderful broccoli is because odds are, consumers will go buy someone else's broccoli. There's simply no profit.

The whole system is rigged against us. The CEOs of junk food companies aren't sitting around thinking of creative ways to contribute to the childhood obesity epidemic. They just need to make money for the shareholders. The system is just set up to reward these behaviors that make people sick. Processed food is a multi-billion-dollar industry. There's a lot of money at stake to keep people confused about nutrition.

Not to mention, only one out of four medical schools have a single course in nutrition. On average, doctors graduate with only four hours of nutrition training. That's out of thousands of hours of preclinical instruction. Those four hours are like the biochemistry of vitamins, not using diet to actually help people. There's no reimbursement mechanism for keeping people healthy because doctors are reimbursed by procedures, pills, and more procedures. That's what they get money

for, not how healthy their patients are. The only way the system will change is if we had metrics that actually rewarded doctors for keeping people healthy.

There's only one diet ever proven to reverse heart disease in a majority of patients—a plant-based diet.

It can also help prevent and even reverse other leading killers like type two diabetes, and high blood pressure.

If that's all a plant-based diet could do, reverse our number one killer, shouldn't that be the default diet until proven otherwise? The fact that it can also prevent, treat, and reverse Type 2 Diabetes and hypertension, all of these other leading killers seem to make the case overwhelming. It's hard to cherry-pick when there's only one cherry. There's no other diet that has been shown to heal our bodies this dramatically.

My faith in our future comes from the democratization of knowledge. In the past, if you wanted to get information about health, you would have to talk with a physician. But now things have changed. Now we have access. We no longer have to have this mediator between us and the body of science out there.

When it comes to safe, simple, side-effect-free solutions, we can take our own health destiny and our family's health into our own hands, and improve it.

"I continue to be amazed by
our bodies' ability for self-repair.
Our bodies want to be healthy.
if we would just let them.
That's what these new research
articles are showing:
even after years of beating yourself
up with a horrible diet,
your body can reverse the damage,
open back up the arteries
and even reverse the progression
of some cancers.
So it's never too late to start
exercising and never too late
to start eating healthier."

—Michael Greger, MD

SHARON

REAL LOVE AND THE ART OF MINDFUL CONNECTION

We all yearn for connection, yet often feel trapped by our sense of isolation, anger, or envy. But there is a key that can free us from this prison of despair.

Love.

The problem? Love is just hard to talk about. Harder to understand. And perhaps even harder to practice.

How do we get it? How do we give it? How do we attract it? How do we cultivate it?

To answer these questions, first we have to define it.

What is love, exactly?

Sharon Salzberg will tell one thing for sure—it's not an emotional state we extract from others. In fact, she would discourage you from thinking about love as a feeling at all. Instead, consider it an ability. Love is an aptness, or a facility, that resides within all of us. It's something that can be cultivated that, when shared freely, leads to profound connections with others, and most importantly with ourselves.

It is that connection that, in turn, nourishes the very sustenance of life itself—and ultimately sets us free.

A towering figure in the field of meditation, Sharon has played a pivotal role in bringing meditation and mindfulness into mainstream American culture since 1974. She is the co-founder of the Insight Meditation Society in Barre, MA and the author of 10 books including *New York Times* bestseller *Real Happiness*; her seminal work, *Lovingkindness*; and her 2017 release, *Real Love: The Art of Mindful Connection*.

Despite her luminary status in the meditation space, conspicuously absent is any hint of pretense. Sharon is down-to-earth. She's very fun to be with. And her approach to Buddhist teachings is modern, secular, and accessible, rendering the wisdom and its practical applications relatable to all.

My conversation with Sharon centers on how we think about and practice love—love for others, love for all, and love for oneself.

It's about unconscious pain and the inherent value of suffering when recognized and properly channeled.

It's about the three most essential life skills—compassion, mindfulness, and concentration—and how meditation can help us master them by training our attention.

And it's a conversation about the imperative of navigating these treacherous, divided times with fierce compassion and unabashed loving kindness.

It's time we redefine our limited interpretation of love. Dispel the misunderstandings that confine and circumscribe it. Plumb the eternal truths within it. And to explore how we can better cultivate and expand our experience of real love in our daily lives.

Let Sharon be your guide—a most wise and gentle steward for all things loving and kindness.

—Rich

SALZBERG

"You can search throughout the entire universe for someone who is more deserving of your love and affection than you are yourself, and that person is not to be found anywhere. You, yourself, as much as anybody in the entire universe, deserve your love and affection."

—Sharon Salzberg

Sharon: What is real love? I am still trying to figure it out. I usually talk about it as a state of profound connection without the adornments and the elaborations western culture puts on it.

There's a saying, "Love is not a feeling, it's an ability." But most of us only know it is a feeling. We yearn for it as a feeling. We think of it constantly as a feeling. But what if we re-conceptualize love as a capacity within us that's not in the hands of someone else, but rather is something we create? Other people may awaken it or enliven it or nourish it or threaten it, but ultimately, it's within us.

In Eastern philosophy, love is quite trainable. It's a skill that's based on how we pay attention. That's all that meditation is—training attention. It's not that you're forcing yourself to feel something you don't really feel or you're covering up some really difficult feelings by suffocating them with sweetness. Paying attention simply lays the ground for love to emerge.

I had a very traumatic, disordered, chaotic childhood. When I wrote *Faith*, I looked back at my journey and realized that by the time I went to college at the age of 16, I'd lived in five different family configurations. Every one of them shifted because of a death or some loss or some profound craziness. My parents got divorced when I was four, then my father disappeared, and it was just me and my mother and her siblings until I was nine. Then my mother died very suddenly and I lived with my father's parents whom I hardly knew.

My father didn't reappear for another couple of years. My grandfather died, and then my father came back for about six weeks and then he took an overdose of sleeping pills and ended up in some mental health facility for the rest of his life, which was pretty extensive. He was either in a VA hospital or nursing home or sometimes on the streets if he would run away. Sometimes he'd be better and sometimes he'd be not so well.

I went upstate to college and I was completely isolated. I was shut down. I was very unhappy but not expressive of it. I didn't even know what was happening within me. When I went to India and started meditating, I began to uncover this rage and fear and sadness I had within myself. It was shocking to me—I didn't know I had those feelings.

When I heard the Buddhist say that suffering is a natural part of life, it was the most liberating thing I'd ever heard. To be born is to suffer. Not that life is horrible, but there's always suffering in someone's life somewhere along the line. That's the truth, and it freed me.

To get to a true or bigger picture of your life, you have to actually move your attention consciously towards good. *Anything good happen today? Is there anything good within me?* That's the kind of elasticity or flexibility of attention you want to foster through meditation. But it begins with seeing the whole story because not only do we tell false stories about ourselves, but others tell stories about us too, and oftentimes those can be very unkind. It takes a great deal of integrity to have a true sense of who you are.

The essence of the meditation is understanding how you're relating to what's happening in reality. Anything can happen in life, but you can experience it differently. You can be more centered. You can be more balanced. You can be more aware. You can be kinder.

RAIN is a meditative technique that is often used when a difficult emotion comes up. Let's say you start to feel anger. Rather than dismissing it or hating yourself for it or plotting revenge, just look at the feeling. That is the first step—Recognize what's happening. The second is Acknowledge it, or accept it. Don't add onto it. Just be with it as it is. The third is Investigate. If we really explore the state of anger for example, we will likely see fear. We will see sadness, and maybe grief. We also see it's constantly changing. Emotions have the tendency to arise and then pass away. Then N, Non-identification means you don't have to fall into the emotion. Just because you feel anger doesn't mean you're an angry person. It is a passing state. This is a much softer way of dealing with the hard things that come up in life.

We're all part of a human family. When you blow it, you're not the only person that has ever done that. Mistakes are part of the human condition.

You can pick up. You can begin again. You are resilient.

EVOLUTION OF A CRO-MAGNON

Weaned on the ailing womb of Scorsese's Mean Streets, John Joseph is a true American original.

It's a life that defies definition. Lower East Side thief. Abuse survivor. Former drug dealer and brawling gutter rat. Hare Krishna monk. CBGB's Street Poet. Punk-rock Robin Hood. Plant-powered Ironman. And a straight-edge, straight talking, modern day spiritual warrior who's astounding path conjures a demented amalgam of Hugh Selby Jr., Jerry Stahl, Henry Rollins, Eckhart Tolle, and Paramahansa Yogananda.

Born into abuse and cast aside to fend for himself on Manhattan's Lower East Side, John's youth was a revolving door of horrific violence, homelessness, drugs, addiction, crime, and prison. In and out of foster care and juvenile detention centers, every day was a struggle simply to survive.

Then things went downhill.

Ultimately music saved his life—and gave him an entirely new one. Best known for fronting the legendary hardcore band Cro-Mags, today John lives a life of sobriety, service, positive mental attitude (PMA), and *ahimsa*—nonviolence.

A Bhakti-yoga devotee, John is also an 11-time Ironman finisher (two of which he completed with a hernia), motivational speaker, and author of three books: *Evolution of a Cro-Magnon, Meat Is For Pussies*, and *The PMA Effect*.

Now 57, he continues to ferociously tour, perform, write, speak, compete, and selflessly serve his fellow man—all fueled on a 100% plant-based diet.

I've never met anyone who has transcended despair as successfully as John and lived to tell the story. And nobody can spin a yarn like the man they call Bloodclot.

I'm proud to call John the best friend I ever had. A man who truly walks his talk, it's been gift to share his many potent appearances on the podcast.

Always leaving me better than before, every straight talk with John is a powerful reminder: no matter how unimaginable one's circumstances, the capacity for wholesale transformation lives within us all.

—Rich

JOHN

JOSEPH

John: Removing violence from my plate was the catalyst that changed my entire life.

When I abstained from animal flesh for 30 days, something morphed in my consciousness, man. Removing that karma from my life, removing that pain and suffering from my body, it fucking changed me. We don't have the right to kill these animals and do this shit that we're doing to them. You could call it hippie bullshit or whatever the fuck you want, but I'm telling you right now, some of the baddest, toughest motherfuckers that I've ever fucking come in contact with, when they abstained from animal flesh, the light switch came on. This ain't hippie shit. This is real shit that we're talking about.

When you come from a life of violence and seeing people's throats get cut in front of you, people getting shot and murdered in front of you, ingesting violence just feels wrong. Anyone who grows the animal, anyone who transports the animal, anyone who kills the animal, anyone who cooks the animal, and anyone who eats the animal gets that karma. Just like you're reducing your carbon footprint, you want to reduce your karmic footprint.

We all have a debt. How the hell do I repay the fact that I didn't go to prison and get fucking killed on the streets for being a drug addict and robbing crazy motherfuckers? How do I repay that? The only way is to constantly be of service and live in gratitude. Reduce my karma. Every day I wake up, I touch my head to the floor, and I say my mantras. I've done that for 37 years, even in my crack period and pill period. I wake up, and

I touch my head to the floor. I say my mantras, and I give thanks for another day on earth.

My happiness is not derived from getting the next thing. Somewhere along the line I realized that having a lot of shit ain't what brings you happiness, cause I never had nothing. And I've given what I did make when I had it. I gave it away. The *Bhagavad Gita* says you have the right to the work. You don't have the right to the results of the work. That's not what you're supposed to concentrate and meditate on.

But the happiness I get from the service I've done, I wouldn't trade it for the fucking world. If you said to me, "Yo, you can go back and I'm going to give you fucking $10 million," I wouldn't take it. And that's God's honest truth. I've turned down TV shows and all kinds of shit, cause it's not along the lines of my core values and what I see as important. My happiness is derived from service.

You may look at where I came from, and where I'm now, but what you don't see is the 37 fucking years of tears, and pain, and fucking bloodshed, and fucking tests that have come, that I've failed, and failed, and failed again. But I was willing to get the fuck back up. And it's not how many times we get knocked on our ass, it's how many times we're willing to fucking pick ourselves up, and push fucking through the next gap between expectation and result. And then the world throws us another fucking curve ball. That's just life in a nutshell. So it comes down to what you want your story to be. I didn't want my story to be, "Oh yeah, he was abused, and he was abandoned, and he was fucking made to

feel like shit. And it's okay that he's in prison or fucking dead. It's understandable." Fuck that, I didn't want that to be my story.

Don't let those events that have happened in your life determine who you are as a character. You can break free from adversity. Really look at yourself, stop looking at everybody else and what they're doing. That don't matter. What anybody else does, don't matter. It's about what's going on with you. That's what you have the power to fix. You don't have the power to determine how people are going to treat you, or look at you, or talk about you. But you sure as hell have the power to stand the fuck up and take care of yourself.

You attract the energy that you put into the world. Start attracting some good shit.

"I made it through the things I did because I had ammunition in the form of knowledge, which I could take shelter of in my darkest hours."

—John Joseph

WE GOTTA ROLL WITH THAT PMA
BY JOHN JOSEPH

There is a reason we've repeatedly heard some of the most badass humans on planet earth tell us that mindset is everything. That's because it's not the circumstances we find ourselves in, but rather how we deal with them

I'm speaking from experience. It took me decades, suffering through addiction and a violent lifestyle to figure that one out. See, I'm what you would call a student of "The School of Hard Knocks."

I was born in 1962 in NYC, son of a violent, alcoholic, professional prizefighter. Actually, my mom never told me that I was conceived out of a violent rape until I was in my late thirties. She left him and he broke into her new apartment and raped her. He continued his violence toward her the entire time we were kids, all through the 60s. I had to watch helplessly as he ruthlessly beat my mother.

My two brothers and I were eventually taken from her by the state in 1969 after she slipped into a deep depression and couldn't care for us. We were bounced around in horrible foster homes, eventually landing in a house of horrors. We were sexually abused, beaten, and made to feel completely worthless. There were days we had to steal their dog's food just to eat. They only took foster kids in for the money. We spent over six years there before the state closed them down for what they had been doing to us and removed all the kids. The thing that hit me, many years later as an adult, was the realization that they never even took one single photo of us. The entire time we spent there we were the ghost children. Forgotten and left to fend for ourselves.

Eventually after a series of more foster homes and institutions I found myself alone on the dangerous streets of New York City in 1976. I had run away from St. John's Home for Boys in Rockaway Beach. I figured the State of New York had failed me, so now I would take my chances and live *my* life.

I resorted to crime. Selling drugs, breaking into stores, and robberies. There was the danger of being on the streets of NYC back then, a kid, alone in an insanely violent world. I saw people murdered and was even shot in the leg for selling drugs to someone's sister. After two years on the run in the fall of 1978, I landed in lock-up with three criminal cases, two for drug sales and one for B and E (breaking and entering). I was sent to the worst place you could imagine for young men 21 and under: Spofford Correctional Facility in the South Bronx. I had to fight daily as I was the only white person in the entire facility and had a target on my back from day one. I even got stabbed in a chow hall riot. I was eventually moved upstate to a lock up for 21 months, which was no better.

Then came my turning point. After lock-up I got out, caught another drug case, and was offered military service instead of jail. I joined the Navy, and I went to Norfolk Virginia. One night I dropped into a punk club and met the Bad Brains, a punk rock band of Rastafarians. The singer, HR, talked about PMA in a song called "Attitude." The essence of the lyrics were that no matter what we go through, if we keep a positive mental attitude, boulders in our path become like pebbles we can just kick away.

That struck a nerve. No one ever told me stuff like that. And even though the seed was planted, I continued my criminal ways in the Navy. I smuggled drugs aboard the ship and sold drugs in Norfolk. One of those sales was to an undercover cop at a bar called the Kings Head Inn. Once again I was facing jail time, so I went AWOL.

Back out on the streets, I made my way to NYC and the Bad Brains were living in my old neighborhood, Alphabet City, on the Lower East Side. I moved in with them and that's when the real change started. No meat, no drugs, no alcohol. Instead it was training, yoga, and meditation. I even started playing with my band the Cro-Mags.

In 1982, I felt I needed to do some real healing and became a Hare Krishna monk for two years. I left after seeing some crazy cult-type shit go down and went back to the Cro-Mags in 1984, living out of a burnt-out building in Alphabet City.

What I brought with me this time was a higher consciousness and a positive mindset on how to deal with things. But I struggled for the next decade, even relapsing in 1988 through 1990 to crack, pills, and booze. I robbed dangerous drug dealers, had several KOSs (kill on sight) orders put out on me, and was nearly killed several times. In 1990, I found myself alone, homeless, penniless, and addicted to drugs. I knew right then I was going to die if I didn't change and slay my inner demons.

I started training again and went back to those lessons on PMA. This time it worked! I'm now clean and sober for decades, and I use my story to help others. I've spoken at prisons, on podcasts, TV, to the press, at high schools, at drug programs, even business conferences and parole facilities around the globe. My message? With the right mindset we can overcome anything in life.

I started really challenging myself when I turned 50 by taking up Ironman races. I've completed 11 so far, including the Kona World Championship twice. I still play music and have penned three books. My latest is *The PMA Effect: How a Positive Mental Attitude Can Make You the Badass You Were Born to Be.* Rich was kind enough to contribute an amazing foreword to the book.

One of the main things I realized in my crazy journey is that the people we associate with are key. My earlier days were spent with violent criminals, drug addicts, dealers, and murderers. Nowadays, I make sure I keep the company of men and women who are trying to stay on the path of PMA. In Sanskrit that's called, "Bhakta-Sangham," or those relationships which are based around higher consciousness. I always feel blessed to be in their association as I continue to learn and grow as a human. I believe that's also how we elevate as human and a society. We need to look for those who have a positive message and lessons to teach, and associate with them. The approach is that we have to keep learning.

It took me years to be able to pen my memoir, *The Evolution of a Cro-Magnon*, because of the shame and embarrassment I felt from what was done to me as a kid. Sure, I had plenty of insane tough guy stories from the streets and the hardcore/punk music scene, but the sexual abuse stuff was off limits. I did not go there, and when I did try to write about it, I'd break down sobbing at my computer for an hour and then shelve the book. I wore a figurative mask in public, as do so many others who have been through abuse, as we try to block it out. But that never works.

Then Robert McKee (my writing teacher) said to me in his class, during a private moment, that it's not what happens to us—it's what we do as a result. That's when it struck me that I had to tell the whole story and get the book done, because I knew it would help others going through similar issues.

In the current atmosphere of 2020 we really need to step up and help each other. We have to collectively come together and work out the issues that haunt us as individuals and plague us as a society. I believe that's done with PMA, with hard work, and with radical compassion. I've learned through my own journey that kindness and service goes a long way, as we simply never know what people are dealing with in their lives when we see them. Actually, it's become my mission in life because by all rights I should be dead. I'm only here today because of my teachers who made time for me. That's an incredible debt I owe them. When I asked how I could ever pay it back, I was told, "BY PAYING IT FORWARD."

MISHKA

THE MISADVENTURES OF A PROFESSIONAL STRUGGLER

Devoted listeners are well-acquainted with my gravelly voiced, chronically self-deprecating, often tortured, but always charming brother-from-another-mother Mishka Shubaly—a guest so frequent on the podcast, it's fair to call him a spasmodic significant other.

A writer oozing talent from his overactive sebaceous glands, Mishka pens true stories about drink, drugs, disasters, desire, deception, and their aftermath.

He began boozing at 13 and college at 15. At 22, he received the Dean's Fellowship from the Master's Writing Program at Columbia University. Upon receipt of his expensive MFA, he promptly moved into a Toyota minivan to tour the country nonstop as a singer-songwriter, often sharing the stage with comedians like Doug Stanhope and musical acts like the Strokes and the Yeah Yeah Yeahs.

But mostly he drank.

It sounds glamorous. It wasn't. At 32, Mishka hit bottom, got sober and laced up a pair of running shoes. In between ultra-marathons, he began publishing a string of number-one bestselling short non-fiction novellas. *The Long Run*, his mini-memoir detailing his transformation from alcoholic drug abuser to sober ultrarunner, to this day remains one of the best-selling Kindle Singles in Amazon history.

Mishka is also the author of *I Swear I'll Make It Up to You*. Brutally honest, fiercely emotional, and muscular in its prose, it's the booze-fueled, opiated account of a precocious young underachiever trying to be good (and failing and failing) until one day he succeeds.

And proving the adage that anything is possible, he somehow hoodwinked Yale University into letting him spend summers teaching young impressionable minds the art of creative writing.

Over the years, our bro-mantic throwdowns never fail to produce conversations equal parts fraught and feral.

Drinking and sobriety. Nihilism and depression. Running and writing. Trading one addict on for another. Music, comedy, creativity, and artistic frustration. Sloth, abandonment, failure, and rebellion. Resentment and revenge. Broken down vans and abandoned cats. Family, love, loss, and forgiveness.

But just beneath the chaotic veneer of these many exchanges rests a profound common theme:

Love.

—Rich

SHUBALY

"Every failure is actually a step forward. That's how you learn to be who you are."
—Mishka Shubaly

Mishka: I struggle with my sobriety.

I haven't relapsed, but I definitely think about that shit a lot. When I get cravings to drink, I know that I am actually just missing being young. I really miss being 22. I'm having a hard time dealing with aging. Being a 40-year-old man is really bumming me out.

My youth is so stitched through with drugs and alcohol that I think in my brain they've become a shorthand or a signal for youth. Alcohol feels like a time machine in a bottle—all I need is a drink to go back there, to being a kid, to hanging out with my friends, to falling down in the river or whatever bullshit we used to do.

Most of the time I love not drinking. I love not apologizing to people every morning. I'm running again. I'm training for a 50K in December and it's going well. I had a real strong 20 mile run the other day where I was just flying. But because I actively planned to be dead a long time ago, I don't know how to live now or how to have fun. But I'm starting to figure it out and get an idea. A lot of people after 38 or 40, they're like, "All right, well now we gain 40 pounds and we quit the band, and we sell the gear. We don't do this anymore, and we don't do that anymore."

I was on that track too. Twizzlers for dinner, Red Bull for breakfast. I was eating just stupid shit. But the thing is I come from the addict school of learning, which is where you don't learn anything until you're in maximum pain and terror. Not too long ago I was feeling depressed and burned out, and knew something was wrong. After getting my blood work back my doctor said, "Well, your blood sugar's high. You're pre-diabetic, and you have the testosterone of a 70-year-old man." This is a month after my uncle died from complications with diabetes. Most of my family is diabetic. I knew it was sort of waiting in the wings for me, but I thought I had at least another 10 years.

This was my own extrapolation, but something told me that if I stopped eating cheese fries and Cheetos and gummy bears and started eating cauliflower and asparagus and flaxseed, my testosterone and pre-diabetic condition would improve. And it did.

Going plant-based wasn't an easy transition, but it was absolutely worth it. If you're on the cusp of trying it, or if you've tried it and failed, try it again, and then try it again and then try it again because it's totally worth it. I struggled with it, but now I got my mind right.

It's going to be uncomfortable. Sure there are ways of cushioning the fall, but understand that it's okay to mess up. If you can get through two weeks of it, on the other side is freedom. There's nothing worthwhile that you get for free, except maybe sunshine. You have to work for the good things.

After 35, 40, things start to slow down and it's harder to do the stuff that you did when you were younger. Does that mean you roll over and give up? Gain 20 or 50 pounds? Netflix and chill for another 30 years before you die? No. You push back. You turn and fight. You say, "I'm not done being a human yet and having a full life. I still got a ton of shit left to do."

Embrace your failures, they are a necessary ingredient for success. Failing is how you learn who you are and who you aren't. Failing helps you decide what you actually want to do with the rest of your life.

I'm still the guy with both middle fingers in the air, but now I'm saying, "Fuck you. You don't need to be drunk and eat shit all the time to be a rebel. If you want to smash the state, why don't you make sure that you have the tools to do it? Why don't you take care of the most important tool you have, which is yourself, if you want to change things?"

Do your best to stick around. Be healthy for a long time. And most importantly, be a pain in the ass for your enemies.

GMAIL IS A CURSE
BY MISHKA SHUBALY

Gmail is a curse. Facebook only exists to reunite you with people you had no intention whatsoever of ever reuniting with, whereas Gmail carefully preserves and catalogues every bit of useless chatter, every conversation you hoped to forget. Every despairing "Baby, please take me back" email, every idiotic late night eBay purchase, even that one desperate time you came dangerously close to doing foot porn for some dude on Craig's List. But Gmail also preserves a few gems. Sitting down to write this piece for Rich's book celebrating the podcast, I searched through my Gmail account and discovered that today is seven years to the day since we first met.

We'd been introduced via email by a mutual friend and agreed to podcast together when Rich was in New York. Still, I was leery. A year and a half earlier, I had published *The Long Run* through Amazon, a short memoir about my radical transition from ultradrunk to ultrarunner without rehab or AA. Its success had subjected my private life to more public attention than I was comfortable with. And having read *Finding Ultra*, I knew that Rich was this data-crunching, performance-obsessed, 12-step, Ivy League, ex-lawyer vegan ultraman. Nothing about my life would survive his scrutiny—my recovery, my diet, my lame ultra-running record, my inability to keep a girlfriend, to say nothing of the squalor of my apartment. I volunteered that we should probably meet at a coffee shop because my apartment was just an indoor slum, more of an orphanage for abused guitars than a place where a human being would actually choose to live. That sealed the deal for Rich—he insisted we had to do it at my dump. Well, shit.

When my phone buzzed—of course our doorbell didn't work, are you kidding?—I ran downstairs to let him in. He was slighter than I imagined, less physically imposing, a wiry coyote of a man with a strong handshake and an easy smile. We walked back upstairs and then sat down on the floor of my bedroom/office/workshop/guitar mortuary and began recording. He had the deep, open, inviting brown eyes of a Jersey cow but there was something behind them—incredible intelligence, yes, but also perseverance. This was a guy who knew how to suffer patiently, with grace, for a long, long time without breaking. He was here to get something from me—my story? New insight into my humanity? A piece of my soul? I don't think either of us knew exactly what it was he was there for but it quickly became clear that he would listen and watch and wait me out until I gave it up.

After a couple of hours, I felt like I had been stripped down to my core. It made perfect sense that Rich was an ultra-marathoner because that's what our conversation felt like. All the mundane banalities, all the platitudes, all the bullshit quickly fell away. It was eerie and unsettling to meet a stranger who had such insight into my internal life. We talked about the big shit: love, death, wounds, scars, alcoholism and addiction, human darkness, the fragility and power of new hope. It was only after he left that I was able to put my finger on exactly how it felt. It felt like I was meeting an old friend for the first time.

I could tell right away that we'd done something worthwhile because I felt raw. I'd let him too far into my head, I'd been too honest, I'd aired publicly shit that people are loathe to think about in secret. I'd trusted him and then exposed myself too much, been too vulnerable. And then the podcast dropped and I was crushed in a wave of enthusiasm, empathy, love and support from his listeners. I was enveloped by his growing tribe, my RRPeeps. Even for the fucked-up shit, especially for the fucked-up shit! What do you know, turns out everyone's pissed the bed, everyone's done horrible stuff, everyone's got secrets and regrets. Even vegans.

Listening back to that first podcast seven years later, I realize I was so freaked out by how much I had exposed myself that I didn't realized the degree to which Rich had exposed himself. Though he had written at length about his alcoholism in *Finding Ultra*, our episode of the podcast was the first one dedicated to sobriety and recovery, themes that would become central to the podcast down the line.

Since 2013, I've done the podcast six times, maybe seven? I've lost track. We ran together in Cali, we did a live podcast and concert in Brooklyn, I got one of his boys a gig in Manhattan, he came and found me in London one shitty summer, I crashed on his floor, his couch, his bed, everywhere. I got to know Robin Arzón and Josh LaJaunie and hardcore superhero John Joseph through Rich. And I got to bring a couple of my folks into the tribe, the profane, divine Amy Dresner and our beloved, fallen ultra-everything David Clark. I've never felt our community draw together like we did to grieve the loss of our friend and celebrate his incandescent life.

The bulk of our friendship has been recorded for posterity. We've spent more time talking on mic than off it, which feels weird to say but also, it's been super cool, so fuck it, we're going to run with it.

Some of you may recall in old cartoons when Sylvester the cat is chasing Tweety bird, he occasionally has a crisis of conscience. A devil cat appears on his shoulder and urges him to do the Bad Thing. He looks to his other shoulder and an angel cat appears there, urging him not to do the Bad Thing. One of my many fatal flaws has been imbalance. Hesitating outside of a liquor store, a devil appears on my shoulder: "Go on, man, grab a fifth of Jameson, you deserve it." I look to my other shoulder for the angel to present the other side of the argument. Instead, it's another devil: "A fifth? A half-gallon is much better value- think of all the money you'll save!" Since the day we met, I have carried Rich with me. Not as an angel on my shoulder, because Rich is not superhuman, he is super human. I carry Rich with me as my trusted friend, my big brother, scoffing and shaking his head and pushing his glasses up on his nose before saying "...man, is that really what you want to do?"

There's no other way to say it: my friendship with Rich has changed my life. My friendship with Rich continues to change my life. This thing he's created, this thing we've created together, him and me and you, especially you, all of you, every single one of you, it's changed his life and my life and I hope it's changed your life, too. I hope we all keep changing together, keep challenging ourselves and each other, keep talking, keep listening, keep disagreeing, keep debating, keep reconsidering, keep moving forward together, as friends, as fellow travelers, as the defiantly hopeful: the RRPeeps.

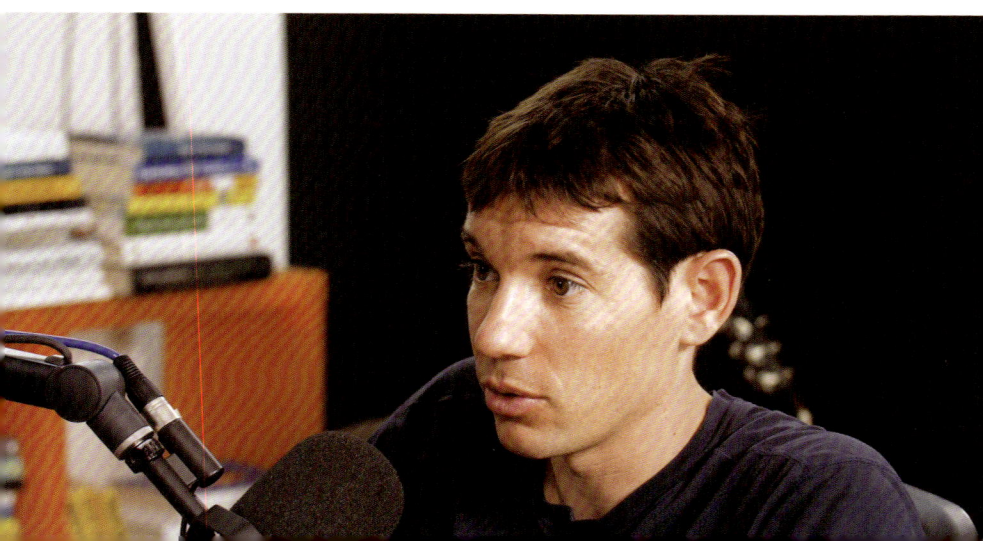

RICH ROLL &
PAUL HAWKEN

Set apart from other education or entertainment modalities, podcasting is a medium of unique intimacy. And yet, it's still fundamentally an abstraction—a mere digital facsimile of true connection.

Moved to better translate those ones and zeros into tactile community, I decided to take the show out of the studio and into the analog world.

So, in Fall 2019, I hosted our first live podcast event at the Los Angeles Wilshire Ebell Theatre. An audience of 1,100 people gathered to share purpose and passion. Cultivate consciousness. Elevate intimacy. And deepen connectivity around our collective humanity—and the important ideas of our time.

An unforgettable moment, the resulting impact exceeded my wildest expectations. I'm still basking in the glow. And deeply grateful for an experience that left me feeling more intimately connected with all of you—and optimistic about the future of our planet.

After a few opening numbers by my stepson's band and a moving, poetic performance by spoken word genius IN-Q (see page 94), I took the stage to share some thoughts before settling into a fascinating conversation with Paul Hawken—one of the world's preeminent authorities on global climate change and a modern-day hero responsible for helping shape my personal perspective on ecological responsibility.

A pioneering environmentalist, serial entrepreneur, and multiple *New York Times* bestselling author, Paul is also an architect of corporate reform who has dedicated his life to changing the relationship between business and the environment. His work includes founding successful ecologically conscious businesses, including the natural foods market Erewhon; writing about the impacts of commerce on living systems; and consulting with heads of state and CEOs on economic development, industrial ecology, and environmental policy.

In addition to penning countless op-eds and peer reviewed articles, Paul has written eight noteworthy books, including *Drawdown: The Most Comprehensive Plan Ever Proposed to Reverse Global Warming*. Based on meticulous research by leading scientists and policymakers around the world, the book articulates the mission of Project Drawdown, a nonprofit Paul founded that is charged with researching and implementing climate change reversal.

"There's no difference between a climate denier and somebody who's literate in climate change and doesn't do anything."
—Paul Hawken

Paul has lectured everywhere, including Harvard, Stanford, and Wharton. He has given commencement addresses at Yale and Berkeley. He has been interviewed by Bill Maher, Charlie Rose, Larry King, and countless others. And his highly anticipated new book, *Regeneration: Ending the Climate Crisis in One Generation*, is slated to hit bookstores in 2020.

Climate change is an existential threat to the future of humanity and the planet at large.

But, to echo Paul, global warming isn't actually the problem. We're the problem. So let's fix us. And together save the world.

—Rich

"*We haven't looked at climate change in a holistic, systemic way. It's the system that causes it and it's the system that cures it.*"
—Paul Hawken

Paul: The climate crisis has been completely dominated by men. Their science and solutions are all about greenhouse gasses—we have to stop putting them in the atmosphere. We have to reduce. We have to lessen. We have to invest in wind, solar, and Elon Musk. Somehow if we do these three, we'll get a hall pass into the 22nd century.

But that's scientific nonsense. It leaves only one and a half things that you and I can do, which is to drive less and put solar panels on our roofs. Agency is totally left out of the male-dominated climate solution. What about teachers? What about schools? What about small companies? What about farmers? What about foresters? What about grazers? What about ranchers? What about cities? What about towns?

We don't need another white, charismatic, male vertebrate telling the rest of the world, "Listen up, I know what to do." The problem we're in now is because white, semi-charismatic male vertebrates have told us what to do and it clearly didn't work. It has to be a "we" not an "I." Let's have a conversation. Let's create community, collaboration, connection. This is the mission behind Project Drawdown. It's a team of research fellows from all over the world, 21 countries, almost half women, half PhDs, all the major religions. It's an amazing group of young people and then 60 outside scientific reviewers to analyze their models.

We've come to find that if we eliminated food waste, we would have more than enough food for not only the population that exists right now, but for the 9-10 billion expected by 2050. Every day we are wasting a third of the world's food, and yet the industrial agriculture companies say that if we don't basically poison the earth and with herbicides and pesticides, we're going to run out of it.

Everybody eats two or three times a day. That's two or three times a day you can be conscious about your relationship to land, food, farming, atmosphere, self, and health. It's not just what you choose to eat, it's where you choose to buy it from. Are the people who are producing your food absolutely honoring and regenerating the soil it grows in? It's so different from the food that comes out of Monsanto soil, which is basically dead lifeless dirt.

The biggest solution to reversing global warming isn't in the city or in our cars or in a lab. It's the soil, forests, and oceans. We can sequester a trillion tons of CO_2 by regenerative farming practices. If we increase by a half percent of soil organic carbon in our grasslands and farms, that's a trillion tons of CO_2. That takes us back to 1870 just to give you a sense of dimension.

In a handful of soil, there's more bacteria, protozoa, and nematodes than there are in all the human beings that have ever been on the planet combined. Soil is the most complex ecosystem in the world. Go outside and pick up a handful of soil—it's more complex than the oceans, and 80% of what's in it is unknown. Scientists don't know. They have gene sequencing and the means to know, and yet they don't. We take it for granted.

This situation that we're in is the most gnarly, super-wicked problem humanity's ever described and may ever face. You can look at it like it's happening to you, feel like a victim, and be pissed off. That's kind of a hell realm. Or you can see it as feedback from the earth. If you look at it from that way, then it's a gift.

Do things that help you connect more to this beautiful, extraordinary miracle we call the living world. That's the gift of climate change. The gift is transformation of self and of the world. The solutions are transformative. We can either accept the offering and the gift or we can go into self-pity.

Is there enough time? Unanswerable question. Will we make it? Unanswerable question. Those questions are irrelevant. What's relevant is our hearts and who we are and what we do. The climate is not the problem. We're the problem.

"Never give up, and believe it can get better no matter how dark the hole is. You can always get out of it. If I've done it, anyone can do anything in life."
—**John McAvoy**

JOHN

PHOTO: THAT CAMERAMAN

FROM ARMED ROBBERY TO PROFESSIONAL ATHLETE
REFORMED THROUGH THE POWER OF SPORT

The metamorphosis of John McAvoy is unequivocally one of the most compelling, improbable, inspirational, and cinematic tales I have ever encountered.

Born into a notorious London crime family—think the Sopranos meets the Krays—John is a former high-profile armed robber who bought his first gun at 16 and quickly became one of Britain's most successful career criminals and most wanted men.

It took two spells in prison and a close friend's death amidst a heist gone awry to birth a desire to change—redemption he ultimately discovered through the transformative power of sport.

Pulling one of the most improbable 180-degree life transformations of all time, John's greatest heist isn't a bank—it's his life.

While serving a double life sentence on the Belmarsh high security wing—space he shared with extremist cleric Abu Hamza and the 7/7 bombers—John decided to take a spin on the prison gym's indoor rowing machine. That experience revealed an unmistakable fact—John's freakish natural aptitude for endurance matched only by an inhuman ability to suffer.

The epiphany was miraculous. And it would forever alter the trajectory of his life.

In short shrift, John broke a cluster of British and world records for indoor rowing while in prison. Upon parole, he began forging a new life as a professional endurance athlete.

Today, John is the world's only Nike sponsored Ironman athlete. He's a stalwart mouthpiece for prison reform. And he's matured into a staunch advocate for the inherent power we all possess to course correct the trajectory of one's life, no matter how dire the circumstances.

A stunning example of the latent potential lurking within us all, may John's story leave you rethinking the limits you impose on your inherent ability to forge the life of you desire.

—*Rich*

McAVOY

"I've nearly been shot dead by the police—twice. I've been to court and handed a life sentence at 24 years old. I've been around some of the most dangerous men in the country, actual psychopaths. . .When I race, I feel tremendously honored that I can compete."
—John McAvoy

John: The most intelligent, articulate, driven, focused young men go wrong when negative people come into their lives. Their intelligence, drive, and focus can be completely and utterly warped. That's why we've got this huge problem in our country with young kids killing each other and getting involved in gangs. They're incredibly ambitious and driven, but it's all channeled into the wrong place because the wrong people have come into their lives. They don't see the destructive nature of what they're doing until it eventually leads to them being killed or spending their lives in prison.

When I was in prison, there were 85,000 men incarcerated. There were 28 of us out of that 85,000 that were deemed as such a risk that we had to be put in a special high-security prison. We were completely segregated out of the whole prison system, because we were deemed to be a threat to national security. We had posed such a risk to the public that escape had to be made impossible.

I was kept in that unit for two years with Islamic suicide bombers. The system wrote me off, and said "We're not stupid. We know people like you will never, ever, ever change." Because, again, I committed serious crime—armed robberies. But if I have managed to do what I have done through sport, why can't the other 85,000 people do it? That's what makes me so passionate about what I do now.

Sport has allowed me to be successful. It's given me everything that I've got today. It's not ever about being a good athlete, it's about the passion and people it's brought to my life.

I'll wholeheartedly say that I was one of the most entrenched criminals you'd ever meet in your life. Sport has allowed me to give that up, and I'm not the only person. There are countless stories of others using sport to become better people.

So never give up and always believe it can get better. Life is so precious and you're alive. You're breathing and one day we won't. Be appreciative of life and just believe it will get better no matter how dark that hole is. You can always get out of it and if I've done it, so can you. Believe that every day.

PHOTO: THAT CAMERAMAN

"Stay positive. Make a change for yourself. Tell others about your change. Feel good and hopefully, the message will spread."

—Gemma Newman, MD

THE HEALING POWER OF PLANTS

For many, the decision to go vegan is rooted in ideology—a moral compunction to ameliorate suffering or live more sustainably.

But Gemma Newman, MD's journey to plant-based advocacy started with evidence-based science matched with rigorous self-experimentation.

After earning her medical degree at the University of Wales College of Medicine, Gemma plied her medical skills across a variety of specialities including elderly care, endocrinology, pediatrics, obstetrics and gynecology, psychiatry, general surgery, urology, vascular surgery, rehabilitation medicine and General Practice.

During her decade-long tenure as a senior partner at a family medical practice in the U.K., Gemma developed a specialist interest in plant-based nutrition and lifestyle medicine.

Today Gemma serves up advisory board duties for Plant Based Health Professionals UK while providing evidence based nutrition, mental and physical health modalities, energetic healing and lifestyle advice to her patients, who have gained tremendous results using the power of their plate to improve their well-being.

In addition, Gemma has been featured in numerous national broadcast outlets and is a regular contributor *Glamour*, *Zest* and *Health* magazines.

Gemma's passion for well-being was forged out of an experience typical for newly minted physicians fresh out of medical school.

As a young doctor in a high-pressure environment, like many she began neglecting her own health. Struggling with her weight, and having bought into the background hum of 'cut the carbs', she adopted a low carb diet. Calorie counting ensued, combined with a modest daily exercise routine.

It worked. Sort of. Dropping from a size 18 to a size 8, Gemma was impressed with the results. Her bloodwork, however, told an altogether different story. Discovering an elevated lipid profile, markers suggesting a tendency to heart disease, raised an eyebrow. But she shrugged it off to genetics. After all, both her father and grandfather died relatively young of atherosclerosis.

It's just something I was born with. Something I just have to live with.

Nonetheless, it nagged her. Gemma just couldn't shake the feeling that perhaps there was something she could do to alter this seemingly immutable fate.

Meanwhile, Gemma's husband Richard picked up a little book called *Finding Ultra* while training for the London Marathon. He decided to give this plant based diet thing a whirl. Being the skeptical doctor she is Gemma was less than enthusiastic

Where would he get his protein? Won't there be nutritional deficiencies? We will never be invited to friend's houses for dinner ever again! How would I feed my family?

> *"If you are trying to find things to be grateful for, it changes your physiology which changes your disease risks."*
>
> **—Gemma Newman, MD**

Undeterred, Richard completed that marathon, slicing an incredible one hour and ten minutes off his personal best.

This got Gemma's attention.

She had already been passionate about researching lifestyle medicine. How changes in stress, sleep, exercise and diet could improve health for a long time. But nothing was to prepare her for the powerful transformations that were possible when people embraced a whole-food plant-based diet.

Hence ensued a deep dive into medical literature, scientific research, and self-experimentation.

It's a journey that transformed her life wholesale. Completely changed how she practices medicine. And left a lasting, positive impact on every patient she treats.

—Rich

Gemma: Like most enthusiastic young medics, I wanted to help people. But as a graduate, I didn't look after myself. I just ate what I was used to eating, and I didn't really think much about it because I wasn't ill. Long story short, I ended up becoming obese. I had high blood pressure, high cholesterol. I felt hypocritical because I was in a position where I had to help people make drastic life changes, and I wasn't doing that myself.

My first foray into the world of lifestyle medicine was thinking, OK, well, I need to lose weight. I need to get healthy. So I turned to popular culture for nutrition, as most doctors do, unfortunately. I went on a low-carb diet, started calorie counting, and started exercising for an hour a day. I got fairly rigorous with it. I went from a size 16 to a size 6.

I worked very hard and I was really smug about it too. But then I decided in my smugness to check my blood profiles, and I still had raised cholesterol and lipid profiles. I had to eat a bite of humble pie at that point and thought, okay, maybe this is just my genetic heritage, maybe this is never going to change for me because my grandfather had already died of heart disease. I didn't know it back then, but my father was also going to die suddenly of heart disease in his late 50s, and he wasn't overweight.

I accepted my fate until my husband ran the London Marathon. He wanted a good time, but he was getting injuries and had to stop training. He was quite disappointed, so he started looking for inspiration. He read *Finding Ultra*. He said to me, "Gemma, I'm going to go plant-based." I was like, "What's that? What do you mean? What is that, plant-based?" I was quite negative about the whole thing.

He ran his next marathon an hour and 10 minutes faster than his last. *An hour and 10 minutes.*

This, of course, piqued my interest and I began to read. I read more, and then I read more. And then I realized that when I read more, there was even more to read, and I kept on researching. I read research paper after research paper, and then I began to feel a little bit silly—why didn't anyone tell me all this evidence existed? If someone like myself who's had years of training didn't know this, then how is anyone else expected to know? It became a passion from that point. I sneakily decided to start eating plant-based without telling anybody because I didn't want to lose face.

After four weeks of my secret plant-based diet, I tested my blood. Over 10 years and two kids later, exercising less than half of the amount I usually did, I managed completely normal lipid profiles. Right then I knew there was something to eating a plant-based diet.

When I spoke to my patients about my findings, the magic really started happening. These were virtually simple changes patients could make to gradually change their own health. It was incredible to see the positive difference it had on them.

My aim in speaking with patients is always to approach them with empathy and compassion. People are trying all these different diets, low-carb, keto, and so on, because they are frustrated and want results. I was there too. The bottom line is, a plant-based diet is the only one that's been proven to reverse heart disease and proven to be very beneficial for people suffering from a variety of different cancers. And we have great mechanistic data to show why that might be possible.

Rather than arguing about the intricacies of a diet trend, what everyone really needs to know is that we're eating more than 50% ultra-processed foods. The national diet and nutrition survey in the UK tells us that there's only an 8% fruit and vegetable intake among us. It's terrifying. So what's the point in arguing amongst ourselves? We need to get people to understand that whole foods, fruits, vegetables, whole grains, beans, lentils, chickpeas, all those kinds of foods, herbs, and spices, are the cornerstone of health. And everybody else can argue over the other bits and pieces.

I like to think of going plant-based as a journey of enlightenment for humanity, rather than as a diet war. We know instinctively that staying close to nature is super important for our health and for the health of our children. Given that one species is dying every 20 minutes, we know we're in the middle of something serious. So something must be done. But overwhelm is not the emotion we need. Hope and gratitude and love are the emotions we need.

Stay positive, make a change for yourself, tell others about your change, feel good and hopefully the message will spread. It's as simple as that.

WE ARE ALL BORN CREATIVE

Conventional wisdom frames creativity as the purview of a certain select few—a rare gift that eludes us mere mortals.

This is a lie. We are all born creative. More birthright than blessing, creativity is a practice. A habit not unlike any other skill or discipline. A muscle every one of us can build, flex, share, and celebrate.

Chase Jarvis takes the notion one step further, asserting creativity as a biological necessity—a transformative force that resides within us all, that when unleashed delivers vitality to everything we do.

Dubbed by *Forbes* as "the photographer everyone wants to work with," Chase is a visionary of images moving and still. His award-winning commercial campaigns for companies like Nike, Apple, Samsung, Google, and Red

Bull have been seen by millions. And his fine art has been lauded by institutions like the Prix de la Photographie de Paris and the International Photography Awards.

As a photojournalist, Chase contributed to the Pulitzer-Prize winning *New York Times* story "Snow Fall" and earned an Emmy nomination for *Portrait of a City*, his documentary chronicling the legendary Seattle music scene.

As an entrepreneur, Chase is the founder and CEO of two influential companies. His iPhone app Best Camera earned "App of the Year" accolades in 2009 from *Wired*, the *New York Times*, and *Macworld*. The first app that allowed users to share images directly to social networks, it is widely credited with kicking off the multi-billion-dollar, global photo-sharing craze. CreativeLive, Chase's current enterprise,

VIS

is the world's largest live-streaming education company featuring the top experts in photography, design, music, and entrepreneurship.

In addition, Chase hosts the wildly popular YouTube series and podcast *The Chase Jarvis LIVE Show* and is the author of three books, including *Creative Calling*—a must-read primer on the power of creativity to infuse your life with greater meaning, purpose, and fulfillment.

As an avid consumer of Chase's high-quality content dating back to the early days of the internet, I had always wanted to meet him. Our encounter exceeded my expectations.

A kindred spirit, call it kismet.

May this excerpt from our conversation leave you rethinking your relationship to creative expression—and how this essential human trait can be leveraged to live your life with greater intention.

—Rich

"Creativity is a muscle. It's a habit, not a skill. It's a process, not a product."
—Chase Jarvis

Chase: We are creating machines—just look around you. Everything, that park bench, the car, the light post, it was all designed and created. Even your route home today, to go this way instead of that way, was an act of creativity. Choosing what to do with your day and your time on a minute by minute basis, and on a life scale basis, are all wickedly, wildly creative acts. Creativity is a muscle. The only way you learn to use it is through practice, which is why I advocate action over intellect. If you're sitting around trying to figure something out and make the perfect chess move, you're just wasting time. It's the action, it's the doing that actually creates learning. It's great to get information, but actually making a move is far more valuable.

Small, creative acts on a regular basis will remind you that you have agency over your life. The goal is to shift gears from being a cork in the tide to being intentional. As you strengthen these muscles and these tools to create your own life, things will start to happen for you rather than to you. It's vital that you recognize your own creativity.

The person that you are inspired by, that you're moved by, that you admire—their life was intentionally created. It didn't happen accidentally. It was consciously crafted. That person set out with a vision for themselves, and slowly got there. It was a creative process, and that creative force is available to you too.

We're social animals, we want acceptance, we want to fit in. Who wants to disappoint the people that they love the most? No one does. But to truly live the life you want, you're going to have to disappoint some people. It's not their script, it's yours. How many lives do you get? One. To put it in perspective, the number one regret of the dying is that they lived somebody else's prescription for their life.

Disappointing others is sometimes required to make the life of your dreams, so embrace it. It is the riskiest time in the world to play it safe. You're leaving so much on the table in terms of identity, earning power, connection with other people, vulnerability, authenticity. You've got to be creative. It's the most practical thing you've got.

Consciously create the next chapter of your life. Don't just be a cork in the tide. Pay attention to the whisper, the calling. You don't have to know exactly what it is, but you have to pull on the thread. Let it unravel and you'll find your path.

"The people that you are inspired by created their lives intentionally."
—Chase Jarvis

TIM FERRISS

SELF-LOVE IS NON-NEGOTIABLE

If you think you know Tim Ferriss, think again.

A relentless experimenter and virtuoso of deconstruction, Tim has spent the better part of his adult life studying mastery and sharing what he has learned on his wildly popular blog and across the pages of his five consecutive number-one *New York Times* bestselling books: *The 4-Hour Workweek, The 4-Hour Body, The 4-Hour Chef, Tools of Titans*, and his most recent offering, *Tribe of Mentors*.

Along the way, Tim became a prominent angel investor and philanthropist, named one of *Fast Company's* "Most Innovative Business People" and one of *Fortune's* "40 under 40." He graced the main stage at TED and been featured in every prominent media outlet imaginable. His work hosting *The Tim Ferriss Show*—the first business/interview podcast to eclipse 100 million downloads with now over 500 million listens and counting—led the *Observer* to call him "the Oprah of audio."

I'm willing to bet most of you are already decidedly familiar with this globally renowned polymath. Like you, I've followed his blog for years. I've read all his books, and I listen to his podcast regularly. It's an understatement to say that Tim's work has been instrumental in helping me forge the life I'm blessed to lead today. For that I am tremendously grateful.

Nonetheless, I never felt like I really knew the man behind the work.

Who is the real Tim Ferriss?

As 2017 neared its conclusion, Tim started asking himself the same question. Turning 40 matched with the passing of some good friends left him pondering his mortality. Fatigued of the Silicon Valley hustle, he walked away from tech investing and the Bay Area altogether, decamping to Austin to slow the pace of his frenetic life.

My conversation with Tim, which took place in December 2017 on the heels of an intense 10-day silent meditation retreat, reflects Tim's evolution into a more contemplative, inward-focused version of the master experimenter. Typically obtuse when it comes to matters personal, I found him remarkably open—a man wrestling with his past, evaluating the person he wants to be, and thinking deeply about what is most important about life.

Intimate and emotionally raw, it was exactly the experience I patiently awaited to have with Tim since the inception of my podcast.

A sincere and intimate conversation that delivered a unique perspective on one of culture's most influential figures, I'm honored to have been its trusted steward—and reminded that vulnerability is not a weakness, but perhaps our greatest strength.

—Rich

Tim: I had some reasonably bad things happen to me as a kid, and I put on incredible armor to protect myself. But in the last few years, I've come to realize that when you put on really protective armor you keep things out—but you also keep a lot in.

I used to view emotion and emotional attachment as weakness, and instead honed myself as an instrument of competition to validate myself and prove my worth. Anything that detracted from that or remotely made me vulnerable was something I disposed of, which led me to develop a high pain tolerance for tackling difficult things.

In the *4-Hour Body*, I wrote about how people should question certain assumptions they've made about what they can or cannot do, and how too many people accept their partial completeness and never challenge it. But I myself never even thought of my long-standing lack of interest in emotion as a gap; I never accepted my own partial completeness. It was this realization that led me to conclude my current state of being was not only unsustainable, but truly not serving me. I had to rewire myself and it involved going back and contending with some really old things.

I learned that my pain tolerance was just a coping mechanism I had been using to silence my inner voice. It was so merciless and such a demon that at any given time if I scored, metaphorically speaking, 99 out of 100, the only thing that mattered was the one thing that went wrong, and how could I be so stupid or so lazy, so inept or so blind, to get that one thing wrong?

There was always something I could've done better. There was always something I screwed up. It was a fear of losing that kept me moving more than any joy of winning. What I thought was a gift ended up becoming a major handicap. Many things that involve some discomfort or pain can be productive, right? But not all things that are painful are productive. You can become a masochist without realizing it.

I still have trouble saying this, but self-love is not an indulgence. It's not just nice to have. It's a prerequisite. Even if all you want to do is feel successful and take care of the people you love the most, to really take care of them you have to put on your own oxygen mask first. If you don't do that, you are short-changing your ability to care for other people completely.

Retreating into your stories, into these loops, can be perilous and punishing and create a lot of suffering. Don't retreat into your old stories. Know you're not alone. Most of the people we think of as superheroes are walking flaws with insecurities and neuroses, who have somehow figured out how to build habits around one or two strengths. They might not talk about it publicly, but trust me—they are all fighting battles that you know nothing about.

DR.GABOR MATÉ

A COMPASSIONATE AND
HOLISTIC APPROACH TO
HEALING ADDICTION

What if everything you presuppose about addiction is wrong?

Enter Gabor Maté.

A world-renowned lecturer, physician, and bestselling author, Dr. Maté is a highly distinguished, in-demand, and at times controversial authority on the subjects of addiction, stress, and childhood development.

With over twelve years of firsthand experience working with Vancouver's hardcore, skid row drug addicts, Dr. Maté has cultivated a powerful yet eminently commonsensical perspective on this devastating affliction. It's a position that contravenes conventional medical dogma—and begins with a single edict:

Addiction is not a choice.

Moreover, addiction has little to do with illicit substances. It's just not about drugs. Or gambling, or shopping, or porn, or whatever behavior happens to, in the words of Dr. Maté, *incinerate* the lives of millions.

Instead, addiction is about the emotional pain behind the behavior. Healing addiction demands grappling with that pain by confronting the past. The goal is to untangle the circumstances that drive the individual to self-medicate in maddening defiance of all reason and logic.

Based on cutting edge science, case studies, and a wealth of personal experience, Dr. Maté concludes that addiction is a predisposition programmed in early years—an infestation that lurks miles beyond choice. A disease rooted neither in genetics nor free will, but rather in environmental factors that hardwire brain neurochemistry during formative childhood development.

Accordingly, those that suffer should not be shamed or criminalized, but instead treated in the same way we approach anyone suffering from cancer or an autoimmune disease—not with blame but rather with compassion, sympathy, and medical intervention.

As an author, Dr. Maté has written extensively on the subjects of addiction, early childhood development and trauma, attention deficit disorder, and the relationship between stress and disease.

His landmark book, *In the Realm of Hungry Ghosts: Close Encounters with Addiction*, mixes personal stories with science to present a radical re-envisioning of addiction not as a discrete phenomenon confined to an unfortunate or weak-willed few, but as a continuum that runs throughout (and perhaps underpins) our society at large.

Based on my own personal struggles with addiction and the many individuals I have personally encountered over my double-decade journey as a sober alcoholic, one thing is certain: addiction is *complicated*.

There is no miracle cure. There is no quick fix. But hope breathes in compassion and self-understanding.

Dr. Maté's work has been revelatory in helping me better understand others, myself and my ever-evolving quest for greater well-being. He changed my life. And I truly believe his message holds the answer to improve the lives of anyone personally or tangentially impacted by addiction. And let's face it—in this day and age that includes almost everyone.

It was a unique honor to hold space with this compelling paradigm breaker—a conversation that commenced with a survey of his life and labors. But then, ever so subtly, Dr. Maté began to gently shift the verbal fulcrum until his focused insight was keenly turned on me.

The interviewer as patient; my own private session writ large.

—Rich

Gabor: A doctor friend of mine said, "It's difficult to get enough of something that almost works."

I believe addiction is an attempt to soothe pain in every case. Cocaine, opiates, heroin, they are all painkillers. Alcohol is a painkiller. Cannabis is a painkiller. Crystal meth diverts you from the experience of emotional suffering by making you feel more alive and excited, temporarily of course. But the question isn't, Why the addiction? It's, Why the pain?

Why would people not want to be themselves? Why are they not comfortable in their own skin? It's because they suffered in their own skin at some point when they couldn't help it.

Addiction in every case, whether it's the severe addiction of the heroin addicts that I treat or the respectable addictions of the workaholic, is always based in trauma. Any attempt to escape the present moment has to do with the discomfort that we incurred as children. Fundamentally, addiction is always an attempt to escape suffering. It's an attempted solution, it's not the primary problem. To say that addiction is a brain disease, which is the official medical perspective that I was trained in, misses the whole point but then again, the medical profession notoriously does not understand trauma.

Drug addiction is only one particular manifestation of addiction. You can be addicted to sex, gambling, online shopping, a whole lot of respectable things like sports. Anything that takes you out of the moment and provides temporary relief from suffering could be addicting. Some people need chemicals to get that relief, other people get it through behaviors.

What shapes the brain and influences a child's trauma is their environment. The necessary condition for healthy brain development is non-stressed parents who can really connect with their child. So you can see in our society why so many people are affected, because how many parents are non-stressed? How many parents have the kind of

support that traditional societies used to provide in clans and in tribes? Not that I want to romanticize the past nor that we can go back to it, but you have to admit that we've lost something.

In this society, which is so disconnected and alienated, 40% of parents aren't even together, and even the ones that are have to work endlessly and are under severe strain economically. They have relationship stress and have a sort of spiritual emptiness in their lives. Kids are being born into situations like this that no longer support healthy brain development. If on top of that they're actually abused, which is what happens to the most severe addicts, their brain development is even more distorted which creates the perfect template for addiction.

I don't cure addictions. In fact, let's just eliminate the word cure here. You're not a piece of meat. You don't have to be cured. You just need to integrate, and that's a lifelong process. As Eckhart Tolle says, for some people it happens as a sudden illumination. That's essentially what happened to him. But for more people, it's work. It's ongoing work.

The first step is to accept that you're suffering. That's the first thing. If you don't know that you're suffering, you're not going to pierce anything. You're not going to look for anything. Once you realize that you're suffering, you can start asking the question, why? And then you're going to look at your own life and you'll look at society and everything else. But it's got to begin with some sense that things ain't right with you. The next step is to make a choice about how you want to relate to your trauma, and how you want to live your life with it. What structures, support, and practices do you want to help you deal with it? Most importantly, you have to resist the urge to check out. Many addicts think that powerlessness

opens you up to being hurt. But surrender is the only way out of the hurt. Our true nature is to be compassionate, sharing, cooperative, and loving. Recovery is returning to who we actually are. It can be a lifelong process, but it's not a bad thing. As with all journeys, if you do it right, it's not about the destination. It's about each step along the way.

"The difference between passion and addiction is that between a divine spark and a flame that incinerates."
—Dr. Gabor Maté

LESSONS FROM THE WORLD'S HAPPIEST PEOPLE

We all want to be happy.

But what exactly is happiness? Can it be cultivated? And if so, how?

Somewhere along the way, you've likely heard of something called the "Blue Zones," a term coined by Dan Buettner in reference to five hidden slivers of the world that boast the highest per capita populations of *centenarians*—people who thrive to 100 and beyond.

Places where people forgot to die.

Interestingly, in addition to living inordinately long, Dan discovered that Blue Zoners also seemed resoundingly *happier* than their fellow Western world equals.

Determined to find out why, Dan shifted his focus away from longevity and zeroed in on the elusive, ever-so-slippery nature of happiness itself.

Overseeing a team of experts, Dan deployed hard science to better define the emotional state we seek most. He scoured the planet in search of the cultures that most exemplify happiness. He examined the internal and external factors that most promote happiness. And he extrapolated the key lessons that can be best applied to ultimately live better and more fulfilling lives.

The result of Dan's quest became a *National Geographic* cover story and the thesis of his *New York Times* bestselling book, *The Blue Zones of Happiness: Lessons from the World's Happiest People*.

A true renaissance man, Dan is a National Geographic Fellow, longevity expert and world explorer with three endurance cycling world records to his name. A multiple *New York Times* bestselling author, he's a seemingly constant presence on *Today*, has appeared on *The Oprah Winfrey Show* twice, and has been profiled on every respected global media outlet from CNN to *Late Night with David Letterman*.

Over the last decade Dan has delivered more than 500 keynotes, including speeches for Bill Clinton's Health Matters Initiative, Google Zeitgeist, and TEDMED. His TED Talk "How to Live to be 100+" has been viewed over 4 million times.

In addition, Dan is the founder of Blue Zones Project, a community well-being improvement initiative. Designed to help people live longer and better through community transformation, his programs have pioneered wellness breakthroughs for municipalities across the nation.

A three-time podcast guest, my conversations with Dan never disappoint. A trifecta of charisma and scholarly experience matched with a preternatural ability to communicate, Dan is the man when it comes to how to live long. How to live happy. How to live well. And how to fuel your life with greater meaning and a sense of purpose.

Hero, friend and mentor, Dan is a rare visionary. The very definition of a modern-day explorer. And an exemplar of service whose life and work has positively, permanently, and quite unequivocally improved the well-being of millions.

May we all aspire to Dan's level of positive impact on humanity.

—*Rich*

DAN

"Follow your bliss, not your material desires."
—Dan Buettner

BUETTNER

> "The more things for which you develop a fondness the richer the life you live."
> —Dan Buettner

Dan: I'm a lifelong explorer; I set three records for biking Alaska, Argentina, and across Africa.

I spent eight years of my life on a series of expeditions that sought to unravel ancient mysteries. After joining the National Geographic team, I set out to find the geographic areas where people live verifiably the longest. In seeking to reverse engineer longevity, me and the team have found what we call "blue zones," or longevity hotspots, around the world.

And now we have cities in America emulating these Blue Zones. The big epiphany was understanding that people make it to 100 and still water ski, stand on their head, and do karate—not because they tried, but rather as a residue of the right environment.

With that insight, we created a program that would help entire American cities live longer—not by convincing people to change their habits, but by shaping their environments so that they're mindlessly and relentlessly nudged into doing the right thing rather than the wrong thing.

So, in every city, we have teams. We adapt food and alcohol policies and build the environment with the city planner so that parks are accessible and there's public transportation, bike lanes, and walk places.

When you bring all of these together, you create the perfect storm. Within three years, in every city that we work in, we see obesity dropping down and happiness going up. Now, in America, those in the top quintile of the happiest people live about eight years longer than those in the lowest quintile. So, when it comes to life expectancy, working on getting happier is almost as powerful as dropping a smoking habit. The original blue zone areas of longevity are within the top 10% of the happiest places in the world.

Savoring, gratitude, meditation—they do all kind of work, but they require a conscious behavior modification. But there are dozens of ways you can change your environment to make yourself happier.

I've found that, in order to have happiness, you need food, shelter, healthcare, education, mobility, and you have to be able to treat yourself every once in a while. No matter if you work at a food stand or sweep the streets, as long as you make an effort to work, you're going to make enough money to cover your needs. They call it "workfare." So we've found that health and happiness go hand-in-hand. And if happiness were a cake recipe, then marrying the right person, getting the right work, being healthy and giving back are all ingredients.

And if you're unhappy, the most powerful thing you can do is move to a happier place. Have meaningful conversations. Volunteer. Getting involved in your community is the secret to happiness. For me, I eat a lot more vegetables. I know the importance of sleep. I make time for my friends. I see the world from my bicycle. Overall, I put a deep consciousness on enjoying my days with the right balance of productiveness that will yield that life satisfaction. In doing this, you develop empathy. You develop wisdom. After all, wisdom is knowledge plus experience—so focus on the art of life.

CURSE? YOU NEVER KNOW
BY DAN BUETTNER

There's a Buddhist fable about a farmer who loses his horse. His neighbors come over to console him, saying they are sorry for what happened to him.

The farmer replies, "What do you mean, you're sorry? You never know."

A few days later the farmer's horse returns with four wild horses in tow. The neighbors return, this time to congratulate the farmer. The farmer responds, "Thank you, but you never know."

A week later one of the wild horses kicks the farmer's son and breaks his leg. The neighbors come over to console the farmer, who again says, "You never know."

While the son is convalescing, army recruiters come through the village to conscript young men to war. Finding the farmer's son with a broken leg, they pass over him. Once again, the neighbors come over to console the farmer. The farmer shrugs . . .

You get the idea. The point of this fable is impermanence: the fleeting nature of all things good and bad.

I've been thinking about this fable lately, specifically about a secondary lesson it holds in these Covid-19 times of uncertainty, mortality and loneliness.

As I write this, the Covid-19 virus has killed over 80,000 Americans and left 30% of workers unemployed. Every screen emits scary news of loss and danger. It's hard to see this pandemic as anything but a curse—But what if we stopped to play out the hand? What if we shrugged off the news and said to ourselves, "You never know?"

Rich Roll is a guy who changed his narrative. For a while, he was a flabby, overstressed, burger-eating, cocktail-swilling entertainment lawyer (I've seen the pictures). He hit rock bottom, confronted his addiction and rebooted his work life. At age 40, he became vegan and shed fat mass the size of a seven-year-old from his midsection.

Bottoming out inspired in Rich the self-work, protean discipline, and brutal training regimen that transformed him. And it's this energy and quest for evolution that he channels in his enormously successful podcasts. His hardship begat success. If Rich hadn't suffered—and learned from it, something tells me Hollywood would have one more fat-cat but the world would not have the *Rich Roll Podcast*.

I'm no stranger to hardship—albeit the self-imposed variety. When I graduated from college, a time when my peers were doing useful and productive things with their lives, I spent eight years biking some 40,000 miles across five continents. I crossed the Sahara without sunscreen, slogged 800 miles across a Siberian bog, and pedaled alone across El Salvador and Nicaragua where I saw human roadkill and a severed head during their civil wars.

I once shared a pot of centipede stew with a Congolese family.
I also contracted my share of Third World diseases: malaria, giardia, dysentery, hepatitis, intestinal worms, and others. These experiences left me with a few lingering health problems but an enormous pain

threshold, a capacity for empathy, and an understanding of our country that comes only from being outside its borders—the qualities of a world citizen.

Later, I went on to identify five pockets around the world where people live the longest. In these "Blue Zones," people survive into their nineties and hundreds largely free of heart disease, diabetes and cancers that foreshorten our lives. They don't achieve this amazing health outcome through platinum health insurance plans or nuclear medicine.

Blue Zone people live lives most of us might not envy: they grow their own food, use their own two feet as transportation, and socialize between six or seven hours a day with friends. They have suffered famines, economic downturns, and agricultural failures. Through it, they've gained knowledge, experience, and resilience. In other words, hardship has yielded wisdom that extended their lives: a blessing.

I now work with 51 cities throughout America to make them more like the original Blue Zones, in that the people who live in

those cities are more active, more social, and thus overall happier. I think too many of us suffer from the affliction of excessive ease and comfort. We've engineered most of the physical activity out of our lives with mechanical conveniences (our grandparents burned about four times as many calories every day in non-exercise physical activity). Every trip requires a car ride, and no one is ever more than an arm's reach from ultra-processed foods. Moreover, we're marketed the notion that if we stay constantly busy, financial freedom will enable us to buy ever more things and achieve success that seems to lie on an ever-receding horizon. In the meantime, we get sick.

Yes, the Covid-19 virus has killed loved ones and created massive economic suffering. Real, true hardship that I don't take lightly at all. But maybe, just maybe, it also opened a window of opportunity if we choose to look.

According to Gallup, only 30% of Americans actually find purpose in their work. Perhaps this forced unemployment will give people a chance to reconsider their job and

to reboot. Find something that better lines up with their values and talents.

The Chinese character for crisis is composed of two characters, one for crisis alongside another for opportunity. Similarly, I think this Covid-19 menace—or whatever hardship befalls us next—provides a hidden gift, perhaps in developing compassion, learning how to nurture relationships, and to reassess our lives and grow.

The next time life sucker-punches you, maybe say OK. Through the pain, maybe say to yourself, "You never know." Like most hardships, it just might materialize as a blessing in the rear-view mirror.

SUSAN DAVID, PhD

DISCOMFORT IS THE PRICE OF ADMISSION TO A MEANINGFUL LIFE

How we navigate our inner world—our everyday thoughts, emotions, and self-stories—is the single most important determinant of success. It drives everything.

Do you allow doubt, shame, fear, or anger hold you back? Do past failings prevent you from believing in yourself? If so, you are among the many who suffer from emotional fragility—and it's holding you back.

Achieving our potential to live fulfilling, purpose-driven lives demands we stop immunizing ourselves against stress and setbacks. No longer can we ignore uncomfortable feelings. To bring our best selves forward, Susan David, PhD contends we must develop "emotional agility"—the facility to confront difficult emotions, gain critical self-insight from these feelings, and ultimately leverage the awareness gained to better align our values with our actions and make changes to bring the best of ourselves forward.

A pioneer in her field, Susan is an award-winning psychologist on faculty at Harvard Medical School, CEO of Evidence Based Psychology, and co-founder of the Institute of Coaching (an affiliate of Harvard Medical School).

In addition, she is the author of the number-one *Wall Street Journal* bestseller, *Emotional Agility: Get Unstuck, Embrace Change, and Thrive in Work and Life*. Based on a concept Harvard Business Review heralded as a Management Idea of the Year, it's a powerful roadmap for real behavioral change—a new way of acting that will help you to reincorporate your most troubling feelings as a source of energy and creativity, and live your most successful life whoever you are and whatever you face.

Susan is a frequent contributor to the *Harvard Business Review*, *New York Times*, *Washington Post*, and *Wall Street Journal*. She is a sought-after speaker and consultant. And her 2017 TED Talk, "The gift and power of emotional courage", has accumulated over 7 million views.

Over the course of our conversation, Susan explains why it's imperative to stop hiding from our stories, our emotions and ourselves. Instead, we must we must identify our core values and face our challenges willingly—as a neutral observer, with curiosity, kindness, and self-acceptance. In so doing, we become empowered, and ultimately greater willpower, resilience, and effectiveness in all areas of life.

When practiced, this skill called emotional agility becomes a superpower. It leads to mastery over our emotions, thoughts, and stories. It helps us and our children become better problem solvers and more engaged learners. And it builds resilience against anxiety and depression.

Simply put, stop avoiding uncomfortable feelings. Because, Susan puts it, the tough emotions are the price we pay for a meaningful life.

—*Rich*

Susan: Society gives us this narrative that says there are good emotions and bad emotions. The good emotions, joy and happiness, these are the ones you should chase. The bad emotions, anger, grief, sadness, these are the ones you should avoid. But our emotions have evolved in us as a human species to help us respond and survive. When we block or suppress or push aside emotions, we are actually stopping ourselves from being meaningful and successful humans. A critical aspect of well-being is moving beyond the struggle with our emotions into this other space where we accept all feelings and see them as normal, not good or bad.

The theoretical acceptance of all of our emotions, our grief, our sadness, our joy, our anger, is a hallmark of resilience and a cornerstone of an effective relationship. That's not to say that because we feel angry, we should act on our anger. But rather, our emotions contain signposts to things that we care about. Instead of judging the emotion, if we can be open-hearted and compassionate towards it, we can then discern the values underneath it.

Our difficulty in seeing our own pain and recognizing our own sadness keeps us from being empathetic, and disconnects us from authentic emotional experiences. One of the most critical aspects of ending this struggle is simply dropping the rope. What I mean by that is just making a conscious choice to notice your thoughts, emotions, and stories in ways that are compassionate, curious, and courageous and to take actions that are concordant with your values.

Life's beauty is inseparable from its fragility. You walk around and you're young. Then, one day, you realize that you're not young. You're sexy. Then, you realize no ones even looking at you anymore. You nag your children to clean their room and then one day, there's silence where your child once was. You're healthy until you get a diagnosis that brings you to your knees.

The reality is, tough emotions are part of your contract with life. You don't get to have a meaningful career or family or leave the world a better place without stress and discomfort. In order to navigate the world as it is, not as you wish it to be, you need to be able to strengthen your capability with the full range of this beautiful, messy, difficult human experience.

OWNING YOUR TRUTH

What is a runner? How do we define an athlete? What does it truly mean to be fit and healthy?

Challenging stereotypes, Mirna Valerio demands that we broaden our limited definition of these terms.

She may not be fast, but she runs. In fact she runs a lot, an impressive slew of ultramarathons to her name.

She's also not skinny. In fact, she's big.

250 pounds big.

But Mirna Valerio is without a doubt a runner.

In fact, the force of nature affectionately known as "the Mirnavator" is one of the most inspirational athletes I have ever met—a prolific purveyor of the trails and a true ambassador of sport—on a mission to empower women of all shapes and sizes to proudly embrace their

MIRNA VALE

"Nothing happens overnight.
So know that whatever your goal is,
it's going to be a journey."
—Mirna Valerio

RIO

bodies, expand their horizons, and own their truth.

Carrying herself with grace, an intelligent self-confidence and a smile so gleeful it brightens all in her path, Mirna's appeal has less to do with her ability to run long distances and everything to do with her unapologetic celebration of herself and others.

Her joyful self-acceptance is both real and rare. It's both authentic and bold. It's as infectious as it is inclusive. And it's incredibly empowering to the millions of people who suffer body-shame issues silently.

When she's not running, the Brooklyn native is a former educator, diversity practitioner, cross-country coach, mom, and author of the remarkable memoir, *A Beautiful Work in Progress*.

Not enough? Mirna is also a Julliard-trained opera singer. To prove it, she concludes our podcast with her angelic voice.

Mirna's story has appeared in the *Wall Street Journal, Runner's World, NBC Nightly News*, and *CNN*. Her writing has been featured on the pages of *Women's Running, Self, Outside, and Runner's World*. And in 2018, she was chosen as a *National Geographic* Adventurer of the Year.

I first came across Mirna's story by way of a viral, pitch-perfect mini-documentary produced by REI called *The Mirnavator*. Hooked, I was determined to share her powerful story with you.

Mirna delivers on self-empowerment and self-acceptance. On the importance of tackling stereotypes, overcoming prejudice, and prioritizing inclusion. And the need to redefine how we think about and define athleticism, the spirit of sport, and fitness in general.

But more than anything, this is a conversation about owning your truth.

—Rich

"Instead of being ashamed of doing what you do or being what you are, I ask two important questions: Why not celebrate it? Why not be proud of the fact that the body you are in can do great things?"

—Mirna Valerio

Mirna: I was driving one day and I started to have terrible chest pain, a type of pain that I had never felt before—right on the left side of my chest. I thought I was having a heart attack because the jolts were so insistent, so rhythmic and sharp.

I made it home and a friend drove me to the hospital. I wasn't having a heart attack, but when I followed up with a cardiologist, he informed me that it might have very well been a cardiac event because I had all this inflammation in my bloodstream. I was overweight and living a very stressful lifestyle that just wasn't sustainable.

I weighed over 300 pounds. My cardiologist told me that if I wanted to watch my son grow up, I would have to make a change. That was a moment of catharsis—I knew what I needed to do.

I made a plan to run a mile every day. The first mile wasn't very pleasant—It took me 17 minutes and 45 seconds. I was so disappointed, but I knew the next day would be different. So I did another mile, and it was a little bit better. The next day, a little bit better. After about two weeks I was running a mile and a half to two miles, slowly returning to my old self. Rediscovering the outdoors had a tremendous positive impact on not just my physical health, but my spiritual, emotional, and mental health too.

Eventually, the weight loss plateaued, and I accepted that I wasn't going to lose any more. I got down to 245 pounds, and that's where my body lives now. I feel really good. Although I plateaued in my weight loss, I wasn't going to stop running because I loved it so much. I wanted to run ultramarathons, and I was going to do it even in my fat body.

When I created my blog, *Fat Girl Running*, I knew the title would be triggering for some people. There's a lot of fatphobia and fat-shaming and I don't think that will ever go away unless there's a huge paradigm shift in our society. I don't struggle with my weight—I am happy the way I am. I wanted to reframe what it means to be fat, and that's what eventually got me noticed.

Having a healthy self-image requires you to appreciate and love yourself. I know that's difficult, especially for people who don't get validation from society or from family members and friends. I'm fortunate in that I've always had a healthy body image, and my family culture supported it. If you don't get it from the outside world, you have to create it for yourself, and that takes deep self-reflection. If you don't have a habit of self-love, if you don't have a habit of stepping out of your comfort zone, you won't experience growth.

My hope is that if you see me running ultramarathons, you can picture yourself doing something just as powerful too. Find something that you might be interested in that you think you can't do, or maybe someone has told you couldn't do and do it. It may require a huge step out of your comfort zone, but you aren't going to learn anything or make any progress staying in there anyway.

Nothing happens overnight. Know that whatever you are changing or whatever you're doing, whatever your goal is, it's going to be a journey. There will be moments of joy and amazement, and there will be moments of awfulness, where you just have to be in the trenches and do the work.

But I promise it will have tremendous implications for success.

MARK MANSON

HOPE, HUMAN DIGNITY, AND THE PERILS OF COMFORT

One day not long ago, I awoke to a bright orange book ubiquitously displayed everywhere I looked.

Provocatively titled *The Subtle Art of Not Giving a F*ck*, a young first-time author had given birth to a publishing juggernaut, custom-tailored for clickbait embrace.

The title also made the book easy to dismiss. In fact I freely admit to downright refusing to read it. But the damn thing just wouldn't go away. Not only did it top the *New York Times* bestseller list, the book stayed there. Four years and over eight million copies later, it still rests at number four—a *full 196 weeks since its publication*.

So who is this Mark Manson guy?

Realizing that my reflexive reaction was perhaps misplaced, I finally relented. I now admit to being pleasantly surprised by what I discovered.

To be sure, the book is both contrarian and confrontational. Chock-a-block with F-bombs. But it's also delightfully refreshing, upending the tired tropes of self-help with an intractable glee. Grappling with real issues, I relished Mark's unique voice—depth meets grit with an infectious philosophical sensibility.

Before he became a publishing sensation (his influence launching countless profanely titled copycat books), Mark began his writing career as a blogger. Sharing personal development advice that "doesn't suck" (his words), he amassed a devoted audience of 2 million monthly readers.

Dissecting our dysfunctional cultural relationship with money, entertainment, and the internet, Mark's latest chart-topper, *Everything Is F*cked: A Book About Hope* is an equally compelling yet more mature follow-up that deftly explores the perils of distraction, comfort, and success.

In other words, what happens when you exceed your every ambition. What then?

Success breeds its own peril. I wanted to better understand the high-altitude, existential crisis visited upon a young man who eclipsed his wildest dreams by age 32.

His answers were found in lessons applicable to all. Learning to maintain focus in an increasingly distracted world. Resisting the comforts of success that erode the soul. And finding ballast in the reservoir of human dignity.

I really enjoyed my time with Mark—and left our conversation with great respect for his profoundly curious mind and keen insights on the human condition.

—Rich

"*Constant stimulation complicates our understanding of ourselves. The more options we have, the less willing we are to compromise what we want to be with somebody else.*"

—**Mark Manson**

Mark: My dream was to have a book deal. But not just any book deal—I wanted to write a bestseller. I wanted to be on the *New York Times* list. I wanted to tour the country. I had this whole checklist of life goals in my head, and *The Subtle Art of Not Giving a F*ck* knocked them all out in two months. I have a lot of pride and gratitude about it, but in a way, it was like getting slammed into a midlife crisis at 60 miles an hour. I had everything I ever wanted and I was only 32.

What surprised me the most about achieving massive success is that I felt exactly the same as I did when I had nothing. In my early twenties, went through this lost depressed period where I was broke, I had no opportunities in front of me, no purpose. But here I am on the other side, the complete opposite situation where I've achieved everything. I have a buttload of money and tons of opportunities, but I feel exactly the same.

We all need to believe that the future can be better than it is today. That's what gives us a sense of meaning and purpose in our lives. But our visions of hope can potentially be destructive. Everything that you hope for, by definition, you hope for on faith. I believed on faith that having a bestselling book would make my life better. I didn't actually know that, it's just something I chose to believe in and it motivated me for many years. We all develop these kinds of faith-based belief systems around what we hope for in the future and tie our personal meaning to them. But at the end of the day, they're arbitrary.

We are reaching a saturation point as a culture—we are beyond overstimulated. We are overflowing with stimulation and it's complicating our understanding of ourselves. When you're sitting in a nice air-conditioned room with 500 Netflix shows, and you can have 20 different cuisines delivered to you in the press of a button, suddenly all these questions about identity, purpose, the meaning of life, and what value you're adding to the world start to surface. Fulfilling desires can actually erode away at our ability to feel as though we have meaningful lives.

Paradoxically, the worst things are, the easier it is to hope for something. If a war breaks out and God forbid California is being bombed, you and I suddenly know exactly what we're waking up in the morning for. But when everything's just fucking great and we're just chilling, drinking some tea, looking at the mountains, it's much easier to think "What do I hope for?"

There's a billion-dollar industry helping people figure out what the hell they should hope for. That is a very privileged position to be in. The first-world creates a lot of trifling problems and that in itself is a problem. Because the truth is, we don't deserve to be happy. We don't deserve anything. If you want to feel something, if you want to have some experience, you have to go out and get it. You have to find some sort of meaningful struggle that earns it for you. You can't just sit in a room and feel fucking entitled to it. It doesn't work that way. Happiness is a by-product of working on the right things, choosing the good struggles. Choosing the right things to hope for.

Self-improvement by its very nature is going to be difficult. No self-improvement feels great. If it feels great, you're probably not actually changing very much. Any real change is by definition, painful, stressful, difficult. This is why I often describe my work as pessimistic self-help. Most self-help books are very idealistic about human nature. They tell you that if you believe, you can do anything, you just need to think positive and manifest it. I don't like any of that shit. I spent enough time in psych-research to understand that we humans are inherently flawed, selfish, somewhat shitty creatures and we don't treat ourselves very well.

So, instead of lying to you and telling you that you can do anything you want, I want you to be a little less shitty to yourself and others. I want you to be aware of your flaws, and really work on them. I want you to understand the lifestyles that do and don't work for you. I want you to take action, to create better habits and disciplines. Let's optimize our time on this planet. We only get one shot.

"It appears that the consequences
for truth are high."
—George Orwell

BRYAN FOGEL

THE PRICE OF TRUTH

How far will we go to be considered the best?

Obsessed with this inquiry, Bryan Fogel decided to answer it for himself.

Struck by the fact that Lance Armstrong never once failed a single drug test, the avid cyclist, playwright, and filmmaker decided to make a documentary with one goal in mind: to prove the system in place to detect doping athletes was bullshit.

What he ultimately discovered was even darker. Simply put, what transpires in the global sports arena cannot be presumed either truthful or fair.

Icarus was premised on an audacious idea: Bryan would undertake an aggressive doping protocol, experimenting with a wide variety of performance enhancing drugs. He would observe the changes in his athletic performance. He would attempt to evade detection. And finally, he would extensively and transparently document the entire experience, sharing the whole endeavor on film.

To guide him through the tenebrous process of doping, Bryan enlists the professional aid of Dr. Grigory Rodchenkov, a renegade Russian scientist and then pillar of his country's "anti-doping" program. As they grow closer, it becomes clear that Rodchenkov is in fact the central figure in what we soon discover is Russia's vast and elaborate state-sponsored Olympic doping program—a nefarious scheme that can be traced to Russia's highest chains of command, all the way up to Vladimir Putin.

When the two realize they hold the power to reveal the biggest international sports scandal in living memory, Bryan's academic exercise in self-experimentation quickly pivots into spy thriller territory—a spectacular high-stakes collision of politics, sports, espionage, and danger more John le Carré than Morgan Spurlock.

An extraordinary portrait of self-sacrifice in the interest of truth, *Icarus* is a taut and gripping exposé that exemplifies the power of film to rewrite history. The Academy agreed, awarding it the Oscar for Best Documentary Feature of 2017—solidifying Bryan as a new and important cinematic voice.

Not only did my conversation with Bryan forever alter my perception of Olympic sport it proved a powerful glimpse into the dark realpolitik of the global sports arena—and its staggering implications for our already deeply strained geopolitical landscape.

—*Rich*

Bryan: Cycling is in my DNA. I got into cycling because I'm 5' 8" and skinny, and the reality was that I wasn't going to be a football player. Cycling for me has been my therapy through life—it grounds me. That passion is ultimately what started me on this incredible journey that became the documentary film *Icarus*.

Now, among all athletes, performance-enhancing drugs are a topic of conversation. I was very curious to see what the drugs did and how they were regulated. I wanted to present to society the questions: *What do we do about this? Should we care? Should we not?* That was the blueprint that I had set out in going to make *Icarus*.

Of course, the film became so much more, with the narrative evolving into a thriller which happened to be true.

I understood that a doping athlete like Lance Armstrong was not the needle in the haystack, but that they were the haystack. I had set out with a hypothesis that the anti-doping system had many problems, but it soon became evident that there was a bigger story to tell. With the help of a Russian scientist named Grigory Rodchenkov, I was able to uncover the single biggest scandal in sport history.

George Orwell had said that sport is war without the weapons. That could not be truer today, particularly in regard to the Olympics, where athletes are gladiators for their country. In the same vein as "doublethink," Grigory—a brilliant scientist—admitted that he had created the anti-venom to his own anti-doping tests, allowing Russian Olympic athletes to pass while other athletes around the world would be caught through the methodology he created.

Russia has been using its sport program to assert itself geopolitically with intent to show dominance and power. This is beyond competing peacefully and in harmony of sport. To me, the issue that we have to look at as a country is, Are we willing to tolerate a foreign power's meddling in our processes?

What you see in *Icarus* is a country meddling in the global affairs of the Olympics and sport to cheat, collude, and create fraud. And the analogy can be drawn into our current U.S. political climate and our recent presidential election. There is an incredibly upsetting takeaway that begs the question: *If a country will do this to win medals, what else are they willing to do?*

Now Grigory's in hiding—and that's really frightening. If the consequences of telling the truth are your imprisonment—your punishment for trying to bring a story that needed to be told to the world—that's concerning on a big level. But, this story is far from over. We are catching history as it is unfolding.

I've learned that as a filmmaker, you can set out on a journey, but you ultimately don't know where it's going to lead. In this case, I couldn't have imagined that it would end up with Grigory and my team exposing a gigantic conspiracy and scandal and, moreover, that I would become so much wiser and understanding of the world that we're living in.

That is very cool about documentary: it can take you on a journey that is not only unexpected, but that can have a serious positive impact on the world.

CHRIS HAU

"We're able to give so much more when we take care of ourselves on a daily basis."
—Chris Hauth

MAINTAINING YEAR-ROUND FITNESS

My early days as an endurance athlete were far from noteworthy.

Below average at best, there was zero evidence that I possessed either the talent or potential to distinguish myself in any meaningful way.

My first stab at a marathon resulted in having to walk the final eight miles. A handful of tepid Olympic-distance triathlon results solidified my middle-of-the-pack status. In my debut half-ironman at Wildflower, I didn't even make it to the run before pulling out, cramped and depleted.

At the time, it mattered little. I loved the experience, which only strengthened my desire for self-improvement. From my staircase moment at 40 that catalyzed a drive to better control my diet, health and fitness, through all my athletic adventures over the last decade, I have constantly strived to continuously improve my body's ability to perform at its best.

When I set my sights on ultra-endurance, I knew I needed direction. I connected with Chris Hauth and never looked back. Picking me up from that Wildflower DNF, Chris patiently rebuilt me from the ground up. With patience, time, and discipline, he ultimately and expertly guided me through three Ultraman World Championships; EPIC5, a boundary-eclipsing adventure in which Jason Lester and I became the first to complete five Ironman-distance triathlons on five Hawaiian Islands in under a week; and the Ötillö Swimrun World Championships in 2017, an event we raced together as a team.

It's a complete understatement to say that none of my middle-aged athletic accomplishments would have been remotely possible without Chris's sage counsel—a coach, mentor, and friend instrumental in turning my crazy dreams into reality.

One of the world's most respected endurance and ultra-endurance coaches, Chris is a sub-nine-hour Ironman, former professional triathlete, Age Group Ironman World Champion, and two-time Olympic Swimmer. In 2006, Chris won the Ironman Coeur D'Alene and went on to be the first American amateur and fourth overall American at the Ironman World Championships in Kona, Hawaii.

When he's not training and racing, Chris hosts the *Weekly Word Podcast* and runs *AIMP Coaching*, mentoring a wide spectrum of athletes ranging from elite professionals—including Ironman and Western States top finishers, Ultraman winners and Olympic Trials qualifiers—to first time half-marathoners.

Whether you are an elite athlete or just starting out, Chris knows how to get the best out of athletes the *right way*.

That way doesn't consider podiums. In fact, it's not even about competition. It's about connection with self. It's about community. And it's about creating a lifelong love affair with movement, adventure, experience, and the outdoors.

A soothing, welcome and recurring presence on the podcast, Chris never fails to drop grounded, actionable advice on every facet of what it means to live an active life.

—Rich

Chris: There are endurance adventures to be found anywhere, whether it's a couple hours away or in your own backyard. Sure, there's people swimming around Great Britain, but there's also people swimming across huge lakes, and curating their own adventures. That's the beauty of people becoming more and more curious of what their potential is: they find their new normal and it pushes their potential even further.

The gear, the Garmin watches, the race entry fees, a lot of people can't afford it all, and it can be overwhelming. So, figure something else out altogether. Where do you live? What can you do to make an exciting, cool, unique, adventure for yourself? Pick something that really challenges you, puts you on the far edge of what you deem is possible, so you have a little bit of fear, a little bit of respect for it. That will keep you motivated. And then train for it. Get excited about it. Connect your community with it or raise funds for charity or something where you're directly impacting your hometown, and showing others, "Yeah, I'm driving two hours to do this crazy challenge in the woods simply because it's worth discovering."

You have to build a long-term roadmap towards this goal. It's about getting consistent, doing a little bit every day. And whatever sport you choose, you have to enjoy it. Sure, sitting in a basement on a treadmill is not that much fun. But there's value in doing it because you're excited about the outcome and enjoy the journey.

The biggest mistake I see athletes make is thinking that they have to keep this perfect string of workouts going. If you get 80% of your week's workouts done, if you get three, four days strung together and done well, it doesn't matter if you miss a day. We're all not going to be 100% on any of this, I'm never 100% on any of this, let alone, most of my athletes. Life gets in the way, and there's no need to judge yourself. The next day, you're going to come back more motivated, more focused, and you'll feel better doing it. So don't look for perfection, look for steady, gradual progress.

Whether you're running or biking or swimming, your training time is an opportunity to check in with yourself. It's so important. When you're truly within yourself, your own breathing, your own heart rate, feeling your body move, it awakens so much within you.

There's only a positive outcome from it: more creativity, more patience, more energy. Our minds start opening up to our unconscious selves and to some bigger thoughts. Everything becomes clearer. When you go out for a run and come back, the answers are somehow there. Some of your best creative ideas come from that time spent in solitude.

It also gives you the opportunity to listen to your body. There's so much static every day in our lives that it's hard to hear what our bodies are saying. Getting a chance to work out no matter what the environment is gives you a chance to reconnect. And it can be hard at first—closing your eyes on a trainer and riding can feel painfully slow. But again, your ability to practice that every day, makes five minutes go to 10 minutes, go to 20 minutes, go to 60 minutes more and more quickly. Whether it's 45 minutes, 30 minutes, an hour and a half a day—that adds up to seven or eight hours of self-reflection a week. If you use the majority of that time to think and be in harmony, you will know so much more in order to put forth a healthier, smarter version of yourself.

We're able to give so much more if we're able to take care of ourselves on a daily basis. It sounds selfish, but your energy, your patience, your vitality towards work, towards family, towards community, all that changes when you get time for yourself every day. Getting a chance to reset your operating system is vital. Don't let anybody take away your joy and journey in training in nature. It's a form of self-care and it's protected time. You deserve it. Don't let anything or anyone rob you of the opportunity every day, to go inside yourself and exhale.

"Whether you're running or biking or swimming, your training time is an opportunity to check in with yourself. It's so important. When you're truly within yourself, your own breathing, your own heart rate, feeling your body move, it awakens so much within you."
—Chris Hauth

THE JOURNEY FOR CONNECTION
BY CHRIS HAUTH

There are so many who appear to be looking for meaning, a deeper connection to themselves and the world around them, a journey that may on the surface not necessarily be thought of as spiritual but as one that is especially fulfilling.

My view may be understandably subjective, but truly I believe that endurance and ultra-endurance events, and simply the world of expeditions and adventures, have gained so much appeal of late because this longing to journey, simultaneously deep within ourselves and far from our known comforts, is a way for connection back to our truest self.

I believe these physical, mental and emotional tests provide a new or renewed sense of purpose and an opportunity to test our potential. These extreme adventures tend to crystalize the realization that there is more to us than sleeping, eating, and working by expanding our notion of who we are.

Our traditional pursuits of work, money, and possessions typically neglect the self. Even though we are enthusiastically barreling headfirst with the reckless abandon of irrational conviction, our compass reading is off. We have lost ourselves along the way and hardly recognize it.

When we bring self-care into our lives, with consistently dedicated time to focus on our health and well-being, combined with a routine that includes muscular activity and an elevated heart rate, a reconnection to nature, along with a genuine willingness to spend time with our thoughts—even deep meditative reflection—something magical happens. We become reoriented with ourselves.

Endurance events allow for all this and more. A connection with nature, with the environment—with its beauty and its ability to revive us. We are hardwired for nature: to be outside, to live in connection with our environment. To feel it, to play and struggle in it, to be challenged by it, and therefore to challenge ourselves. This connective sense of adventure and purposeful struggle, and the realization that we are more fulfilled living this way, is what pulls people toward becoming endurance athletes.

While the journey often begins modestly with small accomplishments that surprise and affirm us, what gets suddenly activated is an internal acknowledgement that we are capable of more. We suddenly connect with ourselves, and the natural world, in a way that is raw and unfiltered. We have a renewed sense of feeling alive, a clarity that everything is active around us in nature, and that we as humans are a part of this nature, part of this vibrant balance.

As we continue to grow into new challenges, which create some uncertainty, curiosity, and even fear, we are again brought back to our rawest selves. We feel most alive when we are truly challenged physically and mentally via nature and our endeavors in it. Nothing can replace that activation, as it makes us more energetic, healthier, happier, more creative, more efficient, more connected and, therefore, more caring individuals.

The stewardship of our natural world begins with love of self. How can one relate to nature (and its destruction) if one feels foreign to it? But when we have felt a oneness with nature as a deeply connected and wired part of us, we begin to unlock this hardwiring and allow it to fire. We become suddenly revitalized for work, family, community and more, because we have made the necessary connections, and our own tank of self-care is full. We are now seeing and feeling our potential, both physically and emotionally.

In order to love others, we need to love ourselves. With this understanding comes a curiosity around our capability, an awakening of the athlete within. The one that is seeking to achieve his or her goals grows to a new level of appreciation of a better, healthier, more confident, beautiful, vibrant, energetic self. This love glows outward because on the inside the fire of that missing component has been lit.

We no longer have these rites of passage that young men and women used to embark out in nature, surviving on their own, surviving off the land for days at a time. This cultural absence has us mystified by outdoor life and adventures, and we long to rekindle our raw ability in the natural world. Why is it common when we see those brilliant landscape photos, or hear stories of epic adventures, that it tugs at us? That it has us daydreaming? I believe we are drawn to it because it is who we are, hardwired from thousands of years of living in the natural world—in balance with it, surviving in it, being challenged by it, and feeling alive in it. Whether on the ocean or in the woods, the mountains or the desert, being in nature activates something within us.

Have we now been sterilized to our fake lighting, fake transportation, fake shelters, fake space we call our property? Where is our danger? Our use of all our senses? Our unease? Where are we truly challenged in body, mind and soul? In play, in the outdoors, your senses come alive; ever so gradually all the components of who you are start awakening and firing. No treadmill or gym can replace this. When indoors, time passes slowly, laboriously. In nature, time passes more quickly because we get lost in ourselves and in our thoughts, listening to our bodies and connecting with our souls. It's all happening there.

How do you feel after a long walk, a marathon, a 50K in the mountains or over some beautiful terrain? How do you feel after a day on the ocean, on the lake—surfing, rowing, sailing, swimming? How do you feel after mountain biking over hills and meadows and across streams? Repeat any of these actions for a few days in a row and your sense of self changes, your priorities shift, your soul exhales and relaxes into what it knows is an integral part of itself.

We all have an impulse to be more. But the journey for connection is in the acceptance of adversity, a self-inspired willingness to take the first step toward our potential. Admittedly, a halting, uncomfortable, even ungraceful movement in a direction of rewards so rich I'd be accused of exaggerating if I told you more.

"Nothing matters except making the world a better place after you've been here."
—David Sinclair, PhD

DAVID SINCLAIR, PhD

EXTENDING HUMAN LIFESPAN AND THE SCIENCE BEHIND AGING

Aging is inevitable. Everybody grows old. Everyone dies.

We accept these statements as fact.

But what if they're just stories based on history and our current understanding of biology?

What if everything we think we know about aging is about to change?

Across the globe, scientists are working on treatments and therapies that are designed to extend healthy human lifespan well beyond what we know today.

At the bleeding edge of such breakthroughs you will find David Sinclair, PhD, one of the world's leading scientific authorities on longevity, aging and how to slow its effects.

A professor in the Department of Genetics at Harvard Medical School and co-director of the Paul F. Glenn Center for the Biological Mechanisms of Aging, David obtained his PhD in Molecular Genetics at the University of New South Wales, Sydney in 1995 and worked as a postdoctoral researcher at MIT where, among other things, he co-discovered the cause of aging for yeast.

The co-founder of several biotechnology companies, David is also co-founder and co-chief editor of the journal Aging. His work has been featured in a variety of books, documentaries, and media, including 60 *Minutes*, *Nightline* and *NOVA*. He is an inventor on 35 patents, has been lauded as one of the Top 100 Australian Innovators, and made *TIME* magazine's list of the 100 most influential people in the world.

In addition, David is the author of *Lifespan: The Revolutionary Science of Why We Age—and Why We Don't Have To*, a *New York Times* bestseller that proposes a radical new theory of aging. As he provocatively writes: "Aging is a disease, and that disease is treatable."

A two-time podcast guest, my conversations with the brilliant and lovely Dr. Sinclair are equal parts philosophic and scientific. On the one hand, they are scintillating and science-heavy primers on all things human lifespan. But they are also meditations on how we think about life and what matters most.

Call him a dreamer, but David truly believes living to over 200 is a plausible reality. If you could double your lifespan, how would this impact how you choose to live? What would it mean for the future of humanity? And for the ecological stability of the planet?

The implications of these questions are profound.

—*Rich*

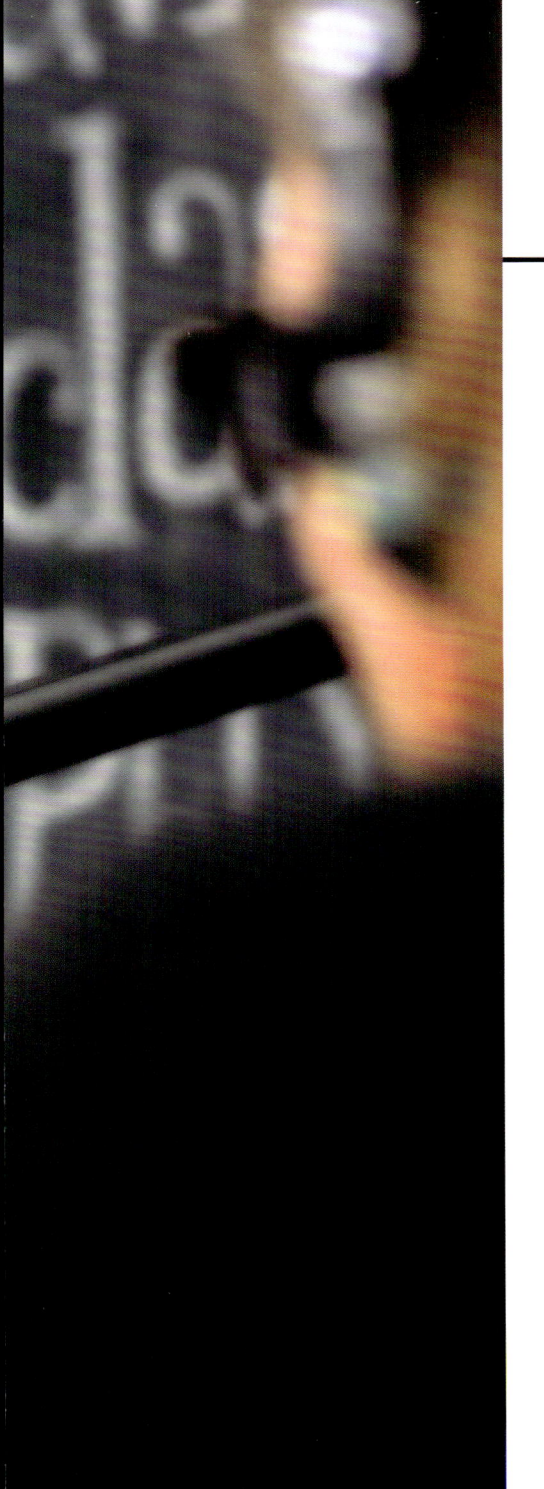

David: Aging is a condition. I will be bold and say it should be declared a disease. That often strikes most people as ludicrous. Let me explain. Early in my career, in the 1990s, we discovered that there are single genes controlling our body's health and longevity. It's not as complicated as we once thought—by simply making one mutation, an organism can live a lot longer ostensibly by mimicking fasting, calorie restriction, and exercise. That was a huge deal, a total paradigm shift in thinking.

Calorie restriction is the most robust way to prevent cancer or heart disease, and pretty much all diseases. The question is how? What we've found is that some of the pathways that we study in the aging field respond particularly to how much we're eating. If we eat a lot of food, they stop defending our body, or stop telling proteins to defend us. If we eat less, these proteins get kicked into action, and do a whole range of things that protect us from disease and can even reverse aspects of aging.

You can also kick them into action by restricting the total amount of protein you bring on board. Eating a lot of steak would be about the worst thing you could do for your body. Never exposing your body to any changes in temperature, another thing. Basically everything that makes your body happy and sedentary and unstressed is bad for you. The reason is, you're not engaging your survival circuits, as I call them.

Exercise also activates longevity pathways in your bloodstream, and has highly anti-inflammatory effects. It's able to change the way our bodies respond to the environment. Exercise is a treatment for the body that puts the entire system in a state

of defense. It's less about getting the blood to flow, and more about getting your tissues to act younger. That's really the huge benefit you get from exercise.

We can stretch out lifespan and healthspan in a way that allows us to have much more say in what we do in life. Stay younger for longer, mentally and career wise. Take longer to find what we'd love to do. Even when we're done with a career, we'll be able, in this new world, to have second and third careers.

I'm not trying to end aging. I don't believe that there's going to be immortality, but I do believe that the way we've been going about medicine for the last couple of hundred years can be improved. The way we've been going about it has been to take one disease at a time, study it, ignore aging and hopefully make a medicine to treat that disease. We've been very successful as a species at making medicines that prevent and treat heart disease for example, but what's that got us? We get an extra couple of years of life, but we end up spending those years with other chronic disease.

To me, it's something you wouldn't even wish on your worst enemies—to extend life but not extend health. We have much more control over our lives than we thought we did. We see that now, that the impact of diet is just incredible. It's the biggest thing we have control over. If there was one thing I could say to you, it would be to eat less. And If you don't have a mission in life, go and get one. It'll keep you happier and you'll probably live longer as well.

"Calorie restriction is the most robust way to prevent cancer, heart disease, or pretty much all diseases."
—David Sinclair, PhD

DARIN OLIEN

A SUPERFOOD HUNTER ON PEAK NUTRITION

What's it like to traipse the furthest outreaches of the planet in search of the world's greatest edible food sources for optimal health? Meet Darin Olien, the Indiana Jones of Superfoods.

Steeped in next-level nutrition insights gleaned from his many immersions with remote Indigenous cultures living in alignment with Native lands and synchronous with nature's rhythms, Darin is a widely recognized exotic superfoods hunter, wellness advocate, supplement formulator, and environmental activist.

For decades, Darin has explored hidden ports of call across the developing world questing for better, more natural pathways to ultimate wellness. Communing with thousands of rural farmers, growers, and manufacturers in remote communities across Peru, Bhutan, the Amazon, the Himalayas, the South Pacific, Latin America, and Asia. Darin is expert in shepherding exotic, high-quality, fair-trade superfoods and indigenous herbal commodities to market.

The co-founder of baru nut purveyor Barūkas and the creator of Beachbody's wildly successful whole food supplement Shakeology, Darin is also the author of *Superlife*, a comprehensive and timeless guide to maintaining health and maximizing potential. He can also be seen costarring alongside Zac Efron in the Netflix travelogue series *Down To Earth*, a Bourdain-esque exploration of health, sustainability and eco-innovation across various exotic ports of call.

Plant-based, ripped, and bearing more than a passing resemblance to his workout buddy Laird Hamilton, it would be natural to presume that Darin has always been an exquisite specimen kissed by the Malibu sun. But he wasn't always this way. A man who has faced many obstacles along his life path, Darin's curiosity, adventurous disposition and commitment to self-experimentation developed only after recurring injuries left him discouraged with the conventional medical establishment. A and pondering a better way to heal himself.

Now a respected authority on the healing potential of food pioneering previously unheard-of superfoods to Western consumers, most impressive is Darin's commitment to doing things right.

Vast swaths of the Brazilian Amazon and Cerrado—essentially the planet's lungs—are being irreparably decimated at an unfathomable rate by well-funded, politically powerful agricultural interests. By fairly, sustainably, and transparently supporting the social and economic long-term interests of the region's Indigenous grower communities, Darin helps preserve these natural ecosystems against the industrialized threat of encroachment.

Mentor, friend, and inspiration, Darin walks his talk. From the foods he consumes to the lifestyle habits he practices, he is the thriving embodiment of what it means to truly own responsibility for your health, your life and the planet we collectively enjoy.

Simply put, where Darin goes, I follow.

—Rich

"*I want people to consume the greatest foods in the world so they can thrive and live the dream life they want.*"

—Darin Olien

"It's so easy to blow off purpose. It's a whisper taken over by a megaphone of what the world tells us we should do."
—Darin Olien

Darin: How does a *superfood* end up in a bag?

A lot of so-called "superfoods" lean on super high vitamin and mineral content—but there's a marketing slant. Companies can advertise a fresh product, but if they haven't observed it, talked to the farmers, or tested the product from a sustainability point of view, then they ultimately don't understand how to deliver nutrient-dense food to the masses.

I was in Brazil a few years ago searching for superfoods in the Cerrado, which is a tropical savanna about the size of Texas. As I drove through this incredible ecosystem, I was equal parts fascinated and holding back tears—the deforestation taking place is heartbreaking. Between 50% to 79% of the Cerrado has been destroyed in the past 40 years.

There's this incredibly robust, beautiful vegetation with extraordinary biodiversity, but it doesn't meet the eye: it's underground. There are 90 million species of insects, hundreds of species of mammals, tens of thousands of plants—but they are all being destroyed for meat. Either cattle are grazing the land, or corn and soy are being grown to feed them.

I've dedicated my life to educating people about superfoods so we can stop deforestation in the regions where they grow, stand up for Indigenous communities, and help people consume the greatest foods in the world so they can actually thrive. My big plan is to influence, help, and heal people by creating a completely transparent superfood conservancy.

I want to teach people that superfoods like moringa, baru, and babassu are necessary in our daily diet. Our bodies *desperately* need phytonutrients to compensate for this underwhelming, nutrient-dead food we have in the West.

In 1992, there was a worldwide soil study that found every continent in the first world is deprived of minerals, which means we aren't getting the same nutrient density in our food anymore. This is one of the most important reasons why we need superfoods in our diet every day.

In addition, we're constantly exposed to toxins that we can't even see—100,000 new environmental toxins are emitted in our atmosphere every year, and of that, not even 10% of them are being tested.

We have elements in our water we don't even know about. We have perfumes we're breathing in that we don't understand. We have all this internal and environmental stress, and the more stress we have, the more micronutrients we need.

To truly thrive, here is what you have to do: get back to your instincts. Eat more vegetables. Get hydrated. Drink a liter of water in the morning, and then pick one meal that you're going to replace with a fresh, organic, huge, vibrant salad. Find activities that you love to do and go play. Find ways to move and be outside with your friends. Then get a bunch of sleep—seven to eight hours minimum.

You have to be patient—lasting change takes time. Everyone wants the quick fix, the pill, the magic powders. But ultimately, you have to take responsibility for yourself and your life and your health, period. You have to educate yourself. This is your body. This is your vehicle.

Take back your power. Vote with your dollar and stand up for your values. Use food as medicine. Don't succumb to spending your whole life ill and depressed—all of that is absolutely changeable.

Habit is health or habit is disease. What's your trajectory?

"Life is going to catch up to your practice."
—*Light Watkins*

LIGHT WATKINS

DISPELLING MEDITATION MYTHS

We all want to be happy.

So why is it so elusive?

The problem isn't information. We all know contentedness is linked to eating right, sleeping well, and surrounding ourselves with those who elevate. We grok the importance of confronting our emotional challenges. We're well aware that life is better when we cultivate gratitude and serve others.

And yes, we know we should meditate.

The science is clear. The evidence is in. And yet for so many, the gap between information and action is an impossibly untraversable canyon.

Perhaps you resist the traditional trappings that swirl around the idea of meditation—the robes and incense a bridge too far. Maybe you can't get your legs to perfectly fold, monk-like, without cramping. You decided you just don't have the time. Or perchance you tried it, only to give up because you just couldn't get your looping

mind to shut off, convinced meditation is just not for you.

Relax. You're not alone.

Light Watkins poses an important question: What if the problem isn't meditation itself, but your approach? In other words, what if it were easy?

Beyond having the coolest name of all time, I would characterize Light as a generous, relatable, and contemplative purveyor of all things mindfulness. Impressively composed and quick with a laugh, he has been practicing and teaching Vedic Meditation for twenty years. Among his thousands of students you will find bankers, artists, politicians, CEOs, care takers, educators, comedians, rock stars, soccer moms and seekers of all kinds.

An in demand public speaker, he's also the founder of The Shine—a global pop-up inspirational variety show that leverages music,

film, philanthropy and storytelling to inspire people to do more, give more, and be more.

Light's latest book, Bliss More: How to Succeed in Meditation Without Really Trying, is a straight-talk how-to book that teaches busy professionals how to enjoy meditation.

Armed with practical tools and a unique knack for dispelling the many myths and misunderstandings that swirl around meditation, Light is the man who will inspire you to finally put your excuses in the rear view and adopt that daily practice that has to date, eluded you.

So let's put all those myths and misunderstandings to bed, once and for all.

Because we can all use a little more bliss in our lives.

And we all deserve to be happy.

—*Rich*

PHOTO: MEGAN MCALLISTER

"I define happiness as having a state of fulfillment and contentedness with where you are and what you're doing."

—Light Watkins

Light: When you sit down to meditate, three things are happening. Number one, you're going to start noticing and forming a new relationship with your mind and with your thought patterns. Number two, your body under the influence of meditation is going to start achieving profound states of rest, which will cause it to do what bodies are supposed to do when they get proper rest: rehabilitate themselves. The rehabilitation of stress from the body is going to cause you to have thoughts, emotions, sensations, and experiences that may be related to old past stressor that are now leaving your body. Over time, this will lead you to not react so intensely to things that once triggered you. The final thing that's happening during meditation is that you're breaking the habit of not meditating.

Start with anything, even if it's just 10 minutes, even if it's just five minutes, start with anything that you can do consistently. Consistency is key when it comes to meditation—if you're not doing it every day, keep experimenting until you find a practice you want to do every day.

In my experience, the best way to approach meditation is to let your mind roam free, or the EASY approach. Easy is an acronym for how you handle your mental and sensational experiences. *E* stands for embrace. *A* stands for accept, *S* for surrender, and *Y* stands for yield to. What are you embracing, accepting, surrendering to, and yielding to? All of your mental, emotional, even physical experiences during the meditation. If you have an itch, you scratch it. If you get uncomfortable, you switch your position. If you have thoughts about

work, that's amazing, don't beat yourself up. Don't just accept all thoughts, actively celebrate them.

We live in a culture where happiness exists in the future. Happiness comes only after you achieve something, only after you get what you want. But I define happiness as having a state of fulfillment and contentment in where you are and what you are doing right now. In any moment, whether you're stuck in traffic or you're at the post office or waiting in line at the grocery store, you can still maintain a level of contentment. You may not like it, but you know that you're right where you're supposed to be. That is how you stay open to all of life's opportunities. You're not seeing anything as an obstacle. You're seeing everything as a gateway to the next opportunity. That encapsulates my idea of happiness because you're no longer wishing you were somewhere other than where you currently are.

Moving in the direction of your intuition is going to take you to a layer of uncertainty. We are all obsessed with control and certainty, so moving towards uncertainty is the last thing most people want to do. If you want to thrive, if you really want to live your Dharma, you have to move in the direction of the unknown. Meditation can help you with that. It can teach you that control is an illusion in the first place. It can teach you to embrace the unknown. Imagine waking up every day and not knowing what the hell was going to happen and being excited about it. Meditation can give you that.

There's nothing special about me. I grew up in the Bible Belt down in Alabama where there have

been more snowstorms than people meditating. I never knew a thing about meditation growing up. I wasn't born enlightened; I wasn't born with this knowledge. I just learned the mechanics and they aren't very complicated. It's no exaggeration when I say that I wake up in the morning and I can't wait to meditate. I don't want to stop, I can't wait until the afternoon to do it again. It has totally transformed me. Once you incorporate meditation into your life, it's easier to be grateful, it's easier to give, it's easier to be patient and slow down.

Everything that happens to you is happening for a reason. There's no point in trying to figure it out, just relax and stay in the present moment and go with it. You're going to see that it's going to turn out better than you could have ever imagined for yourself.

A GUIDED MEDITATION
BY LIGHT WATKINS

Set a timer for five, ten, or twenty minutes. If you're new to meditation, start small and work your way up.

Sit comfortably. You do not need to sit in a rigid posture, allow your back to rest against a chair or a pillow.

Feel your body relax. Soften your gaze. If it feels comfortable, close your eyes.

Take a few moments to ground yourself into this space by practicing awareness.

Start by slowly noticing the sounds around you.

First notice sounds far away, and gradually bring your awareness closer to your body. You do not need to name or recognize any of the sounds. Just acknowledge them and allow them to fade into the background.

Begin noticing the sensations of your body.

Perhaps you feel the gentle sensation of your clothing against your skin as you breathe.

Perhaps you notice tension in your neck or shoulders. As you notice your body, release any muscles that feel tight.

Bring your awareness to your breath.

Do not change or control it; allow it to be as it is.

If it's shallow, let it be shallow. If it is deep, let it be deep. Notice your breath but resist the urge to control it.

Focus your entire awareness on the sensation of your breath as it enters your nose or mouth. Feel it flow in. Feel it flow out. Notice the quality of the air. Maybe it feels cool entering your body, and warm when it leaves.

Keep breathing.

Notice when your attention has wandered away from your breath. It is normal to have thoughts during meditation. Without judgment, bring your attention back to your breath. Feel it flow in and out through your nose. Feel your body expanding. Notice these sensations without controlling them.

Keep breathing.

Every time you experience a thought, sensation, or sound, gently bring your awareness back to your breath. This is the practice of refining your awareness so you can be purely in the present moment. The more you are able to stay with your breath in this moment, the more present you may be in other areas of life.

Keep breathing.

Allow your awareness to focus on the sensation of your breath until your timer signals the end of the practice. Express gratitude for a job well done, and set a time for your next meditation.

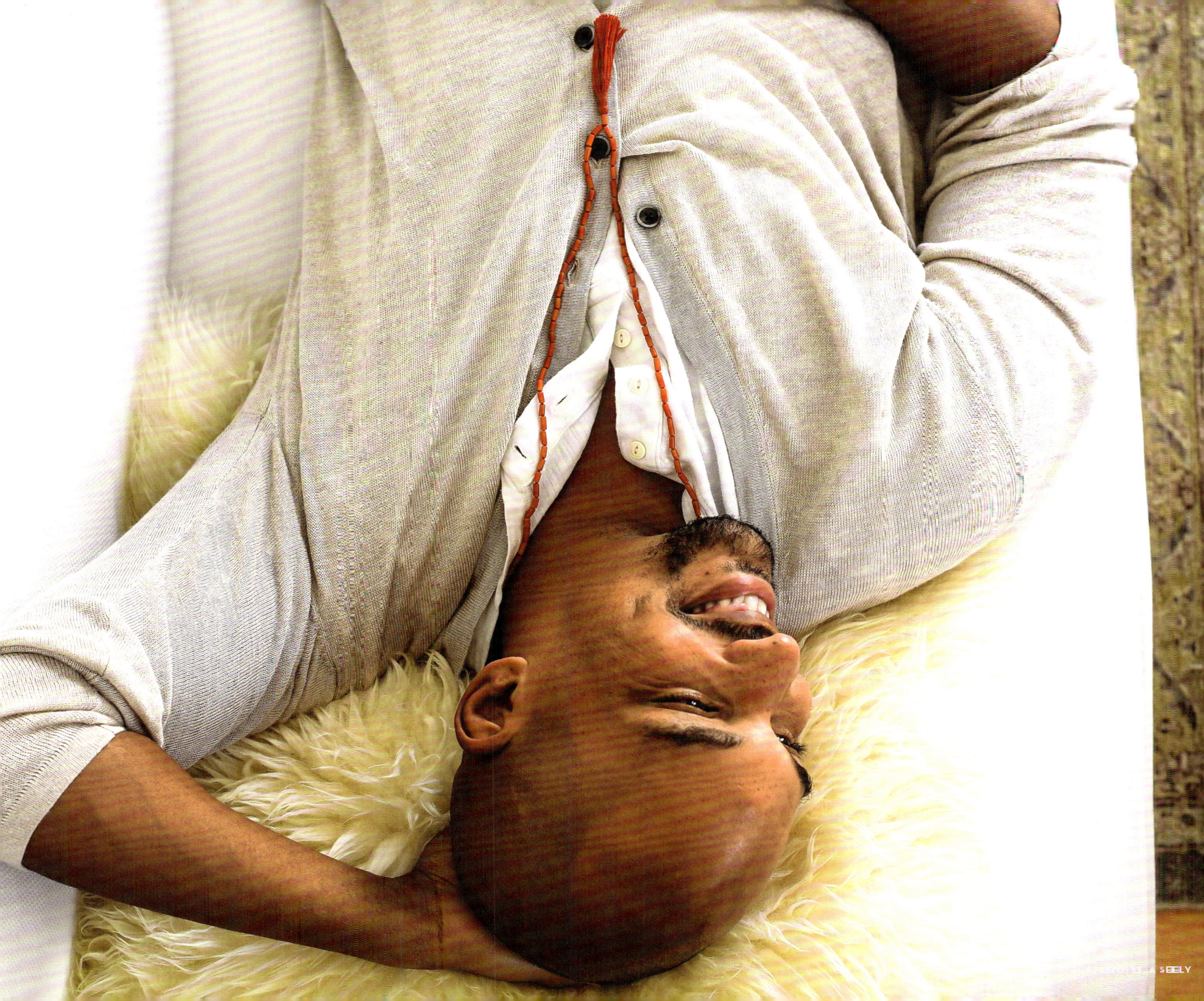

LINDSEY VONN

LESSONS FROM THE WORLD'S MOST DECORATED FEMALE SKI RACER

> *"It's hard to beat the person that won't quit."*
>
> **—Lindsey Vonn**

What's it like to be the very best in the world at something?

Few humans are more connected to this experience than Lindsey Vonn—the most decorated female skier in history and the most decorated skier *period,* man or woman, in US history.

Now retired, Lindsey is a four-time Olympian, a three-time Olympic medalist, the only American woman to win downhill gold, and the only American woman with three World Cup titles. All told, Lindsey accumulated 82 World Cup wins across her storied career, the most of any female skier in history and just four titles shy of the record set by Ingemar Stenmark in 1989.

Off the slopes, Lindsey is a media mogul. A regular on "Most Marketable" athlete lists, she has been profiled in every major media outlet across the globe and graced the cover of publications such as *Fitness, Sports Illustrated, ESPN, TV Guide* and many others.

Not enough? Lindsey sank a hole-in-one during one of her very first full 18 holes of golf. So there's that.

Lindsey's victories are self-evident. Less appreciated are the countless obstacles she's courageously faced and valiantly overcome along the way. Potentially career-ending injuries. Debilitating bouts with depression. And always having to weather the naysayers. In other words, Lindsey's trajectory skyward has been neither linear nor charmed. In point of fact, she has tenaciously fought for everything she has achieved—falling and failing often.

So what drives this champion? And what can we learn from her mindset, process, and experience?

The answer isn't simple. But it has something to do with fearlessness. Relentless persistence. Never being satisfied. And the drive to positively impact on others.

In the wake of our conversation, I'm often reminded of her motto:

When you fall, get right back up. And never, ever quit.

—Rich

Lindsey: I think there's an element of fear that you just can't have if you want to be highly successful at ski racing. You have to be willing to crash at 85 miles an hour and get back up. You're either willing to sacrifice for these things and push yourself, or you're not. There's no complaining, you just shut up and do the job. Most people that are highly successful are not the best at what they do or the most talented at what they do, they're just willing to work harder than everyone else.

It's hard to beat the person that never gives up. Everyone has their ups and downs and obstacles they have to face, but I try to keep things in perspective and understand that I am really lucky to be able to do what I do. I work as hard as I can, and if I'm successful, then great. If not, I'm still doing what I love. There is no downside in trying my best.

The most difficult thing about what I do is being alone. I'm on the road a lot and in empty hotels, in empty houses. I'm lucky that I have many people that support me, but it doesn't take away from the fact that I am still alone. I feel a deep loneliness and it's something that I am constantly working on.

Most people don't know that I have depression, and they say, "Oh, you're successful and you're pretty, why aren't you happy?" All those things don't equal happiness. I have to surround myself with people I love to be content and grounded. I hate the misconception that my life is perfect and that I'm happy and everything's like it is on Instagram—perfect.

The truth is, I am never satisfied. I always feel like I can do better. Somehow one win isn't enough, I need to win two.

I always have this urge to keep going. I want something more, to do something that's never been done before. I want to try something new, start my own company, work with people that no one else has worked with. I have this drive that makes me want to just be better. I don't want to be just a ski racer; I want to have a positive impact on the world and help others accomplish their dreams.

"I don't want to be just a ski racer; I want to have a positive impact on the world and help others accomplish their dreams."
—Lindsey Vonn

"Every day for me is a gift. That's why I get up in the morning and swim. Through this crazy sport called marathon open water swimming, my life has become so full."
—Kimberley Chambers

KIMBERLEY CHAMBERS

THE WORLD'S GREATEST FEMALE MARATHON SWIMMER
ON TURNING ADVERSITY TO ADVANTAGE

Close your eyes and imagine yourself 30 miles off the coast of San Francisco, swimming in the freezing cold, shark-infested waters famously dubbed the Red Triangle. No wetsuit. In the middle of the night.

Most would call this lunacy.

Kimberley Chambers calls this home.

One of the most accomplished record-setting marathon open water swimmers in the world, Kimberley's story is incredibly inspiring, but not for the reasons you might imagine. Instead, it's a tale that astounds because just nine years ago, Kim was not a swimmer at all, suffering from a life-threatening accident that nearly claimed her leg and her overall enthusiasm for life.

The morning started out like every other morning. The New Zealand born former ballerina and rower turned software executive left her San Francisco apartment and accidentally tripped, toppling down a treacherous flight of stairs.

We saved your leg. But it's unlikely you will walk again.

The doctor's verdict presented Kim with a choice: accept permanent disability or prove them wrong.

Needless to say, she chose the latter.

After countless surgeries and an excruciatingly prolonged rehabilitation, a friend encouraged her to try swimming. Although foreign to the water, she immediately took to it. A ticket to freedom.

But the real turning point came the moment she first jumped into the frigid San Francisco Bay. In an instant, she had found sanctuary.

To this day, it's a love affair with cold water and the tight-knit community of like-minded souls who embrace it that changed everything about Kimberley's life and how she lives it.

An inner fire ignited, Kim began to channel her newfound passion into a series of death-defying, envelope-pushing open-water marathon challenges that have redefined the limits of human potential and transformed her into the elite athlete she is today. Among Kim's many accomplishments:

- In 2014, she became the sixth person (and third woman) in history to complete the Oceans Seven—the marathon swimming equivalent of the Seven Summits mountaineering challenge, with each of the seven swims chosen for their treacherous water conditions and potential wildlife risks.
- In 2015, she set a new world record becoming the first woman to swim 30 miles from the shark-infested Farallon Islands off the coast of San Francisco.
- In September 2016, Kim attempted a non-stop 93 mile swim from Sacramento to Tiburon. However after swimming over 24 hours and 54 miles, sustained 30 knot winds rendered it unsafe for her to continue.
- And just two months later, Kim led an international team of swimmers to complete an unprecedented historic swim across the Dead Sea to raise global awareness around the environmental deterioration of that critical body of water.

Delightfully engaging, ever humble, and beautifully human, Kim embodies everything you seek in a modern day female super hero.

—Rich

Kimberley: Every day for me is a gift. That's why I get up in the morning and swim. Through this crazy sport called marathon open water swimming, my life has become so full.

Before, I led a superficial life. But then I was in a freak accident that forced me to rehabilitate my injured leg—and, in the process, refresh my sense of self. Truly, that was the best thing that ever happened to me—it opened a world of possibility; it was rebirth, and I was enrichened for it.

Having been a ballerina for 15 years, I was acutely aware that my post-accident body was misaligned. I felt wrong, I felt trapped, and I wanted freedom. I found myself subconsciously drawn to the water—and when I first got in the pool, my whole body just came alive. It was an electrifying experience that first spurred me to this great adventure, right here in San Francisco. I've been swimming in the bay every day since.

I started to have a love affair with open water swimming. I just wanted to do more. So, I, who had grown up on a sheep and cattle farm in the middle of nowhere, became one of the only swimmers (and women) to complete the Oceans Seven challenge. That feeling of being out there in water that's 10,000 feet deep and being this little person on top of the surface—well, it's intoxicating. Swimming with dolphins, seals, and jellyfish—it's a wonderland!

It's also tantalizing to be right on the edge. I know the sharks are there; I can feel them. In that water, you are at the mercy of mother nature. There is no wetsuit, no shark cage, no thermal cap. And every time I'm out there, I surrender. It's so freeing and scary. But it's everything. You feel like this modern-day explorer-almost like an astronaut.

In my quest to find what I'm capable of, my soul gains more wrinkles. People make fun of me because I'm always so happy out there in the water. I'm like a 12-year-old girl and I'll be swimming and I'll go, "Woo!" It's this expression of pure joy. Now I understand why people climb mountains.

I just hope that by continuing to do what I do, I will inspire at least one girl to see that spark of possibility and decide to take a path she didn't know she could take.

Many of us are afraid to push the limits of our physical and mental selves—but I know that when you push through those fears, you find your sense of self. That's where the real treasure lies—right on the other side of where you're most fearful. So, pick a fear and decide to challenge it face on. When you get to the other side, I guarantee you will have a transformative experience that will serve you for the rest of your life.

After all, tomorrow is not guaranteed for any of us. All we have is now.

ON BREAKING CIVIL RIGHTS BARRIERS

One of the most respected and revered figures in sport, George Raveling is basketball—and so much more than basketball.

A pioneer in transcending the intersections of sports, culture, race, and business, George is the former director of international basketball for Nike and the first African American basketball coach at Villanova, University of Maryland, Washington State, and University of Iowa before closing out a storied career at USC.

He is also an inductee into several halls of fame, including the College Basketball Hall of Fame and the Naismith Memorial Basketball Hall of Fame.

A civil rights activist who has been breaking paradigms since before most of us were even born, George has been outspoken for many decades on a wide array of social justice issues involving race, education, and athletics.

But more than anything, George is a world-class educator. Now 83, he remains a passionate life learner. A man committed to empowering others on the daily. And an extraordinary beacon of light who molds boys into men, and men into better men.

Bottom line? George Raveling is the mentor you wish you had.

But you can just call him "Coach."

Initially introduced to Coach by our mutual friend Ryan Holiday (a young man of many octogenarian companions), I was immediately struck by George's youthful vitality. His insatiable thirst for learning. His passion for ideas. And his devotion to people, human potential, and personal development.

Coach has lived life. He's got stories to prove it. And man, can he tell a story. Tales of breaking racial barriers during the era of segregation. Inspirational musings on owning your

destiny. And the legendary saga of how a young George came to stand alongside Dr. Martin Luther King, Jr. on the steps of the Lincoln Memorial during the March on Washington as Dr. King delivered his historic "I Have A Dream" speech.

A barrier breaker if there ever was one, my conversation with this civil rights legend is a moment I will never forget—a meditation on breaking barriers, self-governance, literacy, and humanity that boils down to one mandate:

Devote your life to making a positive difference in the world.

An absolute gem of a human being, George is a national treasure. So take a knee. Huddle up. And pay attention.

—Rich

GEORGE RA

"The best feedback is what we don't want to hear."

—George Raveling

VELING

PHOTO: JARED POLIN

George: Early on in my life, I began to realize the unique value of information. I used to tell my players that the two most important commodities in the world are information and money. If you've got money, you can buy information. If you've got information, you can get plenty of money.

Little did I know that we'd evolve into a culture that would be dominated by information. So much information is readily available to us that if a person wanted to self-educate themselves, all they would have to do is get a smartphone and ask Google. It's comforting for me to know that I can continue to learn at 79 years old and take myself from where I am now to where I should be intellectually.

As long as someone can control your mind, they can control your body. If we don't allow people to possess our minds, then they can't possess our bodies. How do we achieve that? By filling our head with as much information, knowledge, and meaningful material as possible. At some point, if you read enough, you're going to think differently, act differently, and ultimately be different.

The hardest battle that a person has to fight in their lifetime is to live in a world where every single day, someone is trying to make them be someone they're not. I know who I want to be. I don't need someone to try to make me be something else or live by their values. But I respect their values and their way of life, and I hope they would do the same for me.

I grew up in Washington, DC during the depression, when things like sugar and flour were rationed. When I was 9 years old, my dad died and when I was 13, my mom had a nervous breakdown and she was institutionalized for the rest of her life. By and large, I was an orphan.

My grandmother was the matriarch of our family. She was infallible—whatever she said, went. My grandma worked for this white family in Georgetown and she had mentioned my unfortunate circumstances to them. They were able to get me into a Catholic boarding school in upstate Pennsylvania, and I finished the rest of my education there.

As I grew older, I became more and more aware of the larger world around me. I grew to understand that being Black meant that I lived out the clichés—we were the last hired and the first fired, we lived in ghettos, you get the picture. I never even realized I grew up in a ghetto until I got to Villanova University and took a sociology class. I was perfectly happy with my life, even though most of it was in a boarding school. I began to put my experiences and my pursuits in a broader context. I realized that one of the impediments that I was going to carry with me for the rest of my life was my pigmentation, and people were going to judge me differently because of it.

I also grew to understand that one thing that most people respect about another person is their intellect, whether you're Black or you're white. They might still have misgivings about you, but they will respect you intellectually. I tried to compensate by being an information gatherer, a knowledge gatherer, trying to learn as much as I could so that I could effectively compete in our social system, even if I had all the hardships and the trappings that came with segregation and discrimination. At the end of the day, it was incumbent upon me to figure out how can I successfully compete in this environment? What are the skills I need? What are the things I need to do? And one of those things was to be able to have a courageous voice and stand up and speak out against injustice.

We all can't be Malcolm X, or Martin Luther King, or Stokely Carmichael, or Huey Newton. But at the end of the day, we have to accept that it's a moral obligation to speak out against injustice and inequality. Here we are today, and it's a more sophisticated type of discrimination, not just discrimination against a person because of the pigmentation of their skin. There's discrimination against women. There's discrimination against gays. There's discrimination against Latinos. We have some big problems as a society.

My mission every day is to make a positive difference in as many lives as I can, Black folks and white folks. I try to target young people and share with them my life lessons. As my grandma used to say, "If you listen to me, I can help you avoid some of the bumps and potholes in the road." That's my mission: to help other people avoid potholes, to guide them to their potential, and to encourage them to learn as much as they can throughout their time here on earth.

HOW TO DEVELOP A HIGH-PERFORMANCE MINDSET

What are the consistent behavioral themes across the spectrum of high performing athletes, entrepreneurs, artists, and change makers?

Is there a common thread connecting how the greatest performers in the world use their minds to pursue the boundaries of human potential?

Dr. Michael Gervais has devoted his life to answering these questions. A high-performance psychologist working in the trenches of high-stakes environments, Michael lives and breathes in that special place where there is no luxury for mistakes, hesitation, or failure to respond.

His clientele includes the elite of the elite—the world's most prolific Olympic, professional, and extreme athletes. MVPs in every major sport.

High level military. Internationally acclaimed artists, musicians, and coaches. And Fortune 100 CEO's.

You might recall Dr. Gervais as the guy Seattle Seahawks coach Pete Carroll credits as integral to their 2014 Super Bowl win. The meditation, mindfulness, and other crucial team building techniques Michael helped foster and instill into the fabric of that organization paved the team's path towards incredible success.

You might also remember that Felix Baumgartner's infamous Red Bull Stratos jump from an altitude of 128,000 feet almost never was simply because Felix could not overcome the intense anxiety and claustrophobia he experienced every time he donned the jump suit. It was Dr. Gervais

who helped Baumgartner resolve the issue and get Stratos back on track. *No Gervais, no history-making jump.*

Michael is also the man behind skydiver Luke Aikins, who astonished the world by becoming the first to jump from a plane at 25,000 feet without a parachute or wingsuit and live to tell the story.

While Michael's client roster quietly includes the world's most elite, his ultimate goal is to democratize human potential optimization.

We are all required to perform daily. We all navigate our own high stakes environments. And everybody can benefit with the right mindset training. Towards this end, Michael committed to scaling the principles that drive high performance

DR. MICHAEL

GERVAIS

for the betterment of all. He shares his wisdom each week on his *Finding Mastery* podcast. He works intimately with organizations both big and small through Compete to Create, the mindset training platform he co-founded with Coach Carroll. And together this dynamic duo co-authored *Compete to Create*, an Audible Original blueprint for unlocking potential in high stakes situations.

A man I consider friend and mentor, Michael is one of my very favorite people. Whether you're a high-performance athlete, top-tier executive, nine-to-fiver, weekend warrior, or a stay-at-home parent, Michael is uniquely gifted in helping you be your best.

Because every day, every one of us—irrespective of circumstance—has the opportunity to create a living masterpiece.

—Rich

"There's nothing better than an uncomfortable moment because in that moment we're incredibly aware of ourselves."
—Dr. Michael Gervais

Michael: Most people nod their heads that they want to be better, but they don't want to actually do the work. Understanding what is possible for oneself is difficult. It takes discernment and deep thinking.

Why do people change? In my observation and research, people change because of pain. They change because they are sick and tired of being sick and tired. When people experience a certain level of pain, they will do anything to stop it. But changing for change itself, that's hard.

The journey of self-discovery is what mastery of self is about. Some people use a craft like sport, music, or business to better understand themselves and to better understand people in general. But the craft is really just a tool, a rich experience to learn more about who you are and how you function in the world.

The journey begins with your psychological framework. How do you understand the world? How do you understand yourself? How do you make rational and clear sense of events that take place in your life? One key way is through optimism. What I've found through my research is that most world-class athletes believe that the future is going to work out well for them.

But people are afraid that being optimistic means they'll get soft. Optimism doesn't mean we are all going to hold hands and pick flowers together and everything's going to work out just right. Optimism is at the center of mental toughness. Optimism means you have the mental discipline to stay on course when shit isn't going right.

There are only three things that we can train: our craft, our body, and our mind. I want to help people live in the present moment by showing them not just the value of it, but how to condition their mind to manage the noise, to get to pick up the signal more often. Because the signal, the present moment, is where the most extraordinary experiences in life happen.

Perfection is a constricting thought. It creates tightness, both mentally and physically. It feels awful when we judge ourselves to unrealistic standards. Trust me, you don't need to do extraordinary things to be extraordinary. This idea that we need to do more is wearing us all out. So let's flip the model that we need to "do" more and let's just "be" more. Let's be more present, let's be more authentic, let's be more gracious.

You know when you belly laugh, and it feels really good, and it just totally takes over you? That's space, that's expansion. That's being present to all life has to offer. To me, that experience is priceless. I would trade it a million times over for outward success. Wouldn't you?

"The opposite of addiction isn't sobriety. It's connection."
—Johann Hari

JOHANN HARI

UNDERSTANDING ADDICTION AND DEPRESSION

Why are we seeing unprecedented rates of depression? What's behind our current opioid epidemic? And what can be done about it?

Veteran journalist and author Johann Hari suggests that everything we think we know about both addiction and depression is wrong.

A former columnist for the *Independent* in London, Johan has contributed to the *New York Times*, the *Los Angeles Times*, *Slate*, *Le Monde*, and many other outlets. He was named Newspaper Journalist of the Year by Amnesty International UK. And his TED Talk, aptly titled "Everything You Think You Know About Addiction is Wrong," was viral hit, clocking over 25 million views.

In addition, Johann is the author of two *New York Times* bestsellers. *Chasing the Scream: The First and Last Days of the War on Drugs*, chronicles his three-year investigation and research into the disastrous war on drugs. Propelled by moving human stories and compelling new insights into the nature of addiction, it's a book that profoundly impacted how I think about the disease that impacts me personally and kills countless annually.

Johann's latest book, *Lost Connections: Why You're Depressed and How to Find Hope*, offers an equally radical new lens on depression and anxiety. Probing the causes that underpin these common mental health disorders, he dispels lingering myths. And he discovers why, in some cases, social prescriptions outpace pharmaceutical ones.

If you are familiar with my story, you know that addiction and mental health are subjects of great personal importance. My quest to better understanding the nature of these conditions is a prevailing, recurring theme of the podcast—and the motivation that drove me to seek out Johann for the show.

Powerful, educational, and at times controversial, our conversation explores what drives these malignancies, why they are so difficult to overcome, and how a new approach can plot a more hopeful and solution-based course forward.

Many see Johann's ideas as radical. I can't say I agree with everything he prescribes. But our current approach to substance dependency and mental health—what causes it and how to treat it—is woefully lacking. We have much to learn. Change is necessary. And there is undeniable wisdom Johann's findings.

Chances are you suffer from addiction or depression or care for somebody who does. May Johann help provide you with insight to better understanding the struggle—and a path forward underscored with hope.

—Rich

Johann: If you asked me eight years ago what causes addiction, I would have looked at you like you were an idiot and said, "Well, obviously drugs cause drug addiction." We've been told this story for a hundred years. It's part of our common sense. While there's some truth in it, there's something much bigger and more important going on when it comes to addiction.

The opposite of addiction isn't sobriety—the opposite of addiction is connection and getting your psychological needs met. It's not a coincidence that the opioid crisis is at its most intense in the places where the non-opioid based suicide rate and antidepressant prescriptions are the highest.

The drug itself plays a role, of course. There are chemical hooks that cause physical dependence. But the core of addiction is not wanting to be present in your life because it is too painful. Once you understand that, you can see why imposing more pain and more punishment on people with addictions is such a disaster. There is nowhere in the world that has reduced addiction by imposing negative consequences.

Everyone knows that they have natural physical needs. Obviously, you need food, you need water, you need shelter, you need clean air. But there's equally strong evidence that all human beings have natural psychological needs. You need to feel like you belong, that your life has meaning and purpose. You need to feel like people see you and value you, and you need to feel hopeful for the future.

Our culture is terrible at meeting these deep underlying psychological needs, and this is manifesting in an enormous range of problems. One in three middle-aged women in the United States are taking chemical antidepressants. The suicide rate combined with opioid deaths is now so high that white male life expectancy has fallen for the first time in the entire history of the United States. The average American teenage girl now has the same average anxiety level as a mental patient had in the 1950s. We've created a culture that is unbearable for so many people.

I believe in antidepressants in the sense that people really are depressed. They're not making it up. They're not imagining it. They are terribly depressed and anxious. They need solutions, but if you tell people that their depression is simply a biological problem that can only be treated with drugs, you're essentially telling them that there's no meaning to their pain, and it cuts them off from finding the root causes. So we need to expand our concept of what antidepressants are. Getting people to talk about their values is an antidepressant. Giving people a way to release their shame is an antidepressant. Creating community programs is an antidepressant.

Can you see how this is a radically different story than telling someone there's just a chemical missing in their brain and all they need to do is take a drug?

Your pain makes sense. You're not crazy to feel the way you do. You have been given a really rough deal. We live in a society that's falling apart, where Donald Trump is the most powerful person in the world, where people are profoundly lonely, where they've been taught to value the wrong things, where the inequalities go off the scale, where most people are deeply unhappy with their work.

The most important thing we can do right now is come together. If you can, form a group of people who feel like you do and start seeking answers.

The struggle is the solution, and the act of coming together and caring for one another will help us all immensely.

ANTHONY

ERVIN

THE REBEL OLYMPIAN: FINDING MEANING IN GOLD

"As a competitive swimmer, you feel every heartbeat. You feel as if you're sitting your forearms against your legs. Your heels are touching – you feel that. Being in that state, proceeding from that room, to behind the blocks, to taking your mark, is surreal."

—Anthony Ervin

Imagine winning an Olympic gold medal at age 19 at the 2000 Sydney Olympics: a feat never before achieved by a swimmer of African-American descent. The frenzied media swarms. The only problem? You're only half-Black. You definitely don't look Black. And you simply don't feel authentically Black.

The unrelenting crush of public role model expectation competes with your inclination towards privacy. The pressure and dissonance soon become so intense, you retreat from your Olympic experience not with a lasting sense of pride, satisfaction or happiness, but instead detached. And mostly just numb.

This isn't anything like I thought it would be . . .

Over time, confusion metastasizes into disillusionment. And it's not long before depression sets in.

Lost and lacking the tools to cope, life begins to pivot away from the familiar black line along the pool bottom—a trusted and true arrow that had always guided your path. Adrift, you gravitate towards a dreadlocked blur of rock 'n' roll, boozy, drug-fueled binges, rampant womanizing, cigarette haze, and death-defying motorcycle crashes.

And yet somehow, over the next three years you continue to do the one thing that grounds you: swim. Not only do you continue to win, in 2001 you're crowned the world champion in two events. But these results only magnify what is quickly becoming a profound crisis of identity.

Who am I? Why am I doing this? What does it all mean?

The answers continue to elude you until you find yourself so despondent, so desperate for relief, that you down a handful of tranquilizers. But the suicide attempt fails, fueling a sense of invincibility that only hastens the onset of an even more profound darkness.

So, at the young age of 22, at the peak of his abilities, Anthony Ervin does what he must. He walks away from the thing he used to love. The thing that gave him everything. The thing that made him a star. The thing that betrayed its promise of making him whole.

In a Hail Mary attempt to discover and re-create his life, Anthony travels the world. He meditates at a Buddhist temple. He studies philosophy with a Sufi mystic. He reclaims his body with tattoos. He enrolls in graduate school and spends summers in Brooklyn, where he immerses himself in books, writes poetry, and even occasionally cross-dresses at parties.

The denouement? Hawking his Olympic gold medal on eBay and donating the proceeds to the UNICEF tsunami relief fund.

The only thing Anthony Ervin didn't do during this time? Swim.

Not one stroke.

The next eight years marked a complete divorce from anything and everything swimming. In fact, not one of Anthony's new friends during this time even knew he was an athlete, let alone an Olympic champion. He was just another tattooed, guitar-playing Brooklynite seeking answers to the universe in music, meditation, books, and partying.

But with funds dwindling, Anthony offhandedly takes a gig teaching New York kids how to swim. The experience of service begins to erode his jaded shell and ignites an unexpected spark of appreciation for his former life. A new sense of self-worth begins to emerge, informing the why in Anthony's quest for spiritual self-actualization. Suddenly, love for the sport he so thoroughly placed in his rearview begins to rekindle.

In 2011, Anthony returns to the water. And almost overnight, the impossible occurs.

Twelve years after Sydney, Anthony qualifies for the 2012 London Olympics—his second US Olympic team. Despite his 31 years of age (ancient in the world of swimming), Anthony swims faster than he did at the 2000 trials.

Sixteen years after Sydney, Anthony (then 35) returns for his third Olympiad to captain Team USA in Rio. Bending the laws of physics, he shocks the world by once again claiming gold in the 50-meter freestyle, swimming's crown jewel event.

It's a moment I will never forget. The oldest individual swimming gold medalist of all time, Anthony's accomplishment is astounding—truly one of the greatest moments in Olympic history.

The implausible story of Anthony Ervin is awe-inspiring. One of the most decorated and accomplished sprinters of all time, he's also one of the most interesting and complicated athletes in Olympic history.

What I find most compelling about Anthony is the spiritual and emotional journey he weathered to rebuild the child into not only a champion for the ages, but more importantly, a man.

—Rich

Anthony: I've always loved being in the water. As a kid, I would beg to go to the pool. There's something about the very early years where you have a greater affinity for being in the water. It erodes the longer you're kept from it and as you grow more comfortable on land.

I was seven years old when I won my first swim meet. My parents and my coach were beaming. My family was excited and my teammates were in awe. I wanted more.

My journey in life and in the water are largely one and the same: it's always been about relationships. I had a lull where I was not doing well, not performing well and really struggling as I entered puberty. I only started to find my gift again towards the end of high school.

Mike Bottom, my coach at UC Berkeley, saw something in both my rebellion and my resistance to conformity. I had found my own way to be good without training properly; without adhering to what I called "the way of the establishment." Mike believed he could coach me to the next level, but I wouldn't show up to practice. And I would constantly test whether Mike cared about me, or just my swimming. I made a whole battery of poor choices, forcing Mike to deal with the aftermath. He would try to steer me in a healthier direction, so I didn't need to hit rock bottom if I fell down a few really deep wells.

Going to the Olympics was always a pipe dream—it didn't seem realistic in any kind of manner. Even as I started making these huge breakthroughs my first college season, it wasn't until I broke a world record that I realized I was going to the Olympics.

When I stood up on those blocks for the 50-meter freestyle at the 2000 Sydney Olympics, I don't even remember the race. I took my mark. The race happened. It was just an execution of everything that I had prepared for, and I opened myself up to just swimming free.

I won the gold.

I was beaming. My fists were in the air. I walked down the pool to media, and this reporter Jim Gray puts the mic in my face and he says, "So I noticed you twitching behind the blocks. Was that your Tourette's?" and "What's it like to be Black and win a gold medal?"

I was stunned.

This was something I kept buried. There was no public knowledge of my Tourette's. I am not Black. I am of African American descent. I am very, very white. I couldn't say anything, I just felt the cold stare of the camera. It was excruciating.

The reason I have always loved swimming is that you can't see me, I am just a body moving in the water. There was also something about putting in extreme effort that put my Tourette's at bay. It's an outlet so my body doesn't lash out so much.

After winning my first Olympic gold medal, I never considered that I would have to represent something because of it. I was just focused on racing as fast as I could, faster than anybody. I never thought about the social implications. This mantle was thrust upon me without consent. These old white men were turning me into a story to sell.

Achieving the goal you spend your whole life pursuing is nothing like what you think it will be. The reality eclipses your expectations. Having met my ultimate goal so young in life, I was left with no challenge that could be as noble.

I could have done whatever I wanted. Instead, I ran away.

It took considerable work to finally get my ego to collapse. Once it did, I started to become more me.

Ultimately, I learned that if you don't write your own story, a story will be written for you.

DOMINICK THOMPSON

MASCULINITY OF COMPASSION

When did we decide it's "manly" to repress our emotions, oppress the weak, and deny our shared humanity?

Somewhere along the way the most elevated qualities of masculinity have been denuded by a cultural perversion of the gender norm.

Simply put, caring and compassion should not be gender specific.

Dominick Thompson seeks to reclaim the best of what it truly means to masculine. Because there is nothing more manly than demonstrating compassion over dominance. Protection over prey. Restraint over force. Understanding over judgment. And love over bigotry.

A leading voice in the vegan and plant-based athlete communities, "Domz" is an athlete, activist, and the founder of Crazies and Weirdos—hip, sustainable and eco-friendly clothing made from recycled and organic materials. Devoted to helping people live a healthier, more cruelty-free lifestyle, he's also the man behind the plant-based nutrition meal planner *What Elephants Eat.*

Prior to becoming a social entrepreneur and activist, Dominick was a healthcare executive. A working athlete, Dominick trains like a beast, and typically competes in 10-12 endurance races per year, including marathons, triathlons, and ultra-races.

Recognized for his activism in major news outlets like NPR, ABC, and *Esquire,* Dominick activates his over 200,000 Instagram followers on the daily with a pull-no-punches mix of brutal truth education matched with relatable, uplifting inspiration.

Beyond the magazine spreads and accolades is more than meets the eye. It's the story of a victim of circumstance who faced harrowing hardship and incarceration—formative, hard-knock experiences he ultimately transcended. And it's an unlikely redemptive tale that lends deep potency to his quest to reset and redefine the aspirational qualities of manhood.

In the summer of 2017, I had the honor of facilitating the first public telling of Dominick's scarring back story. A responsibility I didn't take lightly, I still reflect daily on his powerful testimony and the strength of his conviction.

When I think about Domz, I see the best aspects of what it means to be a man and a protector. A human of imposing physical prowess yet devoid of ego. Convicted in a sense of self, but vulnerable with emotions. Equanimous in disposition. Purposeful in the care for others. And selfless in the protection of beings less capable of caring for themselves.

Survivor. Role model. Hero. Awesome human being. Good friend.

Domz is the genuine article—and always delivers the goods on time.

—Rich

Dominick: I grew up on the West Side of Chicago. Anybody that's from there knows what the West Side is about. Some even call Chicago "Chi-Raq" because of all the murders and killings. I lived in a single parent home, no father around or any solid role models—cliché movie stuff. My mom worked her ass off as a nurse. It was just me, her, and my two older sisters. There was a time when it was all four of us in a one-bedroom apartment.

Now that I look back on it, I couldn't avoid getting involved in street stuff. It was a stage in my life I had to go through. The gang life was all around me. Money was tight. I saw these dope boys pulling up in expensive cars, when all I wanted to to was to help provide for my family. I just wanted to put food on the table—but I ended up being able to do so much more.

At 19 I had everything I wanted. I had nice clothes, I was wearing platinum chains and gold watches. I was making money hand over fist, running the streets and having a good time.

But watching my mom work so hard, led me to make some better decisions. I went to college, and when I turned 20, I knew it was time for me to leave the street business. I had the money I need for school, so I focused on that and got a full-time job. My time selling was done.

A few years later, there was a big drought in Chicago. That's what we call it on the streets—a drought, meaning that no one had supplies to produce drugs. When I came back to town, a friend needed a favor and I said yes. It was going to be my last rendezvous, but it turned into a really bad mistake. The government found out about my participation and I ended up getting indicted and pleaded guilty to possession with the intent to distribute.

During my first week of processing, I kept asking myself, Why is this happening to me? I was afraid being incarcerated was going to fuck with me mentally, because every day felt like a Sunday. Every fucking day. I knew what I did was wrong, but I felt like there was

something bigger going on, almost like some energy put me in there. I felt like that was the world saying, hey, come sit down. That was that energy saying, hey, I want to put you in timeout mode so you can really figure out who you are and what you want to do with your life.

I began to feel this connection to animals, like I shouldn't be eating meat. I felt like I needed to give up eating meat and show this energy, and again, I was more religious at the time, that this is the ultimate sacrifice.

I wouldn't destroy anything. Whether it was food or pumping poison, I should not be a part of anything negative. I made that decision right then and there, no more meat for me. My first month of going plant-based, I dropped 20 pounds. No supplements, no drugs, lifting heavier than I have ever lifted. I re-engineered my body and it was all because of plants.

But it's not just what you eat, you have to do your very damn best to not cause anyone harm. The universe will repay you more than you can imagine, whether it be your physical health or your financial portfolio, you get all these new and exciting ideas. This lifestyle has been the best thing that ever happened to me, and If I had to do it all again to get here, I would.

"What we consume as humans should be taken very seriously."
—Dominick Thompson

RUNNING ACROSS INDIA AND WHY SERVICE IS PARAMOUNT

Imagine running a 250-kilometer ultramarathon across the Atacama Desert—one of the driest places on Earth—when your only prior, legitimate running experience is a single ill-fated marathon attempt that left you humbly walking the last eight miles.

Not only do you complete that challenge, but over the course of that same calendar year you also race three more 250-kilometer ultramarathons across the world to become the first female and youngest person to ever run and complete the 4 Desert Race Series Grand Slam, one of the world's toughest and most prestigious endurance achievements.

This is inspiring story of Samantha Gash—ultra-athlete extraordinaire, role model, humanitarian, and generally awesome human.

Initially pursued as a break from her law studies, running unlocked Samantha's latent talent for endurance. Her unique disposition for suffering. And new reservoirs of joy.

Her surprising 4 Deserts triumph left her thirsting for more. So the following year, she conquered a 222-kilometer nonstop foot race across the Himalayas at 6,000 meters above sea level—an event that had only been completed previously by one man.

Bearing witness to the challenges of the developing world led Samantha to leverage her running for a greater purpose. So she got to work and never looked back, raising significant funds for charitable organizations and advocating for humanitarian causes like women's empowerment, social change, and access to education.

Perhaps her most stunning achievement, in 2016 Samantha ran from the west to the east of India—a 3253-kilometer jaunt over 76 days that raised awareness and close to $200,000 to fund children's education programs for localities across India.

And when last year's brushfires were devastating her Australian homeland, Samantha Gash and Nic Davidson created Relief Run—a global, virtual run challenge that went viral, raising over a million dollars for disaster relief.

Samantha has been twice recognized as a finalist in the Women's Agenda Leadership Awards. She has been selected as a delegate for the Australia India Youth Dialogue, and was also nominated for a Pride of Australia Medal.

Samantha's story is one of kinship between suffering and generosity. And it's about the magic that transpires when you have the willingness to entertain the impossible, step outside your comfort zone and courageously leap through fear into the abyss.

But more than anything, her story is a reminder that we find purpose in the call to service—and it's a call to marshal the power we all yield to make a positive difference in the world.

—Rich

SAMANTHA

"We are defined more by our response to something than what happens to us."
—Samantha Gash

GASH

PHOTO: MATT KORINEK

Samantha: Did you know the Latin root of the word "passion" is "to suffer"? Are you willing to suffer the most in your life for that thing that you're passionate about? Because, when you are willing to suffer for something outside of yourself, that suffering doesn't seem so great anymore.

In 2011 I went to India to do a 222-kilometer nonstop run called La Ultra (the High). It was the hardest thing that I've ever had to endure. At the time, I was doing it to see what my own personal physical and mental capabilities were—and, in truth, I was doing it for myself. But it spurred the birth of an idea. I imagined what I could do if I were working for a worthier cause. On that mountain pass, I said to myself, "Never again am I going to push myself so incredibly hard unless it's for something outside of myself." And I haven't since.

Over the last few years, my purpose in running has been to explore the barriers to quality education for children around the world. I think education is the breaking point to the cycle of poverty. Access to education can change a child's life.

With the purpose of visiting 18 different programs and communities, the expedition across India was—for me—not about how fast I did it, but about my observations as I traversed the country. It gave me the world's greatest perspective; I earned a high degree of empowerment and resolve, and, ultimately, I raised over $150,000 dollars for World Vision, funding six education programs.

But I didn't start out as an endurance athlete. In high school, I owned my own wonderful weirdness. I was around like-minded, interesting, bizarre, unique people who were smart and good at sports. It taught me that I can try those things and still be this artsy, small kid who was not sure of her place.

I was studying for performing arts and law degrees, but this didn't stop me from trying my first marathon. I had never really run that much, and I soon realized that it didn't just make me feel physically amazing; I felt the strongest, mentally, that I'd ever felt in my entire life. I was immediately connected with running.

It was after an injury during that marathon that I nearly pulled out of the race. But my friend encouraged me to pull through despite the pain, and it was that near-failure that made me do my first Ultra.

It became an addiction, in a sense. I saw the possibility in the impossible, and I took a leap of faith. Later I ran through the Sahara and Antarctica, and I completed the Grand Slam—which only two people had completed previously, and they were men.

Truly, there's something poetic about playing into what you are naturally inclined to do, and then having to go to the opposite level of it. It all starts with believing in yourself and putting in the hard work.

So put your phone on silent, get outside, find your community, and do things to make a tangible difference.

Live in the moment. Be passionate.

"Put your phone on silent, get outside, find your community, and do things to make a tangible difference."

—Samantha Gash

"Simply put, humans are not wired
to be constantly wired."
—Cal Newport

CAL NEWPORT

ON DIGITAL MINIMALISM:
WHY FOCUS IS THE NEW SUPERPOWER

It's become increasingly harder to just put the phone down. Because the latest apps and digital platforms are specifically designed to addict, we have become slaves to their irresistible allure.

Our precious attention is being hijacked. The ability to focus—to concentrate on that which is most meaningful—simply cannot compete with the magnetic pull of our Instagram feed. No longer need anyone ever be bored. Alone with one's thoughts. Or simply present with one's self.

The result is a global epidemic of distraction. A fomenting of loneliness and isolation. A rise in depression. And a degradation of our humanity.

The solution isn't Luddism. Instead, it's agency. We need not be victims of technology. We have the power to liberate ourselves from the tether of digital dependency. Emancipation from the dopamine rush isn't just the salve to what ails us, it's the gateway to that which we seek most. Meaning. True human connection. And deeper kinship with our innate humanity.

Indeed, there is no substitute for real relationships. Boredom is useful. And focus is the new superpower.

Cal Newport has spent a lot of time thinking deeply about these issues.

A Provost's Distinguished Associate Professor in the Department of Computer Science at Georgetown University, Cal is the author of six books focused mostly on the impact of technology on society. He is a frequent guest on NPR and has been featured in many major publications, including the *New York Times*, *Wall Street Journal*, *New Yorker*, *Washington Post*, and *Economist*.

Regular listeners know I have a penchant for dropping Cal's name with regularity—a habit that began in 2016 after devouring his seminal book, *Deep Work: Rules for Focused Success in a Distracted World*—pages that permanently altered how I think about and apply my attention.

Digital Minimalism, Cal's most recent *New York Times* bestseller, has profoundly recalibrated my relationship with meaning, connection, personal technology, and the digital world.

People often ask me which books have influenced me the most. The aforementioned two rank close to the top—manifestos of great practical import for our modern age.

Similarly, I would rank my podcast with Cal among the most consequential conversations in the eight-year history of the show.

Packed with practical, actionable steps, Cal's message will empower you to free up precious time. Declutter your mind. Connect you more deeply to the work and relationships you care most about. And profoundly improve the quality of your professional and personal lives.

—*Rich*

Cal: What's so unique about our current circumstance is that we have banished solitude. This has never before happened in human history. Just seven or eight years ago, there would be time throughout your day where it was just you alone with your own thoughts. But not anymore. All you have to do is pull out your wirelessly connected device and the boredom and the solitude are gone.

But the thing is, solitude is crucial to the human condition. Freedom from input from other minds gives our brains time to reset. We have to have it on a regular basis. It has nothing to do with physical isolation. It's about what your brain is processing. If you're processing something that was generated from another mind, you're not in a state of solitude. Anytime you're looking at your phone or anytime you have earbuds in, if you're reading something, if you're talking to someone, you're not in a state of solitude. Your brain is in input processing mode. Your brain takes it very seriously and it turns on all sorts of different centers that don't turn on when you're just looking at the things around you.

It's a wild and radical experiment. Let's just say it's not going well.

We've become used to the constant companion model of the phone where we just have it by our side all the time—we think of that as just being fundamental to the technology. But it's actually much more contrived than that. Social media companies radically re-engineered the social media experience from being a way to stay in touch with friends and family, into this stream of incoming social approval indicators. The like button on Facebook, which seems fundamental, was actually a late arrival to social media. It was a boon for the bottom line because the entire dynamic of the platform was transformed. You post something and have to constantly go back to see how many likes it got.

Maybe it received a lot, maybe it received none. But then a little bit later it gets more. Maybe you've been tagged in someone's photo. It's all about receiving this stream of social approval indicators. It feels good to know that other people are thinking about you, right? But these apps are exploiting our psychological vulnerabilities and it's entirely intentional. It's almost impossible to not go back and hit Instagram one more time after you post something. This is purposeful. It's the foundation of the constant companion model of smartphone use. Smartphones went from something that you used as a tool into something that you looked at all the time.

Social media is like a slot machine—this isn't just hyperbolic or metaphorical. Silicon Valley literally engineered these apps to be like slot machines. So many of these massive social media platforms in Silicon Valley borrowed ideas from Las Vegas casinos. In Vegas, they figured out how to actually hard code the reinforcement schedules into the slot machines. But for social media, instead of it being triple cherries, it's 20 likes versus five likes. What I am trying to tell you is that you're not just lazy. The reason why you're looking at Instagram so much is that there are very smart people figuring out ways to destroy your willpower so they can make money off of your attention.

Facebook and Instagram have been accused of artificially holding back likes and favorites.

This keeps you coming back, ensures you keep checking. Behavioral psychology says if you sometimes get the reward, and you sometimes don't, it short circuits the dopamine system in a way that gets you to go back much more than you normally would. If it was a steady stream, it wouldn't be nearly as compulsive.

We wonder why the non-industrial productivity metrics in the American economy have been stagnant over the last 10 years. Even though technology has gotten more advanced, we have fragmented our attention to the degree that we're actually really bad at doing the things we need to do. This is why the people who prioritize really unbroken concentration seem like they have a superpower. It's essentially just relative to everyone else, who are in the state of self-imposed attention residue, which is keeping their cognitive performance artificially low.

But the most unexpected consequence of technology is that it's degrading our humanity. It's holding us back from living a flourishing life. Focusing intensely on something that's really valuable is a huge source of satisfaction and meaning. When you diverge from that with social media, you lose that satisfaction and meaning of intentional and continued work. Doing something that's hard will bring you deep joy. Social media is just distracting you from t

So here's what you need to do: Re-examine what it means to live an intentional life. Start figuring out what you value, so you can start filling your time with it instead of your screen. Aggressively reinvestigate the type of high-quality analog leisure activities that interest you. Just getting a taste for these sorts of higher startup cost activities that give

you more meaning will bring you so much happiness, and help you build the foundation of values you need to actually have a minimalist approach to your technology. Delete all the apps from your phone where someone makes money off your attention. You don't have to quit anything. You're not losing access. Simply choose to not have it as a default in your pocket—only look at those apps on your desktop computer, laptop, tablet, etc.

Once a day, do something without your phone. Take your dog on a walk. Go to the grocery store. Sit in silence for the first 20 minutes of your commute. Just do the things you normally do without the buzzing whirring slot machine in your pocket. Give your brain time to decompress. This is the simplest way to introduce solitude back into your life.

Maximalism is about not missing out on value. It's about spending hours and hours scrolling, so you don't miss that one thing.

But minimalism would say, what you get from missing out on some of those small meaningless opportunities on Instagram, is that you're able to put more energy into things that are far more valuable and far more life-enriching.

I promise it will give you maximum return.

"Digital minimalism definitively does not reject the innovations of the internet age, but instead rejects the way so many people currently engage with these tools."

—Cal Newport

LIFE LESSONS FROM THE WORLD'S GREATEST MOUNTAIN RUNNER

KÍLIAN

Never meet your heroes, they say.

Fortunately, my entire show is based on ignoring that advice.

Kílian Jornet rarely sits for longform press. In fact, he rarely sits, period. Arranging our podcast was no small feat. I still can't believe it happened. But it did.

Everything I hoped it would be and more, my conversation with Kílian made clear one salient point: Kílian is that humble hero we need—a rare and preternaturally inspiring human who convincingly reminds us that anything is possible, and that the boundaries of human capability are truly limitless.

Inarguably the most prolific and dominant mountain runner of all time, Kílian is among the world's greatest athletes in history. Born and raised at 6,000 feet above sea level in the Spanish Pyrenees, at age five he climbed an 11,000-foot mountain—the highest mountain in the region. He adores the mountains with the same ferocity with which he runs them, and has racked up wins in most of the world's most prestigious ultramarathons along the way.

Now searching for inspiration outside the restrictions of formal competition, Kílian has spent recent years focused less on formal racing and more on self-styled adventure challenges. A project he calls *Summits of My Life*, Kílian has been ticking off the fastest known recorded times (FKT) to ascend and descend the world's most challenging peaks, including the Matterhorn, Kilimanjaro, Mont Blanc, Denali, and even the planet's tallest summit.

Not only did Kílian set the Mt. Everest FKT at 26 hours from base camp, *he did it without supplemental oxygen or ropes.* A mere six days later, he did the unheard of and *repeated the performance*—an accomplishment that garnered him Adventurer of the Year accolades from *National Geographic*.

His accomplishments bend the mind. But I wanted to know what drives one of the planet's most uniquely gifted fleet of foot—a man devoted to redefining what is possible, continually pushing the limits of human ability, and never failing to astonish competitors with his near-superhuman fitness and ability.

I discovered that Kílian's motivation isn't what you might imagine. It has nothing to do with race results. And his happiness derives not from victory. Instead, it's adventure that sparks Kílian's joy. Immersion in nature. Living outside the comfort zone. And always, always exploring.

What strikes me most about this otherworldly athlete is his profound humility. Kílian's passion and respect for nature's prowess is earned. Refreshingly grounded, he lives simply, an ethic and aesthetic reflected in the minimalistic purity of his athletic pursuits.

We may not be able to run like Kílian. But his fuel can be our fuel. Because nature, exploration, and adventure are available to all.

I'm glad I met a hero. I think you will be too.

—Rich

JORNET

Kilian: I think conquering mountains is a very, very ironic word. We are not conquering mountains. We can conquer ourselves on the mountain, but we are never fighting against the mountain or against nature—we are part of it.

When you start to do mountaineering, you are afraid of your capacities because you don't know yourself. You aren't afraid of the mountain; you see it as something solid and reliable. The more you climb it, the less you are afraid you are of yourself, the more you learn your capacities, your techniques. You gain experience and confidence, but the fear switches: you become more afraid of the mountain than yourself. You learn that the mountain is moving and it's dangerous. You can control yourself and trust yourself, but you cannot control nor trust the mountain. You can think logically about your route, but then an avalanche might come where it's not supposed to or some rock might fall in a zone you deem safe. That's part of mountaineering—accepting what you can and cannot control.

Sports are all about ego. You win a race and stand on top of a podium—it's so artificial. Why are you better because you run faster than the guy that is second? Or the one who is third? Or even the one that is last? Sports encourage an egocentric mindset. It's easy to believe that you are better than others. But in the mountains, that kind of external mindset is very dangerous. If you are doing a race and you are not one hundred percent present and humble, you are going to have a problem. And that problem isn't that you are going to lose the race—the problem is you might die. The consequences are big. The mountains teach you that you are nothing.

At the beginning of my career, I was completely driven by competition. I wanted to win races and become a world champion. That is what motivated me, and it's easy to train very hard if you have this mindset. But when you achieve the goal, the satisfaction only lasts a second. And then you are on to the next thing. You are never really satisfied.

Everyone wants to leave a legacy and be remembered. We all want to do something important. But when you realize how insignificant you are, you see how wonderful it is that you exist at all.

> *"Conquering mountains is an ironic phrase. We are not conquering them. We can never pretend to be fighting nature because we are part of it."*
>
> **—Kilian Jornet**

PHOTO: LYMBUS LIFE SL

"I don't want to be 'the eating disorder recovery girl,' I don't want to be 'the athlete.' This is just me. I'm super flawed, I'm super complex, just like everybody else out there."
—Amelia Boone

AMELIA BOONE

THE "QUEEN OF PAIN" REFRAMES UNBREAKABLE

The most dominant and decorated female in the history of obstacle course racing (OCR), Amelia Boone is persistently lauded for her grit and preternatural ability to suffer.

More impressive is her dignity—and the courage she has demonstrated navigating her most daunting challenge yet.

A Spartan Race World Champion and three-time World's Toughest Mudder Champion, over the course of Amelia's celebrated athletic career she has amassed over 50 podiums and 30 victories. The ultimate weekend warrior, she's done all of this while balancing a full-time career as a corporate attorney—first at the prestigious Skadden Arps law firm in Chicago and currently at Apple.

Dubbed the "Queen of Pain," it's a skyward trajectory that's landed her magazine covers, major publication features, national television gigs, and a legion of adoring fans across the world.

But Amelia's dominance also came with pressures that drained the fun out of competition. And a mask that obscured a deeper dysfunction lurking beneath the surface.

Amidst the celebration of Amelia as an unbreakable champion, prodded for her daily habits, morning routine and training regimen, she privately battled an obstacle more daunting than any race she'd endured: *an eating disorder she kept hidden for the better part of two decades.*

I celebrate Amelia not for her accolades, but for a different kind of courage—the vulnerability to face her disorder. Forge a path to wholeness. And leverage her public profile to change the way we talk about a condition that debilitates millions.

I first met Amelia a couple years ago. I freely admit my projection of her steely disposition, framed by glossy magazine profiles, left me intimidated. But that perception later shifted when she began to publicly share the unvarnished details of her private, protracted struggle. I connected with her guilt and shame. Her honesty and courage only deepened my respect.

The facade gone, I fell for the human—and felt compelled to help amplify her powerful and important message.

Eating disorders currently afflict over 30 million people in the U.S. alone. Many suffer this pernicious disease in silence. But there is a solution. The path to wholeness begins with breaking that silence.

I appreciate Amelia entrusting me with her story. It's an honor I shoulder with both empathy and compassion.

—Rich

Amelia: I don't have anything to blame for my eating disorder. I don't have any trauma. My parents were super supportive. We had very normal relationships with food growing up, there was never any diet talk. No one I knew was trying to lose weight. I had a wonderful life, wonderful parents, a totally functional family and yet, I have these demons in my head and I don't know why.

I was a very good athlete growing up. I was the fearsome pitcher that nobody wanted to face in softball—until I lost a lot of weight and grew very, very weak. I became so weak that I was unable to compete anymore. When I finally told my parents about my issues with food, they took me to a doctor who checked my vitals. I was so sick I was immediately sent to the hospital and that night my heart actually stopped beating. My parents almost lost their daughter, and that still pains me to this day.

Eating disorders thrive in shame. I was very ashamed of what I looked like. I was very ashamed of what I was doing. I would try and hide my body by putting on two or three pairs of tights under my jeans. I didn't like what was happening to me, but I just—I didn't know how to change. These habits were ingrained in me.

I have a 20-year history with this, and if I am being honest with myself, I know I haven't been in a good place for the past six or seven years. Practically the entire time I've been in sport. I told myself I was okay because I was doing well. I was winning races and world championships, so how bad could my disorder be? But I was just barely managing it. Barely. I was on death's door for most of that time.

My life was so hollow. I would come home to my apartment after work and all I had was my disorder. I had walled myself off from relationships and totally disengaged from those around me. I would go to all these races, but I wouldn't want to go out to dinner with everyone because I was terrified. I had to be in my safe space even though it was lonely. I got tired of spending so much time obsessing about food.

I knew there was more out there, and that I could have a more fulfilling life if I worked through my disorder.

I have a great support network now, but I have to make sure that I actually use it. That is the most important thing I learned in treatment: to out myself and not marinate in shame. I learned how to say, "Hey I'm having bad disordered thoughts right now, and I just need to tell somebody." When I put it out there it doesn't hold as much power over me. The shame dissolves.

If someone in your life is struggling with an eating disorder, don't comment on their weight. Instead, point out their changing behaviors. Check in with them regularly. Many people struggling with eating disorders will withdraw socially, and simply saying something like, "Hey, I've noticed you've been not showing up to group runs or group dinners. What's going on?" Sometimes you might have to be the bad guy if it is necessary for them medically. But ultimately, you can't force them to recover. You have to accept that. You can only support them the best you can.

> *"Finding ten things a day that I'm grateful for is a tool in my toolkit on a daily basis."*
> **—Amelia Boone**

DAVID EPSTEIN

WHY LATE BLOOMERS WIN

> "You don't change your identity overnight. You have to start with little keyhole experiments until something you thought was just an interest becomes a real passion or a vocation."
> **—David Epstein**

Conventional wisdom dictates that mastery demands an early start. Relentless focus on developing a specific skill set at the exclusion of other pursuits. As many hours of deliberate practice as humanly possible.

Be it violin, painting, basketball or boat building, there's simply no substitute for a life wholly devoted to developing that narrowly defined skill.

Hence the "10,000 hour rule" zeitgeist embrace—an edict divined by psychologist Anders Ericsson and made famous by Malcolm Gladwell.

But is this actually true?

David Epstein wasn't convinced, so he put this theory to the test. A relentless researcher, he scrutinized the personal histories of top performers across a wide variety of disciplines to discover a most counter-intuitive truth: early specialization is actually the exception to the rule.

It turns out that the most successful among us are those who developed a broad base of interests and skills while everyone else was rushing to specialize.

Our greatest masters—professional athletes, Nobel laureates, musicians, inventors, and scientists—all resist siloing themselves in a single field. Instead they think broadly. Embrace diverse experiences. And constantly cultivate new interests.

Step aside, Malcom. It's the generalists who are the ones most primed to excel. Because breadth is actually the ally of depth—not the opposite.

A journalist and multiple *New York Times* bestselling author, David is a former investigative reporter for both *ProPublica* and *Sports Illustrated* with master's degrees in environmental science and journalism. Three of his stories have been optioned for films. And his TED Talk, "Are Athletes Really Getting Better, Faster, Stronger?" has been viewed over 9 million times.

David is currently best known for his two smash-hit bestsellers, *The Sports Gene: Inside the Science of Extraordinary Athletic Performance* and *Range: Why Generalists Triumph in a Specialized World.* A number-one *New York Times* bestseller, *Range* is arguably the must-read breakout hit of 2019—a book as much about parenting as it is about performance.

He's also exceptional runner. At Columbia University, he set the school record for 800 meters. And despite his intellectual tête-à-tête with one Mr. Gladwell, it brings me joy knowing they are not only friends, but running buddies. Count me jealous.

In a world that favors specialization, that celebrates the nose-to-the-grindstoners, it's actually the jacks-of-all-traders and frequent quitters that inherit the Earth—and blaze a path to greater success, happiness, and fulfillment in both career and life.

Because failing isn't just good, but the best way to learn.

Not convinced?

I didn't reach my athletic peak until I was 43.

I didn't write my first book until I was 44.

I didn't start my podcast until I was 45.

At 30, I thought my life was over.

At 54, I feel like I'm just beginning.

This is one is for the dreamers. For the dabblers and tinkerers. No longer shall you be castigated as dilettantes. Perhaps, like me, you are but a late bloomer. And, as David so thoroughly and eloquently contends, it is us late bloomers who ultimately prevail.

—Rich

"It doesn't have to be a flying leap to start learning new things about yourself, but you do have to be a little uncomfortable"
—David Epstein

David: You learn who you are in practice, not in theory.

This is why we have to embrace experimentation. There are of course basic skills that everyone should learn, but a part of developing young people should also be facilitating some experimentation and helping them find the place where they fit instead of just putting everyone—through the same damn conveyor belt. You have to start with these little keyhole experiments until something that you think was just an interest becomes a real passion or a vocation.

There are many different ways to get to good outcomes. There are many different possible paths as there are people. But if you want to be a journalist, study something other than journalism. Find other interests. You're going to need stuff to write about. One or two years of experimenting can pay big dividends. If you're going to be in journalism for a long time, having another model of how to think about things is really, really useful. That can really set you apart. Because the way to find interesting stories is to live an interesting life.

So this is what I do: I have what I call a book of experiments. I use it the way I did when I was a science grad student. I pick something I'd like to learn about myself, and ask, Am I interested in this? Do I think I could be good at it? Do I have access to training in it? And then I'll try it and be a scientist of myself and write conclusions and reflections.

Start your little book of experiments. Don't worry about finding the thing that lights your hair on fire. Identity doesn't change overnight; it changes a little piece at a time. Reach out to the fringe of your network. Take a class in something you don't know about. Start exposing yourself, systematically to little things. Having the book of experiments will force you to reflect on them. Did it ignite a new interest? Is it something that might cater your talents?

When you hit on something where you want to get a little deeper, go ahead and do that. But also keep that experimentation process going. It doesn't have to be a flying leap to start learning things about yourself, but you do have to be uncomfortable. Because you're going to dabble in things that you don't feel competent at, yet.

There are some short parts of my life, like when I lived in the Arctic, or when I lived on a ship; these stages of my life weren't that long, but they felt long because they are important and impactful memories to me. They were so uncomfortable and so unusual. It's everyone's choice, but for me, that's the kind of life I want to live.

BOOKS OF SMALL EXPERIMENTS
BY DAVID EPSTEIN

I've written two books. Each time, the process has felt to me like running the 800-meters did in college: spine-tingling and nerve-racking just before the start, difficult but extremely compelling in the middle, torture toward the end. And yet, if I ran a personal best, the memory of torture would soften in phases until it inevitably became: "Well, that wasn't so bad. Let's try it again."

In my best races, I tended not to remember what exactly it was that I had done. Perhaps in those races I was so in the moment that I didn't have time to encode memories. Whatever the reason, the strange fact is that when I ran well, I would have little memory of what actually occurred in the race. For me, that memory lacuna is another parallel to book writing. I can't reconstruct, in detail, the daily process of writing.

After my first book came out in 2013, I was frequently asked about my process. I had a few trusty systems I could share, but the most important work—the winding path of exploring my curiosity—was impossible for me to recreate. Once when I was asked, I passed the buck to my wife. Could she remember how I had worked? "You went upstairs and came back down two years later," she said. Not quite what I was looking for.

Without a formula to return to, I felt like a rookie in 2016 when I started research for a second book, but this time with an obstacle that had not existed the first time around. The first book was about sports science; I was the sports science writer at *Sports Illustrated*. My day job and my book job coexisted seamlessly. By the time I began the second book—which is about the strengths of generalists and late bloomers in an increasingly specialized work world—I was an investigative reporter at *ProPublica*. With a few exceptions, my day job had nothing whatsoever to do with my book.

The divergence presented a problem that I did not immediately recognize. A year into working on the book, I only knew that I wasn't happy with the draft I had. I wasn't really sure why. I just didn't like it. I decided to stop writing for a while, in the hope that I could continue research and return to the draft with fresh eyes.

On a whim, I decided to take a beginner's fiction writing class online. I don't know what I was looking for, but it turned out to be a minor revelation. First, the class made me feel incompetent, which was horrible and wonderful all at once. Until then I hadn't realized how comfortable I'd grown with magazine writing. So comfortable that I was on autopilot, not pushing myself enough to explore new writing structures and styles. Competence had bred complacency without me even noticing.

In the online class, nothing I had previously done mattered; everyone was a beginner. Everything felt daunting, but everything felt possible. I thought of the Zen concept of beginner's mind: "In the beginner's mind there are many possibilities, but in the expert's there are few." As I had become more skilled at magazine writing, I had unconsciously stopped doing what helped me grow in the first place: experimenting. In the fiction class, everything was an experiment for me.

One homework assignment was to write a story using no dialogue at all. It helped me realize that I had been leaning on quotes way too heavily in my book draft. I had, after all, been writing investigative articles, which tend to be quote-heavy. But at the length of a book, it's exhausting to read page after page dense with quotes. Plus, I was frequently using quotes to convey ideas that I wasn't confident I understood well enough to explain in my own words.

I dove back into research on those topics. It was an enormous amount of work, but when I was satisfied that I really had a deep understanding, I went back, stripped quotes, and replaced them with narration. I think the book that resulted is one that is clearer, more compelling, and that I enjoyed creating. (I mean, it was torture toward the end. But maybe it wasn't so bad.)

Getting out of my comfort zone in that online class reinforced a lesson in my own book that I hadn't given enough attention: difficulty is not a sign that you aren't learning, but ease is. I had initially defaulted to a style of writing that came easily to me, even though it wasn't the right style for the job. And now for one last 800-meters parallel: if you do the same exact training day after day and year after year, you might not get worse, but you probably won't get better either. Writing is similar.

The more experienced I became as a runner, and now as a writer, the more I had to seek out new challenges to improve. After taking the fiction-writing class, I started keeping what I call my "book of small experiments." I write down a hypothesis—a guess about some topic I might be interested in or some skill that I'd like to explore—and then I force myself to try something new so that I can reflect on the hypothesis. Some of those experiments have been fruitful, others forgettable. But I had no idea what I might learn when I took the fiction class. I don't know what experiment or experience might next stretch me in just the right way. I don't know, and I can't know. And that's why I have the book: to make sure I keep looking.

LAUREN FLESHMAN

ON EMPOWERING WOMEN ATHLETES

"I changed my body for sport. No girl should."

—Lauren Fleshman

What is the current state of gender parity in sport?

Ask one of the greatest middle-distance runners in American history and she'll tell you that women and girls are no longer content just to have a chance to play—they're demanding that sports be rebuilt altogether.

Meet Lauren Fleshman—a former world-class athlete with a legacy of breaking both records and paradigms.

After collecting state championships as a standout high school runner, Lauren matriculated to Stanford, where she garnered five NCAA titles, 15 All-American honors, and a spot in the Hall of Fame.

As a professional track-and-field athlete, Lauren's accolades include two USA Championships and five World Championship berths for Team USA.

But it wasn't all podiums and medals. Lauren's career is also noteworthy for its devastating setbacks.

Holding the painful distinction of most likely being the best American distance runner never to make an Olympic team, Lauren's dreams were repeatedly impaired by injuries that had her on crutches at the wrong four-year intervals.

But hard knocks produce life lessons. Lauren leveraged her misfortunes to develop a philosophic perspective on running. A unique take on human potential. And profound belief in transformation.

Now retired from competition, Lauren the very definition of an active mom of two. She serves up coaching duties to the elite women runners of Oiselle's Littlewing Athletics. A prolific and talented writer, she is co-author of the *Believe Training Journal* series. And she's hard at work on a hotly anticipated book.

As an entrepreneur, Lauren hosts the Wilder Running and Writing Retreats. She's the co-founder of performance nutrition company Picky Bars alongside her (recently retired) professional triathlete husband Jesse Thomas, who graced episode 442 of the podcast. And together they host the *Work, Play, Love* podcast.

How Lauren's successes and failures fuel her as a coach, parent, businessperson, and role model are instructive. But what compels me the most is Lauren's committed, stalwart advocacy for advancing female equality, empowerment, and prominence in sport.

Simply put, Lauren Fleshman is the role model we've been looking for.

—Rich

Lauren: As a top Nike athlete, it was hard for me to talk about what was really going on behind the scenes. I was vulnerable to the adults in my life and their input on what it would take to be the best. I took a small step in the wrong direction and I probably would have taken many more if I had been in the Nike Oregon Project. I was one of the most promising athletes in history coming out of Stanford in my event, and a lot of people thought I had the complete package to put women's distance running back on the map.

When Alberto Salazar founded the Nike Oregon project, his intention was to use every single method just on this side of legal to put his athletes on top. That wasn't controversial at the time—it was applauded. But his intent was to get an unfair advantage. Can you see how dangerous that was? The biggest and most influential sports brand putting their marketing dollars behind this group and their performances was incredibly impactful on the future of clean sport.

Because the truth is, the altitude tents and inhalers and thyroid treatments were all just stepping stones to other things. Bad things.

Think about it: Nike spends so much time on branding initiatives that have to do with the purity of sport, and yet they have never taken a stance on doping. They've never launched a brand campaign about clean sport and only using the body you've got. They have the power to make sweeping changes culturally, but they won't. Why is that?

I believe in the future of ethical, clean, and fair sport. I am pushing for it because it eats at me. My seventh in the world finish with all these suspicious people in front of me weighs on me constantly. Was everyone else doping? What would've happened if they weren't?

It's going to be hard a process because it needs to be nuanced. Here's what we need to do: One, we have to drop the black and white view of it all. No one's going to come out and talk about their experiences if they are going to be immediately demonized. Two, we have to end the zero-sum game of competition and encourage fair labor practices. Why does it have to be that only people who win medals can actually make a living? Why is it the athletes go to the Olympics and don't get paid at all for going there while the IOC makes billions of dollars? If everyone on the team was financially compensated, teammates and competitors wouldn't get so desperate and turn to drugs. The Olympics depends on free labor—athletes are deprived to the point where they're at each other instead of trying to change the system that is oppressing them in the first place. To have fair and ethical sport, we also need to even the playing field for men and women.

There are these important milestones that start with men: the sub-two marathon, the sub-four-mile, but there is no female equivalent. What could we do that is equally exciting or transcendent culturally to get people pumped on the women's side? It's upsetting for me when I think about the biggest sports brand in the world deciding where they're going to put their marketing dollars; it's mostly men in those rooms and they're only interested in other men's performances. How do we get more women into those rooms?

Similarly, how do we better support pregnant women athletes? Being a professional woman runner, you kind of view your motherhood plan based on your job. That's true well beyond sport. But the way athletic contracts are set up, there is no mention of the word 'pregnancy' specifically. Pregnancy is treated as an injury. Generally, athletes have some sort of a clause that says if you don't compete within a certain number of days, you get a contract reduction of 50%—or you get dropped.

As a younger woman looking at my contract, it didn't look like babies fit in there anywhere. I thought I'd race for about eight years, retire, start a family, and that'd be it. It pushes athletes into such a non-creative space, and they lose all this great talent right when they're entering their prime. Kara Goucher's story is very compelling—she was suspended when she got pregnant. Nike didn't pay her that whole year but required her to do appearances. She was on the cover of Runner's World. She actually became more famous than ever that year. She wasn't getting paid at all, but she was working for them, and she was not allowed to seek payment from anyone else.

We have to make these changes in sport, but we can't stop there. Sports are just one of many industries where unfair labor practices exist, where discrimination against people of color, women, and especially pregnant women or nursing women, exists. It's endemic to our society.

So to create lasting change, you have to be involved in your community. You have to stay engaged and informed. It's the only way for progress to be made on these major issues around gender equality, racial equality, and clean sport. Disseminate information and speak up. Your voice matters.

Let's do something about it.

"You can write your own story. You make your story worthwhile."
—Lauren Fleshman

"You are here now.
Make the most of it and
change what's not working.
It's crucial."

—Jeff Gordinier

JEFF GORDINIER

PERFECT PLATES, PUNK ROCK, AND PROLIFIC PROSE

Why is great food important? How and why did restaurants become culturally significant? And what life lessons can be gleaned from the world's greatest chef?

There is no more enthusiastic ringmaster currently holding court on such questions than Jeff Gordinier, the merry man of food and pen.

A writer, journalist, and author who inhabits the converging intersection of food and culture, Jeff is a frequent contributor to the *New York Times* and currently serves as the Food and Drinks editor at *Esquire*.

A graduate of Princeton University where he studied writing and poetry, Jeff is a former writer and editor for *Entertainment Weekly*, editor-at-large for *Details* magazine, and over the years has written about music and culture for a multitude of national publications, including *Travel + Leisure, GQ, Elle, Creative Nonfiction, Spin, Poetry Foundation, Fortune,* and many others.

Last year Jeff released *Hungry: Eating, Road-Tripping, and Risking It All with the Greatest Chef in the World.* Equal parts midlife crisis autobiography, adventure travelogue, and biography, it chronicles the four years Jeff spent traveling with René Redzepi, the renowned chef of Copenhagen's Noma, arguably the world's greatest restaurant. And yet, the book really isn't about food. A meditation on risk, re-invention, creative breakthroughs, and human connection, it's among my favorite reads of 2019.

I first met Jeff in 2015 when he visited our home for a *New York Times* feature he was penning on the rise of veganism. Dubbed "Vegans Go Glam," the piece caught fire, including a day spent as the most e-mailed story on the entire *New York Times* website. It was a big moment for us, and the plant-based movement at large.

In the wake of that experience, Jeff and I struck up a friendship. He sent me an early copy of *Hungry,* which I devoured. It left me wanting to know more about Jeff. About food culture. About the mysterious René Redzepi. And what can be learned about life from this charismatic, cult-like genius redefining cutting-edge cuisine.

Our podcast was a Vulcan mind-meld. What I took from our exchange—beyond the sheer joy of conversing with someone vibrating on my specific wavelength—is the importance of investing in experience. Never shying away from reinvention. And the significance of deep human connection—to others, oneself, and the environment we share.

About a week after our podcast, I got a text from Jeff:

"Table for 2 booked at Noma. Are you in?"

I've never been one for extravagant impulsiveness. But an opportunity to eat at the world's greatest restaurant? That's an adventure likely to come knocking only once. Especially at Noma, where the waitlist rivals the phone book.

Every instinct told me the idea was ridiculous. First, I live in Los Angeles. Noma is in Denmark. And second, the reservation was mere days away. Too expensive. Too last minute. I couldn't possibly justify it.

"I'm in."

The trip exceeded all expectations. Produced once-in-a-lifetime memories I will forever cherish. And to this day serves as a constant reminder:

Life is short. Always say yes to adventure.

—Rich

Jeff: I think some people are drawn to writing because they have a pulsing, gnawing need to tell a specific story. It could be a story of pain from their youth of abuse, it could be an immigrant story that involves a lot of challenges and uphill battles. Speaking candidly, I'm not coming from that place. I was drawn to books because I loved language. I just loved stories. I loved sentences. I found them exhilarating. The Lawrence Ferlinghetti book or a Frank O'Hara book, I liked that the words jumped all over the page. I liked that they were breaking the rules of punctuation and grammar. That seemed fun. That seemed kind of punk rock.

I started to see Joan Didion, Tom Wolfe, Gay Talese, John McPhee, do these incredible pieces for magazines, sometimes profiles of stars. But sometimes more reported essays about cultural movements or whatever. Isn't that one hell of a job? It's basically subsidized adventure. You get to weigh in on the culture, you get to move the needle, you get to meet all these captivating people and somebody else pays you. That's what gets me high. I don't even buy new clothes, as my wife would tell you.

I don't even wash my clothes. So I apologize if I'm stinking up the studio, but I don't care about those luxury things in any way. I care about new vantage points on life and that sense of rush in your head. It can come through a poem for me, it can come through a song, it can come through time with my children. If life is not working

out for you, change it. That's not a brand new statement. We hear that from Silicon Valley entrepreneurs and we hear that from spiritual figures. It's just true. It may be your relationship, maybe your line of work, it may be your health as you know. Change it. Do the work. Say yes to it.

When I first got a reservation at Noma, I got a table for two. I had all these friends who knew that I'd met René Redzepi, and they told me, "Okay, listen to me dude. Seriously, I will move fucking mountains. If you ever get a table at Noma, text me, I will buy a ticket immediately." And when I got the table, all of those people, some of whom have unlimited resources and money (which I do not) said "No, I gotta rake the leaves, man. I'm supposed to get a haircut."

It was really interesting to me how people, for absolutely sensible reasons, do not say yes to the greatest experiences in life. I couldn't afford that dinner at Noma. But I found that I needed to. I needed to say yes to it and I realize it's an extraordinary set of circumstances that I happened to meet René and everything, but I do think that these opportunities come about all the time.

Friends of mine are dying. I'm starting to lose people in my life or they're getting sick. So let's get together. Let's go for a hike. Let's have a weekend together. Say yes to that. I'm not trying to make some snotty argument, like, everyone should eat in Denmark. It's about how you are here now, make the most of it and change what's not working. I think it's crucial.

JAMES ASPEY

A VOICE FOR THE VOICELESS

Why do we love dogs, eat pigs, and wear cows?

Dr. Melanie Joy coined this phenomenon: "speciesism."

James Aspey bluntly calls it what it is—just plain wrong.

Motivated to raise greater awareness for the planet's voiceless victims, in 2014 this passionate, young, Australian animal rights activist took a 365-day vow of silence. After an entire year without uttering a single word, James broke his fast on Australian national television with a moving plea for animal compassion. Amassing over 7 million views, it's an iconic interview that overnight cemented James as a charismatic new force in the fight for the ethical treatment of animals.

Ranked number three among the "Top 25 Most Influential Vegans" by *Plant Based News*, James has cycled 5000 kilometers across Australia to prove that vegans can be fit and healthy. He got tattooed for 25 hours straight to raise $20,000 for charity. And in 2019, he campaigned for Parliament in the state of New South Wales, running with Australia's Animal Justice Party.

Over the years, James has been featured in a multitude of prominent mainstream media outlets; given countless free speeches; attended local activism events, slaughterhouse vigils, and street outreach events all across the world; and transparently documented all of it online to a massive tribe of global followers.

Enthusiastic, accessible, and highly skilled behind a podium, James is inspiring a new generation to change how we eat and live in communion with the animals that share this home we call Earth.

But there's so much more to this young man's life than meets the eye. At 17, James was diagnosed with leukemia and told he only had six weeks to live. He beat the cancer only to slide into a life of drugs and alcohol punctuated by a profound eating disorder. It was a chance encounter with an Indian man that would forever change the trajectory of his life.

It has been said that the greatness of a nation can be judged by the way its animals are treated.

History will not look fondly upon our track record.

It is therefore with pride that I help amplify this passionate voice for the voiceless.

—Rich

James: When you make the connection that there's no need to kill any animals to survive, that you can get every essential nutrient you need through a plant-based diet, then all the merciless violence we inflict on billions of sentient beings every day seems so futile and so glaringly wrong.

We love dogs. We love dolphins. We love whales. But we think nothing of killing and eating pigs, cows, chickens, fish. It's not because those animals are less intelligent, or have less value, or feel less pain, it's simply because they're the ones we've chosen to eat—we like the taste of their flesh.

I used to eat as much meat as I could. I was one of the biggest meat eaters out of everyone I knew. I'd wake up in the mornings and have steak for breakfast. My favorite meal was ribs or lamb chops. I didn't think that a meal was a meal unless there was meat. I didn't believe it was possible to be healthy without it.

But within days of going vegan, I noticed *improvements* in my health. My energy was at an all-time high, and I was training harder than ever in the gym. I learned that not only can you be healthy on a plant-based diet, but you're likely to live longer and reduce your chances of developing diseases and ailments.

This all came as a shock to me.

Eating meat is such a normal part of our culture. We are told that meat is manly and that we need meat for protein and dairy for calcium. These are lies that we have been duped into believing. When you buy a meal with meat in it, you're not just paying for

the bacon, you're paying for everything that happened to that pig in order to get to your plate. Most people would never be okay with even a tenth of the violence and the suffering that is inflicted on these creatures.

We simply should not be killing animals if we don't need to.

Going vegan is a process. You don't just change your whole life and unravel decades of conditioning overnight. Some people go vegetarian for a year. Some people do it for three months. Some people start eating vegan for breakfast, vegan for lunch, then vegan for dinner. Some people do meatless Mondays. The point is just to start somewhere. Maybe all you do today is buy soy milk instead of cow's milk. There are not that many steps to go vegan. It's actually quite easy.

If it was hard, there wouldn't be thousands of people around the world doing it every day.

CHARLES EISENSTEIN

THE CORONATION

There is a potent silver lining to our perilous global moment of pandemic and political upheaval. It's the opportunity to snap the denial that humans exist separate from each other—and the biosphere that supports all life.

Like an addict's moment of clarity, we are awakening to our intrinsic interconnectedness—with others and the world at large. An epiphany both humbling and beautiful, it is now incumbent upon us to rethink, reimagine, and recreate the story we tell ourselves about who we are and aspire to become.

This is an initiation. An opportunity to reset. A call to reclaim our inherent divinity as spiritual beings having a human experience in intimate relationship with every living thing. An occasion to expand our awareness beyond self-interest and elevate the collective consciousness—so that we can chart a more compassionate, sustainable and community-empowered new normal going forward.

A crucial voice in this important conversation is Charles Eisenstein, one of the deepest integrative thinkers active today.

A speaker, writer, and social philosopher focusing on themes of human cultural evolution, economics and consciousness, Charles is the author of several books, including *Climate—A New Story*, *Sacred Economics*, *The More Beautiful World our Hearts Know is Possible*, and *The Ascent of Humanity*.

A graduate of Yale University, where he acquired degrees in both mathematics and philosophy, Charles is a counter-culture intellectual and a proponent of alternative political and economic narratives that combine ecology, biology, philosophy, and spirituality to challenge our current system.

Current events, both pandemic and otherwise, have cast a cosmic panic I am not interested in amplifying. Nor do I feel it appropriate to deliver an empty dose of conjectural optimism.

I don't hold myself out as knowing exactly what is happening.

I can't give you a prediction or a prescription.

What I can offer is perception. Some perspective. A broader aperture to reckon with the many ramifications of planetary events that are equal parts unusual and entirely predictable. How to make sense of the devastation they have produced. And how to discover the hidden gifts they bequeath.

My deliberation on these themes was initially inspired by "The Coronation"—Charles' insightful and well-considered long read on how to think expansively about our current moment. It's a piece that has stayed with me. And one deserving of further exploration.

In the vein of my many exchanges with Dr. Zach Bush, my conversation with Charles—which transpired near the beginning of the coronavirus pandemic—is a deeply thoughtful and at times metaphysical meditation on completely redefining our definition of normal.

In an age of division, it's about the potential energy of this shared experience to unite humanity.

It's about asking questions. Challenging the dominant narrative. And taking a hard look at our institutional failures and the systems that perpetuate them.

As we delicately wade the muddy waters of political calamity, media distrust, social upheaval, racial division, economic disparity, environmental devastation, police brutality, and fake news, let Charles' voice linger in your conscious awareness, gently reminding us to listen. To feel. And to connect our senses with the quiet call that change is actualizing.

Without minimizing the severity of what may or may not befall humanity and the planet we collectively inhabit; this truly is our opportunity to cast a new world.

May Charles Eisenstein be our gentle steward.

—Rich

Charles: We are not just these discrete individuals floating through the world—the world is a part of us, and we are a part of it. When the world falls apart like it is now, we fall apart too. Crisis gives us existential vertigo: Now that the reinforcing circumstances of our lives have disappeared, who are we? It's disorienting but also empowering. Crisis reminds us of the things we took for granted both externally on a social political level, and personally in our own lives. Things like seeing friends, grocery shopping, going to the park, were once unconscious programs that now feel more like conscious choices.

This pause in normality gives us the opportunity to ask, Do we want to go back to normal?

Every response to COVID-19 is an intensification of something that was already happening in society. Social distancing for example—people are congregating less in public spaces and living more online. The migration of commerce onto the internet. The migration of education onto online forums. The restriction of civil liberties, the monitoring of our whereabouts at all times. The regime of paranoia about germs. This was all starting to happen even before the pandemic. Our reflexive response to a crisis is to impose and extend our control over the world. And when that generates further crises, we respond by extending even more control. It's an addiction pattern. We see it played out in every realm, as applied to school shootings, terrorism, foreign policy, agriculture, medicine, and so on.

It's part of a very deep myth that defines our civilization, which is the myth of technological utopia. We started out as these superstitious, primitive, helpless, ignorant creatures, at the mercy of natural forces, barely surviving amidst all the competition in the natural world. But thanks to our big brains, we developed science and technology, and gradually, century by century, exerted more and more

dominance over the animal kingdom. Someday this grand project will be complete. When science develops a theory of everything, when nanotechnology and genetic engineering allow us to extend our control down to the smallest level, only then we will be completely safe.

But human life, in a lot of ways, is getting worse. Is safety worth it? Are people actually healthier and happier now than they were a generation ago? Not according to depression statistics, obesity, addiction, suicide, and anxiety statistics. Ironically, longevity is even starting to decline—what do we do about it?

There are more important things than living as long as possible. There's something that you might call living as beautifully as possible, living a good life, living an aligned life. That is hard to recognize when we are immersed in a quantitative mindset. It's hard to value those things numerically. It's hard to fit them into costs and benefits.

Here's where we are going: a world of isolation, distancing, separation, polarization. A world where there is a major concentration of wealth, a world with no human contact, no community. We've been silently, helplessly, unconsciously moving toward this realm as if it were an inevitability for a long time. We have to reclaim our sovereignty and our collective ability to choose our future rather than merely adapting to something that we see as inevitable.

We don't have to go back to normal. Normal sucked. Normal was like a road to Hell. Things were getting worse and worse—not just for people, but for our ecosystems, soil, water, the whales, the elephants. Now that normal has been interrupted, let's make a conscious choice to go in a different direction.

I am hopeful. We've got an amazing opportunity. It's something that we can choose. It's alive. It's the future. Together, let's take the path to a more beautiful world.

Gratitude is elusive. Nor, for me, does it come naturally. Indeed, gratitude is a practice. In its adoption I have found that life expands in proportion to its exercise. The more consistently pronounced the gratitude, the more life delivers things to be grateful for.

—Rich Roll

Allow me to disabuse you of the notion that writing a book is a solo affair. It is not. In the case of *Voicing Change*, I am but one player on a large team comprised of very talented people who have worked tirelessly—and merit a standing ovation—for creating this special work of art.

Let's start with a step back. The book wouldn't exist without the podcast—another team sport affair created week-in-week-out by a collective of devoted souls more than deserving of recognition.

In early 2016, a stream of messages from Jason Camiolo began to flood in my email and social media inboxes, lobbying for the job of podcast audio engineer. I respect persistence. Jason's was undeniable. We gave him a shot and never looked back. Beyond editing the podcast, Jason has grown to shoulder critical responsibility for the weekly production. Jason, thank you for growing into an instrumental member of the team. For your friendship. And allowing me to persistently invade your weekends and evenings. Always good to go, I can't remember the last time you didn't answer the phone when I called, or respond to a text within minutes. I'm reminding you that it's totally okay if you need to call me back later.

When the time came to take my amateur audio production to the video level, David Zammit travelled from Malta to document the show behind a camera. Reece Robinson inherited the post before handing the baton to Margo Lubin and Blake Curtis—my tag-team dynamic duo that enervated our video presentation with the professional gloss you today enjoy. Thank you.

From images moving to images still, thanks belong not only to David and Reece, but to Ali Rogers and Davy Greenberg. Your work elevates every episode you shoot, and always makes me look better than I actually do. Thank you also to Shawn Patterson, our first graphic designer. Your art pioneered the show's aesthetic and set a new bar for podcast production value. Further thanks are deserved by visual artist Brian O'Hara for crafting the interlocking "R" logo that has become the show's signature asset. And let's throw some love in the direction of Jonathan Retseck and Ben Ende at RXR Sports for helping us pull off a stunning live podcast event with IN-Q and Paul Hawken, a 2019 highlight.

Of course, the RRP of today is but a legacy of those who helped originate it. A debt of gratitude is owed to Chris Jaeb for creating the space for me to launch our first shows—I will always love that warehouse and its glorious echo. To my stepson Tyler Piatt, who took pity on my lack of technical acumen and became a steady partner throughout the early years, contributing original music (which he still does today) and deftly managing weekly engineering and editing duties with the skill and maturity of someone twice his age.

We can't forget credit for that melodious series of tones with its clickity-clack bike chain linger. Originated as a temporary scratch track for the first few episodes until the boys could concoct a more polished theme, the audience became irrationally attached to it. Thus it persists, often to my chagrin. Thanks to my nephew Hari Mathis (I still remember you holding a microphone to my bike chain), who wrote and banged out the ditty in an afternoon alongside my stepsons Tyler and Trapper.

Art requires commerce to thrive. David Kahn is the steam in our engine, fueling us with the best financial partners for the show. My friend for over twenty years, it's a rare gift to work with those you care about and trust most. Thank you, DK. For your hard work. Your loyalty. And belief in our shared mission. You are truly the lifeblood of the RRP.

Thanks to Adam Skolnick, the latest team member and my "Roll On" co-captain for all matters "ask me anything." Your fresh enthusiasm has breathed renewed vigor into our ongoing format experimentation. Thank you for the meticulous preparation and sagacious commentary—and for providing me with confidence and the bandwidth to express my perspectives more broadly.

Onto the book, a project for which I deserve credit the least.

Inheriting graphic design duties from Shawn Patterson, Jessica Miranda quickly set about advancing the visual composition of the RRP, divining a gorgeous new look and distinctive feel that truly sets the show apart, and is the professional envy of my fellow podcasters. The elegant and exquisite aesthetic of all things

Voicing Change can be credited to Jessica and her collaboration with designer Jennifer Garrett, with assistance from Andrea Mendoza, Andrew McBride, Erick Torres, Katie Simpson, and Margaux Piñero. It's an understatement to say that this book would not be what it is without your collective artistry. Thank you all, with apologies to Jessica for inundating you with messages on Slack.

At the heart of this volume are the actual words proffered by the guests profiled. Selection was an arduous process that entailed mining countless transcriptions in exhaustive search of the most precious treasure, and translation into palatable written form. Gold medals for detail go to Georgia Whaley, Michaela Thompson, Lisa Marquart, and Geoff Hyatt. Georgia also serves up a weekly copywriting assist on the podcast, helping to craft scripts, hone ad copy, and compile show notes.

A jigsaw puzzle with a thousand moving pieces to assemble, properly managing the production of this book demanded leadership. Our captain was Chris Swan. A trustworthy jack-of-all-trades in service to myself and the podcast throughout the early years, Chris now assumes responsibility for overseeing podcast matters legal and financial. Managing the daunting task of securing permissions from all our guests and photographers alike fell to Chris. No small feat, Chris. Thank you.

Speaking of photographers, the book is rife with many gorgeous portraits and editorial captures, once again courtesy of our in house, go to talents—Ali Rogers, Blake Curtis, David Zammit, Reece Robinson, Leia Marasovich and Davy Greenberg—and the collective contribution of many other photographers who graciously allowed us to share their guest portraits: Alex Wood, Andrew Castro, Andrew Kelly, Arika Bauer, Becca Wyant, Brett Hillyard, Bruce Viaene, Clayton Boyd, Daniel Johnson, Eric Ray Davidson, Eric Voake, Fabio Filippi, Jared Polin, Jenny Wohrle, Lila Seeley, Lyndon Marceau, Matt Korinek, Matti Bernitz, Megan McAllister, Michelle Craig, Nick Fancher, Rachel Wass, Simon Emmett, Tawni Bannister, Tomasz Jakubowski, That Cameraman, and Tom Medvedich.

Great book covers are rare. Few things are harder to get right. Jennifer Garrett and Jessica Miranda nailed this one with a design that is timeless—a proud addition to even the most discerning of coffee table book collectors.

Thank you to my friend and loyal literary agent, Byrd Leavell. Although we went the self-publishing route with one, I foresee many book project collaborations in our future.

Not only is this book a collaborative affair, it wasn't even my idea. Credit for that rests with Greg Anzalone. My business partner and mentor, Greg is that friend we all need. The guy who's always in your corner, with your best interest at heart, but unafraid to deliver uncomfortable truths when needed most. Thank you for your vision. For playing four-dimensional chess when all I see is checkers. And for being an unwavering source of constant support. Your foundation provides the space for me to create. And together, we have built something truly meaningful. Your example inspires me to be better. An expression of appreciation will somehow always feel inadequate as a measure of my admiration and gratitude.

And finally to Julie, my greatest love and partner in all matters material and ethereal. For the last eight years, I have disappeared every Sunday afternoon to spend hours putting the final touches on the week's episode, lost in minutiae I'm certain only I cared about. Thank you for standing alongside me in support of an expression that not too long ago seemed crazy. For always believing in me, especially when I didn't believe in myself. For expanding my awareness and deepening my connection with consciousness. For co-creating a life of our dreams. And perhaps most of all, thank you for showing me the meaning of true intimacy.

In closing, thank you to all of my podcast guests over the years. You inspire me in ways you will never fully appreciate. Trusting me with your stories, your wisdom and your vulnerability has been a gift I have endeavored to receive and share with humility, and sometimes even a little bit of grace.

To all my fellow podcasters, I salute you. I'm proud to be part of a community striving to have conversations that matter. You too give me hope that together we can create a better world.

And finally to you. The reader and the listener. Without you, none of what I do matters. Together, you are my lighthouse. You keep me honest. And motivated to constantly improve my advocacy. Thank you for your attention—a privilege I don't take lightly. I am, and remain, at your service.

In Gratitude,

Rich

PODCAST INDEX

LISTEN TO THE FULL CONVERSATIONS AT RICHROLL.COM | YOUTUBE.COM/RICHROLL

PHOTO CREDITS

ABOUT THE AUTHOR

Simply put, Rich Roll likes to run far and talk long.

Named one of the "25 Fittest Men in the World" by *Men's Fitness* and "The World's Fittest Vegan" by *Men's Health,* Rich is a globally renowned ultra-endurance athlete, wellness advocate, bestselling author, husband, and father of four.

At age 40, Rich made a decision to overhaul the sedentary throes of overweight middle age. Walking away from a career in law, he reinvented himself as an ultra-distance endurance athlete, clocking top finishes at the Ultraman World Championships and cementing his place in the pantheon of endurance greats by becoming the first of two people to complete EPIC5: five Ironmans on five Hawaiian Islands in under a week.

Rich shares his inspirational story of addiction, redemption, and optimal health in his number-one bestselling memoir, *Finding Ultra,* and the cookbook and lifestyle guides *The Plantpower Way and The Plantpower Way: Italia,* which he co-authored with his wife Julie Piatt.

Rich has been featured on CNN and on the cover of *Outside* magazine, and has been profiled everywhere from the *New York Times* to the *Wall Street Journal.*

When he isn't lost on a trail or spending time with his wife, four children, and two Great Pyrenees, he hosts the wildly popular *Rich Roll Podcast,* one of the top 100 podcasts in the world with close to 100 million downloads.

CONNECT WITH RICH

 @RICHROLLFANS  @RICHROLL @RICHROLL   RICHROLL.COM

RICH ROLL
ENTERPRISES LLC

2630 Conejo Spectrum Street
Thousand Oaks, CA 91320
RichRoll.com

VOICING CHANGE™
Is an ongoing series. This is Volume One.

Library of Congress Cataloging-in-Publication
Data available.

Founder: *Rich Roll*
CEO: *Greg Anzalone*
Administration: *Chris Swan*

Staff:
- *Ali Rogers*
- *Blake Curtis*
- *David Kahn*
- *Jason Camiolo*
- *Jessica Miranda*
- *Margo Lubin*

Editorial:
- *Georgia Whaley*
- *Michaela Thompson*
- *Lisa Marquart*
- *Geoff Hyatt*

Design:
- *Jessica Miranda*
- *Andrea Mendoza*
- *Andrew McBride*
- *Erick Torres*
- *Jennifer Garrett*
- *Katie Simpson*
- *Margaux Piñero*

Photographs Courtesy Of:
- *Abundance 360*
- *Alex Wood*
- *Ali Rogers*
- *Andrew Castro*
- *Andrew Kelly*
- *Arika Bauer*
- *Becca Wyant*
- *Blake Curtis*
- *Brett Hillyard @HillyCollective*
- *Bruce Friedrich*
- *Charles Eisenstein*
- *Clayton Boyd*
- *Daniel Johnson*
- *Darin Olien*
- *David Sinclair, PhD*
- *David Zammit*
- *Davy Greenberg*
- *Dominick Thompson @domzthompson*
- *Dotsie Bausch*
- *Eric Ray Davidson*
- *Eric Voake*
- *Fabio Filippi*
- *Dr. Gabor Maté*
- *Jared Polin*
- *Jenny Wohrle @Oiselle*
- *Leia Marasovich*
- *Light Watkins*
- *Lila Seeley*
- *Lymbus Life SL*
- *Matti Bernitz / Lymbus Life SL*
- *Megan McAllister*
- *Michelle Craig @ZionAdventurephotog*
- *Nick Fancher*
- *Rachel Wass*
- *Reece Robinson*
- *Robin Arzón*
- *Robynne Chutkan, MD*
- *Samantha Gash*
- *Simon Emmett / Trunk Archive*
- *Susan David*
- *Tawni Bannister*
- *That Cameraman*
- *The Nantucket Project*
- *Tomasz Jakubowski*
- *Wim Hof*
- *Yuval Noah Harari*

ISBN: 978-1-7354458-0-9

Printed in China
Global PSD, *Steven Goff*
1 0 9 8 7 6 5 4 3 2

Special Thanks to all the guests from the
Rich Roll Podcast, without their stories this book
would not be possible.

IN-Q, "Father Time" and "Learned Fear,"
Inquire Within, Poems by IN-Q, reprinted
with permission by HarperOne, © 2020

Also available from Rich Roll:
- *Finding Ultra*

Also available from Rich Roll & Julie Piatt:
- *The Plantpower Way*
- *The Plantpower Way: Italia*
- *This Cheese is Nuts*